CAPPUCCINO AND PORRIDGE

Harris and Tuscany – the Lands of our Fathers

CAPPUCCINO
and PORRIDGE

Tuscany and Harris -
the Lands of our Fathers

Duncan MacKenzie

Registered Charity SC047866

First published in 2020 by Acair,
An Tosgan, Seaforth Road, Stornoway, Isle of Lewis, Scotland HS1 2SD

info@acairbooks.com
www.acairbooks.com

Cover paintings and illustration by Ailie Osborne
Subtitle handwriting by Alessandra Gori MacKenzie

Text and cover design by Margaret Ann MacLeod, Acair

A CIP catalogue record for this title is available from the British Library.

Printed by Hussar Books, Poland

ISBN: 978-1-78907-079-8

Dedicated with profound thanks to
Alessandra's surgeon, David Anderson,
MB ChB, FRCS (Ed), FRCS (Gen).

Acknowledgements

They don't know which of them first thought of it, but Ale and our sons all seemed to share the view that I should try writing. The bedtime stories I used to make up for the boys about three Harris sheepdogs were perhaps what they had in mind. Once I began, encouragement came from relatives and friends on Harris, on the mainland and over in Italy. It was most welcome.

I am indebted to Allan for information on the Balavil bomber crash and for putting me in touch with the London Scottish. He, Liz and Joan kindly read over the section on their dad, Joan also reading two entire drafts.

Special thanks is due to Nazareno for sharing his recollections with me in his beautifully clear Italian. My visit with him to his former family home and its surroundings was unforgettable.

My brother and DI Macleod were particularly positive about my first draft. Without their enthusiasm, I doubt that I would have attempted to go beyond my initial intention which was to produce an account only for the younger generations of the three families. I also much appreciated Mairi Sutherland's kind comments and most helpful suggestions.

Reading one of their publications had prompted a visit to the website of Acair Books whereupon I put them at the top of the very short list of publishers that I might approach. No unexpected visitor bearing an unsolicited synopsis could have hoped for a kinder reception than I received in Stornoway. Their manager, Agnes Rennie, interrupted her work to read my synopsis and to ask me about the background. From that moment on I have received thoughtful advice and much encouragement from Agnes. I am very grateful to her and to her team including designer Margaret Ann MacLeod.

Margaret MacIver, also from Lewis, made our discussion of commas and relative pronouns both fascinating and fun. She even taught me the Gaelic for 'Too much information.' Thereby hangs a tale. What an enjoyable experience the editorial process proved to be.

It is a delight for me to see Ailie Osborne's superb drawings and paintings in 'Cappuccino & Porridge'. We have a family connection with her niece, Catriona, being my daughter-in-law. Added to that, we are both Scots who are married to Italians. Our collaboration feels doubly appropriate.

To all of the above, mentioned by name or otherwise, I record my sincere gratitude.

Lastly, to the one who will understand my dedication of this book better than anyone...grazie, Ale. Ti amo.

Contents

Introduction 12

EDINBURGH
Restorative Colinton Dell 15
My Brother, Stepbrother and a P45 24
Our Frequently Asked Question 26

MY DAD'S WAR
Talking with my Father 29
His Diary: A Window to a Father and a Grandfather 35
Tobruk 45
Siege 56

ITALY
Tregozzano, Tuscany 65
A Fisherman's Tale 68

ALE'S DAD'S WAR
War Zone Survival 74
The Allies Arrive 83
The Fire 90

REV JOHN FLETCHER
The Highland Padre 94
The Silent Toast 101
Nazareno's Hunt for John F 102

ALE AND I MEET AGAIN
My Positive Premonition 107
Christmas Eve 1983 114
The Italian Wedding 117
August Dobringer: The Austrian Connection 122
Iain Alick Helps Nazareno 124

BALAVIL, KINGUSSIE
'Finlay's Pool' 127
'The Tromie' 134
Lessons Learned and a Rare Sight 138
Highland Retreat 144
Short and Sharp 148
MacKenzie's Farewell to Balavil House 150

THE LANDS OF OUR FATHERS
A New Chapter in Harris 161
The 'Flodabay Five' 166
Poultry Problems 172
Quidinish, Isle of Harris: Early Memories 176
Quidinish: A Continuing Legacy 187
The Bond Deepens 192
Sons, Crabs and Urchins 197
Two Eagles and an Irritable Seal 200
A Six Island Road Trip 203
Berneray: Camping and Contemplating 212
Anniversary Trout 218

Quidinish to Bavaria 221
Woolly Pigs and an English Garden 224
A Road Well Travelled 229
Marina di Pisa 234
Acclimatising for Two 236
Nazareno's Farm and another Italian Wedding 242
Eat to Stay Young 251
Nazareno and John F – Walking in their Footsteps 254

AUSTRIA
Our Favourite Hotel 263
Nazareno's Wee Housie 265
Highlanders in Austria 272
Upper Austria: Courtesy and Tradition 275

REFLECTION 281

SOURCES 284

INTRODUCTION

'So, how did you two meet each other?' A couple from different countries which are neither neighbours nor similar in terms of climate and culture can expect to be asked that question regularly.

Our mothers used to talk of writing the story behind our meeting. Language teachers both, the Scot and the Italian conversed in French with a common enthusiasm for correct grammar. Neither needed to be a beginner in the native tongue of the other. It worked very well. Sadly, however, their proposed writing was never begun before we lost them both in the same year. Some years later, unexpected leave of absence from my work prompted reflection and provided me with the time to take up the idea that the two mothers had shared.

Paying fond homage to our mothers, this telling of the story is in tribute to their husbands, that is to my father, my stepfather and my father-in-law whose very different experiences in the Second World War would eventually have a remarkable influence on my life. In preparing to write this account, I have come to know all three men better through, respectively, a long-lost war diary, excerpts from a regimental gazette and spoken recollection some of which was shared with me on location.

Throughout the story, I have recalled memories, distant and recent, of the places each one introduced to me, places which my family and I still enjoy so much.

My late father, from the Isle of Harris in Scotland's Outer Hebrides, encouraged in me a deep attachment to his island and to the village of Quidinish in particular. That this bond survived his premature death is due in no small measure to the 'welcome home' I received as a teenager from his people there. Since then, they have made me feel as one of their own. The bond continues to grow with my every visit to Harris, the frequency of which reflects both my wife's understanding and her own affection for my relatives there.

My late stepfather, although from the Isle of Skye in the Inner Hebrides, introduced me to Balavil Estate on Speyside in the heart of the Scottish Highlands. Happy holidays and weekends were spent there over many years and the welcome given us by my stepbrother and his wife at neighbouring Croftcarnoch remains second to none.

My father-in-law's ongoing gift to me is the hospitality of his home region of Tuscany in Italy plus the opportunity to enjoy a beautiful area of Upper Austria. His family in Tuscany and his friends in Austria have welcomed me as warmly as my wife, Alessandra, has been welcomed on Harris and on Speyside.

We are fortunate to live close to Colinton Dell in Edinburgh where its wooded river valley offers both tranquillity and an abundance of wildlife within the boundaries of Scotland's capital. It was during long walks with our dog in these woods that I began to think about writing.

Duncan MacKenzie.

EDINBURGH

~•~ Restorative Colinton Dell ~•~

Scudo MacKenzie was up to his chest in freezing, fast flowing water, looking up at his walking companion who was standing on the bridge above, completely ignoring what was becoming an increasingly perplexed stare. Being totally disregarded did not come easily, especially from the middle of a river, to one who could normally command the attention of the other through the merest meeting of eyes.

Stabilising his stance among the slippery rocks of the river bed, Scudo looked over his shoulder to see what his dry-shod partner was gazing at of such interest, only to find a dumpy little bird sitting on a large branch which had become wedged amongst rocks in the roughest stretch of water. Edinburgh's Water of Leith or 'silver thread' was running more of a caramel colour that morning, and quickly at that, through the stretch of the 'ribbon of green' that is Colinton Dell.

A year earlier, it would have been a glance at the bird before hurrying on over the bridge and along the river bank, but Scudo's companion was a changed man now, his hands clasped on the duck-head shaped handle of a staff, chin resting on hands. The duck-head was the result of quite a few visits to the workbench under the house. Mention of me and a workbench in the same paragraph had, until very recently, been unthinkable. I did become rather attached to that staff.

The dumpy little bird's technique was much more impressive than his appearance. He dived into the foaming water and stayed submerged for about ten seconds, before returning to the branch for what should have been a rest, but instead, looked more like a celebration involving much bobbing up and down. The bird then changed tactics and executed a series of short visits to the riverbed, before hopping back on to the branch for more bobbing. It must have been a successful style of hunting, as the energy spent seemed enormous in that fast-flowing section of the river, yet that little bird certainly did not give the impression of ever having gone hungry. The white-throated dipper looks like a pudgy little butler, but it has developed the remarkable technique of using its wings in the flow of a stream like the fins and spoilers on a racing car. Downward pressure keeps the little bird on the riverbed for food and the racing car on the road with better grip, so I was later told by a nature loving friend who happened also to be steeped in motor racing.

When the bird left for another stretch of river, there was a whistle and off we went too – my dog, my duck and me.

A couple of my rugby and football friends, formerly nuggety prop and uncompromising central defender respectively, both otherwise pragmatic and streetwise gentlemen of a certain vintage, had recently lost long-standing canine companions. These former sporting warriors had come over misty eyed to me as they bemoaned their loss of dogs that had been able to read their minds, they said, and vice versa. This has been a mild source of relief to me, as I had convinced myself that I could read my dog's mind and was, therefore, pretty certain that the dog could read mine. If these former tough competitors could think in that way, it might just be ok for me, too.

Scudo MacKenzie is a very fortunate dog in that, although he lives in the city of Edinburgh, he is only around two corners from one of the entrances to Craiglockhart and Colinton Dells. What is more, the family he looks after have relatives in the Highlands and on the Isle of Harris. They also have friends in Bavaria and Austria plus a huge network of family in Italy. Initially thinking that his name was Scudo MacKenzie Si i i t, he got the idea quickly enough and soon came to understand commands in both English and Italian. One or two Gaelic commands have crept in too, now that he has been invited to help expel raiding sheep from a Harris croft. His working springer and working collie parentage, coupled with two languages in his head, might have been more than enough of a challenge, but he has also had to learn that the Scot and the Italian look for different things in a dog, or perhaps it's just a man/woman thing. He can still find it taxing.

Scudo's master is very Scottish, my wife, Alessandra, more often called Ale, being very, very Italian. Both English and Italian are spoken in the family home and our three sons, John, Seumas and Finlay are all fluent in their mother's language, not that anyone would guess that from their names. These names bear witness to their father's strong sense of his Hebridean heritage and also to their mother's benevolence, although it was understood that she was hoping for a Marco, Giampiero, Giuseppe or Fabio MacKenzie in the next generation.

Ale had wanted an Italian name for our dog and she got to choose. The choice of names for the children, graciously, was never raised by her during any discussions on the naming of the puppy. Scudo is the Italian word for a 'shield' and it was chosen as the puppy's white chest fur was like a shield in shape.

Both Scudo's parents being working dogs, he does get the inclination to hunt sometimes and to help with sheep at other times. Either way, he needs to be careful to avoid the wrong genes kicking in and getting him into trouble. Letting the rabbiting genes loose when there are sheep around would not be helpful. Although it cannot be easy for a half collie, he has perfected a sheepish expression which he can call upon in mitigation when he has been caught chasing one of our own cats in the street.

We had bought the family home without knowing that Craiglockhart and Colinton Dells existed. Often referred to in the singular, the Dell is a heavily wooded river valley which can be entered only 300 yards from our front door. The Water of Leith does not have the most rustic of names, but it is both clean and varied, with fast shallow runs and deeper, slow pools. The sides of the valley are steep, but there are five flat, open areas in our local section, where you can happen upon a tent (contrary to regulations), a picnic (permitted, but no fires) or a varied pack of dogs with their equally varied owners (very sociable).

Just as the river can be a 'silver thread' or a coffee coloured turbulence, so does the Dell change with the season and the weather. Varied, too, is my emotional association with the Dell, it having been for me a place of happiness and discovery, of distress and fear, of refuge, recovery and friendship.

In the early days, Ale and I delighted in helping our boys to hone their bike skills on the Dell woodland paths where there were few other cyclists and only a fraction of the number of dogs that are walked nowadays. Years later, however, during a winter walk along a level stretch of path, Ale's plea for me to slow down crystallised in my mind the dreadful possibility of her being seriously ill. I had only been walking at the steady pace of one who carries his golf clubs on the course and prefers not to pressurise the players in front of him. Very worrying it was, but that incident was perhaps fortunate in that it hastened Ale's referral to her consultant. Despite my initial serious concern, I had then, for only the second time ever in grave circumstances, allowed optimism to hold sway. I had persuaded myself that we would be told, in a few days, that our worry had been excessive and that the symptoms were only infection based. I allowed myself, rather easily, to be persuaded to attend a partners' meeting at my firm's head office, albeit an important one during the very difficult economic circumstances of the time, instead of accompanying my wife to her appointment with the specialist. After the consultation, she called from the City Bypass as she drove home, her voice vibrant, if a little forced. She had got on well, she said. A very few days later, when Ale went into hospital for tests to 'rule out anything nasty', I went to work as usual. I had got it badly wrong.

Ale had been trying to protect the husband who was already struggling and had not told him that the hospital tests were actually to confirm the consultant's initial diagnosis. It was her close friend, Jane, who brought Ale home from hospital. On my return from work, during a tender embrace, my wife whispered, 'It's not good news,' and doubtless felt the jolt that these words sent through me.

What I did next was either quite sensible or the act of a coward; my jury is still deliberating. The expression on Seumas's face told his father that his mum's news had already been received by our middle son. Eldest son, John, was away, but

Finlay was due to arrive home from school at any minute. Doubting that I would be able to match my wife's faith and bravery when it came to her telling our youngest son, I made my fears known and asked if it would be alright if I took Scudo for a walk. As it turned out, young Finlay was also immensely brave, while down in the Dell, moving on autopilot, I started to receive calls of support from my brother, niece and nephew.

That I associate the Dell with recovery and restoration is in great part due to Ale's joyful display of health and stamina a few years later when, having passed through the Dell on several training walks, she completed the marathon length Moon Walk, with Jane at her side all the way. There had been no slacking at a golfer's steady pace that long night.

In April 2015, having fought many a skirmish, over several years with those equally menacing 'cousins', Anxiety Disorder and Depression, body and mind refused at what appeared to me as an impossibly high Puissance Wall in the shape of a return to work after a week's holiday in Quidinish, my late father's home village on the Isle of Harris.

The medical advice was clear and given with a confident firmness that brooked no discussion, never mind argument. There would be no quick return to work.

Our alarm was kept at its working day setting and I got into the routine of joining my wife on the morning walk with Scudo in the Dell. Both Ale and the dog kept a watchful eye on me. I, on the other hand, kept a watchful eye on my surroundings, determined to keep my mind occupied with the nature that we are lucky to have so close to home. These woods soon began to show promise as being an ideal place in which to set out on the road to recovery, at least for one whose earliest years had been spent in rural Banffshire, then in a tiny village on the banks of the River Annan and for whom the move to live in Scotland's capital had been far from voluntary, but rather as the result of an assisted place at boarding school, offered to an eleven-year-old soon after his father's death.

The Dell can feel like real countryside, boasting, as it does, a river and a wide variety of trees. Holly is abundant with ash, birch and elm plus oak, yew and beech. There is also hornbeam which was brought in specially as its wood was helpful in the old mills which used to operate along the banks of the river. According to the Water of Leith Conservation Trust website, over eighty species of birds have been spotted around this 'silver thread in a ribbon of green', the kingfisher and large heron being the family favourites. As for animals in the Dell, Scudo has frequently been called back from trying to make the close acquaintance of roe deer, not that he would have much chance.

Gradually, I took over sole responsibility for the daily dog walk and soon found myself in demand to walk some of the other dogs in the wider family. Of those dogs, pride of place goes to Effie, a Parson's Jack Russell/Lakeland terrier cross; an elegant Jack Russell on stilts who can, nevertheless, be a little nippy and yappy, she is fully deserving of the accusation of being a drama queen, occasionally, but warmly, levelled at her. She is much loved in the MacKenzie family where her efficiency in rat control is also greatly admired. She carries out these duties on a farm in Dumfriesshire rather than in leafy Craiglockhart. Effie's owner is Catriona, wife of Seumas and whose parents have a farm near Thornhill.

Effie spends most school days at our house. Seumas and Catriona live in a former farm cottage in East Lothian, but Catriona teaches quite close to our home, so the idea of Effie's spending a couple of days a week with us seemed sensible when it became clear that I would be absent from work for quite a while and even more so when my absence became early retirement. Her stays soon became five days most weeks.

Effie and Scudo do get into a bit of bother together, but reference to Scudo's expression, when it happens, suggests that this is totally inequitable and entirely due to the ignorance in the family of the situation under their very noses.

The back garden of our home is enclosed by a high fence beyond which are mature trees and bushes. The legal boundary is beyond all of that, being the mid-point of a burn which flows past the garden and on down to the Water of Leith. Until recently, the family has had little idea that the burn, with its high trees and bushes on either side, is a complete wildlife superhighway for all manner of animals, some less popular than others. Foxes, rats, roe deer, badgers and otters are back and forth all the time, even during the hours of daylight. The foxes are far and away the worst; smelly and sleekit, not to mention vicious, especially when they think they have the upper paw. 'Never a backward step with that lot,' appears to be the Scudo motto. The family consider that he earned his spurs by charging into the front street one evening while one of our then cats, Tina, originally from Rodel, Harris, was facing up to a large vixen. Tina was holding her own, but under severe pressure, until the fox bolted on the gallant Scudo's high-speed arrival, but not before sinking its teeth into Tina's face. The wound went septic – that says it all.

The family reckon that Liath, another of our cats, was taken by a fox. She never, ever left the garden, but disappeared one Saturday morning. A rescue cat, Liath was neither bright nor bold, but she was definitely affectionate; no Scudo to the rescue that time, sadly.

The roe deer are worthy of mention. One snowy Christmas morning, roe deer were spotted in the neighbouring garden with four of them in full view from the patio doors in the kitchen. The fact that I, the least technically efficient of the household, managed to capture the four deer on my old phone was a bit of a triumph.

The local residents get quite excited about mention of otters. Having had four deer on one side of the house, news came from the other that Alan-next-door had lost his second pond-full of fish, the refill having been of a cheaper variety, thankfully. He spotted the culprit in flagrante, not one of our cats, but a creature he described as being like a giant rat. He was wondering about how to break that particular piece of news to his wife, when he realised that he was looking at an otter. That would almost be alright, then. From his description, however, I reckon he had been looking at a mink. I have only seen two, both in Harris, but have seen film of them shot on the banks of our local stretch of river. They are definitely to be found in this area. Wisely, Alan has not restocked since.

Winter evenings offer excellent opportunities to the human residents for the spotting of wildlife. One such sighting happened after I had backed the Land Rover into the driveway at about 11pm on my return from six-a-side football. I don't exactly leap out of the driver's seat these days; it's more of a post-match creak than a leap. I had switched off the engine, but still had the clutch pedal depressed when, out of the corner of my eye, I saw a movement and assumed it was one of the cats coming home for the night. They often appear at the sound of the engine. Wrong. Here came a badger padding his way casually down the pavement past the end of the front path. The tiny sound of my releasing of the clutch pedal caused the badger to stop and stare up at the windscreen. He then gave the badger equivalent of a dismissive shrug, pure Italian it was, and ambled on down the pavement, entirely comfortable in his own fur.

~·~ My Brother, Stepbrother and a P45 ~·~

My other most regular Dell walking companions became like parts of the furniture in the MacKenzie house over an eighteen-month period of extensive and varied orthopaedic surgery for their owner. What began as a couple of walks each week became three long periods of boarding for Beezer and Cassie, a father and daughter black Lab team, belonging to my brother, Uncle John, referred to as such because we have several John MacKenzies to differentiate.

Beezer and Cassie work in the field of customer relations, or perhaps client liaison. They specialise in 'meet and greet' while their owner, based in the centre of Edinburgh, specialises in family law. Two friendly black noses, poking where they possibly shouldn't, can go a long way towards easing the first few minutes of a perhaps stressful initial consultation. Scudo also did a fair bit of this kind of work at one time and it did seem to help, especially with those clients who were as anxious on entering a lawyer's room as they might be when approaching the dentist's chair.

When Uncle John was taking a friend to a client's estate up in Lochaber, the purpose of the visit being the selection of a black Labrador puppy from a litter, it was probably inevitable that he would fall for a puppy himself. Welcome, Cassie! She is a lovely dog, well behaved, affectionate and no trouble whatsoever. She cannot really have taken after her dad, Beezer. He came with a bit of a reputation, fine with humans, but not at all good with other dogs.

On the sale of the Lochaber estate, Beezer had trouble adjusting to having to spend much of his time in kennels. The poor dog was bored stiff. By pure chance, his owner, who was spending most of the year abroad, arranged a move for Beezer to Balavil Estate, Kingussie, home of our stepbrother, Allan Macpherson-Fletcher and his wife, Marjorie. One of their boys, Nicholas, took Beezer over.

Beezer was supposed to be a gundog, but he hadn't really reached the required standard in what is a serious business with no room for indiscipline or lack of interest. Rumour has it that Beezer believed grouse and pheasant were being shot for his breakfast – not exactly, Beezer. Furthermore, other dogs on a shooting estate are there for work and pleasure, not for canine gladiatorial combat. Beezer had failed to grasp the basics.

After a short time, the Balavil feeling was that Beezer was, if not too aggressive, then certainly too boisterous. Their well-trained working cockers could be relied upon not to clatter wine glasses off occasional tables with an alligator-like swipe of a powerful tail.

In the end of the day, it was looking as if Beezer was just not settling in as hoped, so Uncle John suggested taking him for the weekend to see how he got on in the same household as Cassie. Everything then fell into place and Uncle John, not for the first time, had two dogs.

Beezer was a bit of a nightmare down in the Dell, but the story of his being handed his P45 as a gundog went down well with other dog owners who showed great tolerance which, coupled with much patience from Uncle John (and me), encouraged Beezer to become a pleasure to host and walk. The short stay at the vet might have had something to do with his improvement too!

~•~ Our Frequently Asked Question ~•~

The convivial atmosphere in the Dell is such that conversations can be struck up even on the first meeting of dog owners. On one such occasion, Ale and I were both out with Scudo when two large huskie type dogs emerged from the trees. The first impression was that they had the distinct aura of timber wolves about them, but they proved calm, obedient and gentle in their acceptance of a biscuit. The meeting was, however, memorable more for the owner's recognition of Scudo's name; he even produced the Latin origin which is 'scutum'. Before long, the owner and I were trading Latin names for weapons, but it was clear that Scudo's master had met his match when the other fellow countered my 'pilum' for javelin with 'onager' which was both a wild ass, with a big kick, and a Roman catapult, also with a big kick, used in sieges.

There can be some rather erudite conversations during a Dell dog walk, but perfect quotation of Latin names for weapons was a first. The huskie owner wasn't a Latin teacher, but rather a former member of a Roman army re–enactment group and went on to ask us, 'So, how did you two meet each other? University?' It is not a question one would normally ask of complete strangers, but the friendly dog with the Italian name, well versed in dog/dog and dog/human diplomacy, often encourages conversation which, in turn, leads to Ale's mention of her nationality. I answered the former 'centurion' with what had become my stock response of 'World War II', but it felt particularly glib that day, a bit smart Alec. My wife was by my side and nobody was more aware than she that our story merited much better than my well-worn flippancy.

That day, I made up my mind never again to trot out that trite, disrespectful response.

Having been born roughly ten years after the war, reference to it features amongst my earliest memories. Goodness knows how young I was when I first began to understand words like 'surrounded', 'surrender', 'prisoner of war'. At the very early age of nine, I came to feel that the war had dealt a massive blow to a young mother and her two little boys. The thought that millions of others had suffered similarly and even worse was not the direction a nine-year-old mind would take. 'Why him? Why us? Why me?' was much more like it.

The ultimate effect of what my father suffered in various Prisoner of War (POW) camps during the war shattered my very happy little world, much of which involved what had already become a very strong attachment to Harris.

It certainly never crossed my mind that anything bringing happiness to my life could ever have a war connection, far less have its roots in events which took place while my father was struggling to survive the deprivation he was facing in captivity.

But, while my father was suffering in Germany, in a little village in Tuscany, an Italian family was forming a friendship with a man of the cloth from a little village in Skye.

MY DAD'S WAR

~·~ Talking with my Father ~·~

*"I thought, when the shelling stopped and we surrendered,
the nightmare would be over. I did not realise I was
about to enter Hell."*

These are the words of Peter Coombe, Royal Engineers, who was captured at Tobruk in 1942 and who spent the rest of the war as a prisoner in Italy and Germany. They were quoted by his son, also Peter, in a World War 11 Today website comment I happened upon. There were many such comments; most were by children and grandchildren of men who were among the 33,000 Allied prisoners taken on the fall of Tobruk and most of them alluded to the reluctance of their relatives to speak about their experiences. There was chillingly frequent reference to post-war, premature death.

My father, John MacKenzie, was the son of a fisherman. He was born at Sruthmor on the Isle of Harris where he is referred to by his patronym, Iain Alick, or simply as Iain. I have always liked the use of his patronym or patronymic and will use it as an alternative to father/dad.

Sruthmor is part of Quidinish, but with the post office having been in Finsbay, it was Finsbay which appears to have prevailed in the address. The general area is known as the Bays of Harris.

I cannot remember at what age I first became aware that my father had been in the Royal Air Force during the war and had been taken prisoner. Like so many others, it seems, my dad spoke little about it, although he did order up his medals for me and told me that, due to poor eyesight, there had never been any prospect of his flying a plane. The little boy had been disappointed to hear that, instead of flying a plane, his dad drove a lorry. I also recall being disappointed back then, to learn that his personal weapon as a lorry driver, at least at the start of the war, was no more than a pick-axe handle, but felt better on hearing his candid assurance that he was nevertheless highly accurate with a rifle, although he had gone on to say that he had never actually fired a shot in anger. Somehow, there was further disappointment on hearing that. Guns were my favourite toys.

Iain Alick's response to his young son's question on how he had been taken prisoner was to explain that he and his comrades had been surrounded by the enemy.

'But, why did one of you not just grab a machine gun and spray bullets right round in a circle, Dad?'

'It wasn't really like that, laddie.'

Neither it was.

Iain Alick did tell stories from the war about going fishing with hand grenades. It does seem that fishing is in the blood of the MacKenzie family, but I only remember going fishing with him once; no hand grenades, just rod, line, hook and worm.

As a very little boy, I was also told of prisoners of war being forced to work, without gloves, on railway tracks in freezing conditions, causing the skin of the hands to stick to the metal. My dad told me to think how the fingers stick to the tray of ice cubes in the freezer section of the fridge and then to imagine it a hundred times worse.

My brother and I have remembered having to finish all the food on our plates, whether we liked it or not. Severe hunger had been suffered by our dad throughout his captivity. By way of complete contrast, our mainland granny's encouragement was for us to leave a little on our plates...for the birds in the garden. Iain Alick had been told, on his eventual release from captivity, that his stomach had shrunk to the size of an orange. How anyone worked that out was a source of puzzlement to his son, back then and still now. After her husband's death, our mother, Margaret, with quiet pride told her young boys that their dad had been put in charge, by his comrades, of Red Cross parcels for the POWs, because he was the most scrupulously fair in his hut, when it came to the sharing out of food from home.

Iain Alick also told his young sons that he had been liberated by the Russians, but although I obtained my dad's Royal Air Force (RAF) record, I did not immediately manage to work out where he had been held as a prisoner of war. There was a place name, handwritten, but it appeared to have been scored out. One of the comments left on the Tobruk website by a granddaughter gave her grandfather's journey from prison camp to prison camp through Italy and Germany after his original capture at Tobruk. Maybe my dad's journey had followed a similar course. The list gave me a bit of a start, as I had been to the following in the course of my own visits to Italy, Austria and Germany viz- Leghorn or Livorno; Genoa; Milan; Trento; Bolzano; Innsbruck; Rosenheim; Linz; Passau. Could my own father have been transported via some or all of these places?

I have a handwritten family tree going back through Iain Alick's forebears to the early 1700s. Place names appear beside very many of the individuals and are almost entirely on Harris or on the islands off its coast. Great interest is taken in ancestry and family connections in the Hebrides. Bill Lawson's Croft History, Isle of Harris, Volume 3 covers, inter alia, Quidinish and Finsbay. In the late 1800s and early 1900s it seemed commonplace for there to be five, six or seven children in a family. Double figures were reached in two MacKenzie households in the Finsbay area. As a result, Iain Alick had many first cousins. Those best known to the young MacKenzie boys were addressed as 'Aunt' or 'Uncle' and considered as such. It was much less cumbersome than offering up 'First cousin once removed Murdo!' Many of them became very important to and much loved by Iain Alick's sons. They will be referred to as aunts and uncles throughout although, for the sake of family accuracy, only Johnnie, otherwise Seonaidh Alick, and his wife, Maggie, at Sruthmor were Harris uncle and aunt.

At one time Uncle Norman, in Ardvie, Finsbay, had provided some very valuable information for me regarding my dad's return from captivity, namely that he had been released through Odessa. There seemed to have been political reasons for a delay in the return of the POWs who were released through that Black Sea port. Far worse than mere delay, my research resulted in some very unpleasant reading. I counterbalanced that by recalling how my father had been teaching himself Russian during the last year of his life. I had noticed, at the time, that he had not chosen to study German or Italian.

Uncle Norman spoke of how Iain Alick was due to arrive home on the boat bringing back the very last of the Harris and Lewis POWs. It was running late. When the steamer finally made it to port in Stornoway, the pipers who had been detailed to pipe the boys ashore were apparently 'tired' and had to be propped up by a couple of mates each, to keep them steady. They played triumphantly all the same.

So very little was said by Iain Alick about his war experiences, during the few years that he survived the birth of his sons, that any little snippet of information was gratefully received by us until, some forty years after our father's death, we made a surprising discovery whilst we were going through our mother's papers. She had sung professionally before, as a newly married couple, our parents had moved to Banffshire to take over a primary school together. On her eventual retirement from the teaching profession, our mother had returned to singing and had gathered, therefore, a considerable collection of music. From amidst some sheet music, Uncle John suddenly raised a notebook which he immediately handed to me with the comment that I might be better to have a look at it, doubtless due to the obvious Italian flavour of its cover.

The notebook was, in fact, a school jotter and had a quote by Mussolini on the top of the front cover below which was a picture of 'Il Duce' himself which blended down into a picture of a crop being harvested by sickle. At the very foot was the Italian word 'Quaderno' (jotter) after which Iain Alick had added in his own hand 'di' (of or belonging to) 'J. MacKenzie Hut 23.' On the back cover there was a very basic map of the Mediterranean and the Latin words 'mare nostrum' printed across the sea. Within the notebook, incongruously, were three of Iain Alick's school reports, one of which showed a Latin exam score of 96% with the teacher's comment that it was one of the best exam papers he had ever marked. On that evidence, it would have been easy for Iain Alick to recognise that the ancient Roman name for the Mediterranean meant 'our sea'.

For whatever reason, neither son had ever been given any indication by their mother that their father's war diary was in her possession. It had obviously survived Italy, the transportation to Germany, the liberation and return to Harris through Odessa, post-war Glasgow, then Banffshire, then Dumfriesshire followed by three different houses in Edinburgh. Had it been misplaced amongst that music in their very early days together and assumed to be lost? We brothers will now never know.

As soon as I saw Mussolini, I realised the origin of the notebook. I remembered my mother telling me that my father had been captured by Germans and then held by Italians, adding that the latter kept the prisoners short of rations and tormented them by pouring drinking water on to the sand, from behind the safety of a large fence, as the parched Allied servicemen looked on. Father had obviously told our mother much more than he had told his sons, but that was as much as she had shared. Articles I have read painted an even blacker picture of the behaviour of some Italian soldiers. I have since been very glad to read also of great bravery, ingenuity and kindness shown by Italians in helping Allied POWs later on in the war.

The jotter was a diary giving an insight into the thinking of a young man from Harris who had learned English at school and very well at that. When I read it, I recalled my mother telling me, more than once, what beautiful English my father had spoken. That was praise indeed from a Modern Languages teacher whose own love of language was lifelong and infectious, not to mention of great academic assistance to her sons and grandchildren.

His Diary:
~·~ A Window to a Father and Grandfather ~·~

The diary opens in October 1941 with a declaration of utter boredom following two years of service, albeit mainly spent in the very pleasant Harrogate area. Iain Alick tells of his having heard much about overseas service, leaving him completely dissatisfied with the monotony of his situation and he writes of how he hadn't volunteered for overseas service having made his mind up early on never to volunteer for anything while serving. This decision resulted from his hearing a Flight Sergeant asking, 'in a very sweet tone (pure camouflage)', for anyone who could play the piano. Five keen men had stepped forward only to be detailed to go and shift a baby grand.

The news of his overseas posting came to Iain Alick out of the blue and with it came twenty days of embarkation leave which allowed him a second visit home to Harris in the space of three weeks. That visit home was followed by a period of preparation and frustrating delay.

He describes the initial train journey, during which the main impression on him was that of complete silence in the carriage, where nobody was even reading and there were certainly no card games being played. He could tell that several of his companions did not relish the prospect of serving overseas, their faces betraying their emotions. Several were leaving established families behind, others having just married during the period of embarkation leave. With these men in mind, he dared to examine his own feelings and concluded that, while not thrilled, he felt pleasant anticipation as he was leaving boredom and monotony behind. He then felt self-critical for not feeling sad or homesick, before he justified himself on the grounds that he was a single man with few home ties.

The P & O liner 'Viceroy of India' was berthed at Glasgow, waiting for these young men to transport them to a destination overseas, to them as yet unknown.

Not for the last time in the diary there was, at this point, reference to what must have been very heavy smoking, Iain Alick enthusing over the bountiful supply on board of all popular brands of cigarette. No doubt many of these young men already smoked. If they didn't on embarkation, they might well have begun by the time they next docked. The Harris boys seem to have gone in for smoking in a very big way. My father told me that he had started aged twelve with Uncle Kenny MacKenzie, at ninety-three, recently claiming to me the age of eight for himself and also the absence of any ill effects!

Absolute secrecy was the keynote of the departure. Although some of the Glasgow men could actually see their houses, there was no one on the quayside to wish them a 'Bon voyage.' Iain Alick writes, 'The scene gave weight to the argument that modern warfare is a science, cold, systematic and entirely unsentimental.'

Once the vessel reached open sea, sea sickness began to afflict many. The detail which Iain Alick provided in his diary is not repeated here, where it will suffice to say that he did not succumb to seasickness himself, instead noting wickedly that the worst case was suffered by the son of a retired sea captain. The young man clearly took after his mum but, after a week in sick quarters, any thought of such banter, at the expense of the young fellow, was replaced by sympathy.

The 'Viceroy of India' formed part of a convoy which sailed due west, the rumour amongst the men being that they reached within a few hundred miles of the Canadian coast. The convoy moved in three lanes at an average speed of thirteen knots. At any one time, around twenty of the forty ships could normally be seen. The escort was formed of eight destroyers with HMS 'Resolution', a Revenge-class battleship, boosting the feeling of safety.

Most of the voyage seems to have been uneventful, but complaints about the food come over loud and clear. The initial promise offered by the first meal on board did not materialise, with scant allowance being made for the change in climate as the convoy turned south. Morning porridge followed by thick barley soup were described as unpalatable in the heat, while stewed rabbit for one lunch caused a massive strain on the sick quarters. Freshly baked bread with bully beef and pickles seems to have been a favourite meal, providing grounds for some positive reference to the diet at sea.

Monotony seeped into my father's life again and he seems to have enjoyed describing it. With scant reading material being available and lecture subjects being of little interest, out came the playing cards with Frank, Jimmy and Peter being Iain Alick's card playing partners... all afternoon and all evening.

Eventually, word filtered through to the men that there would be four days ashore at Durban and that they would be disembarking, ultimately, in the Middle East. The diary then gives a description of Freetown harbour with the locals attempting to sell iffy fruit from small boats and thereafter offering to dive for thrown coins. A few 'ersatz Glasgow tanners' in the shape of halfpennies covered in silver paper were thrown in the water. The discovery of the deception led to the divers' issuing of a loud torrent of swearing with strangely strong Scottish accents. Possibly of more interest to Iain Alick was the specimen hammerhead shark he enjoyed watching as it smoothed its way regally to and fro alongside 'Viceroy'.

The next entry in the diary revealed a liking for the pipes and a knowledge of Wordsworth. One night, the distant strain of bagpipes brought my father up on deck to find a bright moon in a cloudless sky with not a ripple on the sea, each ship showing all her lights to be reflected by the still surface of the water. 'Resolution' was lit up like some large, floating hotel. The distant strain developed into a full skirl as a motor launch swung around the stern of 'Viceroy' before cruising in and out among the anchored ships. On board was not a sole piper, but a complete pipe band. 'The Road to the Isles' was the tune being played as the launch headed for shore, its band fading slowly out of earshot. Iain Alick wrote that, like Wordsworth, he could truly say, 'the music in my heart I bore long after it was heard no more.' I had not previously been aware of my father's liking for the pipes or his enthusiasm for the works of Wordsworth.

My dad was clearly relishing taking in the experience of his voyage by this stage, there appearing to be no hint of anxiety as to where he might find himself at the end of it. He records that departure from Freetown prompted an atmosphere of energy, excitement and anticipation aboard 'Viceroy'. Even the entertainment improved. In this leg of the voyage there was organised sport and music, but best of all seems to have been the 'brains trust' sessions. For those, a padre took the chair and the 'trust' comprised a King's Counsel (K.C.), a surgical specialist, a county cricketer (and Welsh rugby international trialist) and lastly, a stage/screen star. No names were given. The K.C. seems to have impressed father most, with his years of thinking on his feet in court giving him the ideal preparation for dealing with some awkward questions.

On arrival in Durban, Iain Alick and his card playing buddy, Jimmy, appear to have benefited greatly from being befriended by the combined families of two regular sergeants major. The Hall and Moore families had followed their soldiers to India, Palestine and Egypt, but on a posting to the Middle East, the families had been transferred to Durban for the duration of hostilities and that at the expense of the British government. There, they were regarded by locals of non-British descent as 'evacuees'. Although far from the theatres of war and immune from attack, the 'evacuees' found it impossible to obtain work of any importance. The families took the opportunity of extending both real welcome and kindness towards two young Scottish servicemen. This, my father recorded with heartfelt warmth.

As his ship entered the Red Sea, Iain Alick noted a large vessel moving very slowly while attended by two tugs. He was told it was the 'George' which had, some months earlier, been bombed and set on fire off Alexandria in a very determined German attack. The reason for the ferocious and sustained attack was sitting on the deck of the 'George', or rather, it wasn't. The new model of German tank, which the British had captured in the desert, had been put on board the 'George' to be conveyed to Britain for scrutiny by experts. A very early attack on the British ship had suggested that the enemy knew of its special cargo, so the tank was quickly removed, with a cardboard replica being parked on the deck in its place. Further attack on the 'George' was inevitable, but the real German tank made it back to Southampton for detailed British examination.

Finally, the 'Viceroy of India' docked at Port Tewfik which is now known as Suez Port. From there, it was into the back of a Crossley lorry for a high speed, rough road trip to the Middle East Reserve Pool at Kasfareet where Iain Alick had to adopt the strange tactic of dressing up to go to bed and undressing on rising, so cold were the nights and so hot the days. At this large transit camp, he was introduced to the Middle East troops' menu which he obviously found very agreeable. The midday meal or 'tiffin' was usually bully beef, cheese, raw onions, tomatoes, lettuce and a variety of fruit. Dinner was at 4pm when the heat of the day had dropped a little and a cooked meal could be more appreciated.

The Suez Canal was only a short walk away from the camp and it allowed the men to enjoy some swimming. Other entertainment was available at a nearby RAF maintenance unit where there was an excellent canteen and a cinema. It was here that Iain Alick from Harris, on his only visit to that cinema, first came across Gaelic on film. They were showing a travel talk about the islands around Britain which included an Outer Hebridean fishing scene. Each island has its own distinct accent and there are differences in vocabulary, so my father knew the scene was shot off Uist, but he didn't specify whether it was North Uist or South Uist, a surprising omission of detail on his part.

The next entry in the diary refers to an order to leave for A.M.E.S. Reserve Pool at Almaza which I reckoned was a reference to Air Ministry Experimental Station, meaning it was to do with radar. It was ten miles out of Cairo.

Of Cairo itself, Iain Alick wrote that it wasn't mosques, pyramids, a sphinx or other relics of ancient civilisation which grabbed the attention, but rather the excellent catering. Opportunities to eat well abounded at all hours of the day and night. He listed a meal of several rashers of bacon, three fried eggs, chips, grilled tomatoes, lettuce/tomato salad, tea with bread, butter and jam, all for less than £4 in today's money.

I do not recall ever knowing what kind of cuisine my dad liked, but the diary does suggest that the young Iain Alick enjoyed his food, as detail is given of both good and bad meals. There is no indication as to whether or not he was reasonably well fed at the time of writing the diary. If he wasn't, the detail of his recollections must have been painful to record. In any event, Iain Alick and two of his friends seem to have hit Cairo pretty hard on their first evening, but not before fortifying themselves with a large meal of chicken with mayonnaise sauce. He records that they ended up 'a very jolly trio' and from what he writes that seems to have been commonplace at the time, with the desert being quiet and Cairo being full of servicemen who ended up in various levels of intoxication, behaving in various degrees of order. The word was that the 'Tommies' were managing to spend two million pounds a week in the city. That is the figure quoted in the diary. Apply an inflation calculator and the result is mind boggling.

It did not come as a surprise to me to find that my dad's diary evidenced a real liking for dogs, as there was a collie in the family home while I was very young. Chasing cars and rolling in manure seems to have been Scamp's favourite entertainment. The suspicion is that my mother will have negotiated (insisted upon) Scamp's re-homing, possibly with one of her husband's crofting or farming cousins. The dog in the diary was bought in Cairo by friend Jimmy who was sufficiently 'relaxed' one evening to find a puppy for sale outside a pet shop utterly irresistible. It might have been the pink ribbon the poor thing was being forced to wear round its neck. In any event, Jimmy was not to be dissuaded and beat the seller down to a few pennies.

Things looked up for the puppy straight away, as it was escorted by three British servicemen into the Café du Nord to be served a saucer of milk and broken biscuits by a straight-faced waiter. The puppy then became the centre of attention in the café and Jimmy the recipient of numerous offers of purchase. His love at first sight for the puppy seems to have faded as quickly as it had blossomed, as he decided to put Iain Alick in charge to auction off the little animal. An Australian produced the winning bid, representing a 250% profit for Jimmy. In the meantime, however, the excitement had accelerated Jimmy's intake of alcohol which, in turn, had revived his attachment for the puppy. He refused to part with the wee thing at any price. The three friends then seem to have separated, with my dad, after aggressively surviving a local taxi driver's attempt to rob him, eventually making it back to camp, only to blunder his way into an officers' tent. Finally, he found Jimmy and the puppy fast asleep in the correct tent.

All ended well for the puppy, as it was looked after very kindly until the time came for posting whereupon it was presented to a member of the permanent staff to become camp mascot.

Finally, on 1st April, my father was given word that he was bound for AMES Tobruk. He wrote, 'The mention of Tobruk was sufficient to send a thrill through me. During my last months in England, the siege of Tobruk occupied the headlines and was the main topic of conversation. The heroic defence by the British and Australian troops had become an epic of the war. It was discussed in homes, in clubs, in pubs and at work; it had strengthened the morale of the people more than propaganda or promises ever could and it had inspired every man in uniform to emulate the handful of their comrades in arms who were holding out stoically against the most incessant bombardment that the world had ever known. While on embarkation leave, I was often asked where I was going; I didn't know, but to the usual rejoinder of "Where would you like to be sent?" it is no wonder my reply was, invariably, "Tobruk." The desire on my part did not arise through any thirst for danger or adventure, but rather through curiosity to see the town and meet some of the men who had for so long stood together cheerfully among privation and suffering. As a matter of fact, by this time, the pendulum of war in the desert had swung west again, the 8th Army had linked up with the Tobruk garrison again and the element of danger was considerably reduced.'

Close buddy Jimmy had been posted near Cairo and Iain Alick found himself as a transport driver in a draft of seven who were complete strangers to each other. After two years together, he was sorry to part company with Jimmy.

On his way to Tobruk, my father spent much time in the company of a young Rhodesian who had been serving in tanks since the start of the desert war. While they passed through the Nile basin, the young man entertained with stories of his experiences, told with an air of humour, but not a hint of boastfulness. He had an abundance of tales about the personal prowess of other men and when he spoke of 'Jock' Campbell V.C. (Victoria Cross), under whom he had served, it was with the enthusiasm of a man who worshipped and adored his leader.

Several times, the young Rhodesian broke off, saying that he was going to check on a mate who was towards the front of the vehicle. Iain Alick eventually met the mate who was the elder of the two and who had clearly been badly affected by the war. The thought of returning to the front line had prompted him to attempt to bolster up his nerves with an overdose of liquor, but the effect was that, until sleep took him, he sat in the corner and wept silently. Iain Alick wrote of the patience and devotion of the younger Rhodesian which 'told of that deep knowledge and understanding of each other which comes only to those who have faced danger and death together.'

As they neared Tobruk, my dad noted that the landscape was dotted with the relics of desert battle – overturned lorries, wrecked cars and motorbikes, burnt out skeletons of trucks and planes. The ferocity of past fighting was demonstrated by the state of Sidi Barani which, through pounding from the air and artillery, had been reduced to a mass of ruins with not a single habitable building left. A nearby cemetery held the graves of fifty British officers and men who had fallen on the same day during the battle of Sidi Barani. Side by side, Iain Alick noted the graves of two brothers who had fought and died together.

Iain Alick's description of the scenes he came across is just that, a description. Factual. No hint of any effect on him or on those travelling with him is offered. Indeed, he moves on immediately to record his first of several encounters with scorpions.

~·~ Tobruk ~·~

The first impression of Tobruk was that of an air of peaceful tranquillity over both the town and its long, narrow, sheltered harbour. In fact, at first sight, the scene was devoid of any suggestion of war, but a closer look revealed the havoc which had been wreaked. What had appeared to be shipping in the harbour proved to be a collection of derelict ships outstanding among which were the Italian liner 'Marco Polo' and cruiser 'San Georgio'. The masts of several ships could be made out where destroyers and cargo ships had been sunk in deeper water. Tobruk itself was much bigger than imagined by Iain Alick and he had also much underestimated the damage, as he soon found that, in the middle of the town, not one building could boast an intact windowpane. Three quarters of what had been the town centre was reduced to a jumbled mass of fallen masonry which had been gutted by fire into the bargain. His unit's billet was on the northern edge of Tobruk in buildings which, in peace time, had housed the Italian military police.

My father clearly relished relating the next part of his story which brought a smile to his twenty first century reader who found the word 'scrounging' being introduced as if it were a novelty.

When the Italians were driven out of Tobruk, they left behind a massive amount of equipment. There were about a dozen motorbikes, mostly of Italian make, but with a few British Nortons and a German BMW amongst them. Some of these machines, found dumped in a wadi, were mechanically perfect, but the majority had been built from parts by the Italian men themselves.

Every room of the billet had a wireless set, built up from odd bits, but of most use was the supply of machine guns twenty of which were placed at intervals on the flat roof. The most popular machine gun was the small Italian Breda while the rest comprised Bren, Lewis, Browning and Vickers. I now know where my interest in guns came from and had a look for information on the Breda to find the view that this light, Italian machine gun suffered the risk of jamming and premature wear in the deserts of North Africa. It could overheat, causing a bullet in the chamber to ignite without the intention of the gunner and thereby put him at risk of injury or even death. The suggestion was that the Breda was distinctive in appearance, but widely viewed as poorly designed, one opinion describing the gun as nearly unusable in North African desert sand and dust.

In his diary, Iain Alick describes the working with guns, the scrounging of parts for a motor bike and generally the building of any sort of machine as being a hobby for the practically minded man with such enthusiasm as to refer to a spell in Tobruk as being like a first-class holiday! On reflection, this did not come as a complete surprise to me, as I recalled a pedal car built for me, while a very small boy. The memory came to me whilst sat at my solid, six-drawer, wooden desk, also built by my father around the same time.

My father describes how one of his new comrades, Eric Barrington, set about building a cook house, with his own contribution towards the building project being to ferry Eric and a work party, as often as required, to uplift bricks, tiles, wood and cement, all of which were available in abundance. It was on preparing for such a trip that he had his first experience of what he calls a 'Stuka parade.' Although there was a lull in the land fighting, the Luftwaffe hardly ever failed to pay Tobruk a daily visit. Such visits occurred mostly at dawn and were concentrated on the harbour area, especially if there was shipping in. His first experience was unforgettable. Initially, there was ack-ack fire in the distance, then the drone of enemy planes became louder and more distinct and finally, the whole defensive battery opened up; 'all Hell let loose.' Guns of all description pasted the sky with shells while the 'crump-crump-crump' of bomb salvos formed the background. During all this, the room shook and shivered as though about to collapse. On the hill behind the billet there was a Bofors gun post of the harbour defensive battery and, every time it fired, the concussion knocked plaster off the wall and on to my dad's bed. Such raids, however, did little damage with the view being offered that the anti-aircraft defences were the strongest in the world under the possible exception of those protecting Malta.

It was on a hot, still Saturday morning that Iain Alick took his Crossley lorry down to the cement store and sat having a smoke in his cab while the work party dealt with the loading. He had been enjoying a sunny, quiet and peaceful scene for a while before realising that he was catching the unmistakeable drone of approaching aircraft – lots of them. Up to that point, the only noise had been the distant rumble of another lorry and the light tapping of a hammer from the ordnance yard next door. He heard ack-ack opening up and stepped out of his cab to look up and see a group of '87s', escorted by Messerschmitts, approaching at height from the north. He joined the work party in the dubious shelter of the cement store and, with the raiders starting to dive, every gun opened fire. The ordnance yard, right next door, was clearly the designated target for this particular raid and bombs were soon screaming down and exploding on all sides. With each explosion, the men were thrown to the ground and so lost count of the bomb bursts. Their intention had been to try to match the number of whines of falling bombs with the number of explosions, so that they could tell whether any delayed action bombs were in use.

After twenty minutes all went quiet, so my father immediately got the work party into his lorry. Never before had he been so acutely aware of the clumsiness of his vehicle than on that attempted rapid departure. On reaching the billet, his Commanding Officer (C.O.) offered him a cigarette, in flagrant breach of the regulation against smoking anywhere near a transport vehicle. In response to the C.O.'s comment about an exciting morning, Iain Alick replied that the work at the cement store was not finished, but that he thought that a couple of time delay bombs had been dropped. At that very moment, two massive explosions proved him correct in what must qualify as a very close call for him indeed.

The men were only allowed a pint of water a day and looked for every opportunity to add to that meagre ration. For washing purposes, they often scoured the vicinity of the town in search of wells to supply a fifty-gallon water drum which they had positioned outside their billet. Muddy well water would settle in the drum, eventually, allowing the chance to syphon off a decent supply of clear water. Newcomers had noticed early on that that lack of water for washing did not seem to bother the more experienced servicemen in the unit. The latter had found that petrol formed an effective washing agent. We do hear of a 'bright spark' (!) who thought he would take things a stage further by heating his petrol. As you might imagine, this ended badly with an emergency visit to hospital.

Despite Iain Alick's earlier assertion that he volunteered for nothing, he writes that, in an effort to provide extra water for the building of the new cook house, he volunteered to be lowered into a well which was twenty feet deep. He was the smallest in the group and thought he had better offer, but only as a last resort. By this method all the drums were filled, but the only rope with the party turned out to be rotten and snapped as Iain Alick was being hauled back to the surface, leaving him to fall back down the well. For him, the second attempt to haul him out seemed to last forever until he was able to grip the narrow neck of the well and escape.

My father's diary entries often bemoan the desert conditions and their effect on the vehicles, while strongly asserting that the members of the transport section did their very best in the circumstances and were completely without blame. The lorries had to be driven over rocks and boulders, up and down hills and through wadis, leaving hardly a tight bolt on any of them. The only Commer in the section had no doors, starter or engine hood. Without its starter, it had to be parked on the hill facing the billet and the golden rule was never to stop the engine, at any time, other than on a downslope.

The daily swimming run to the hospital beach was a popular duty for which the Commer was used, the passengers often having to push start it. The beach was sandy and sheltered and, between two and four each afternoon, it resembled a popular holiday resort except that the hospital nurses kept to one end, jealously guarded by their escort of officers. Iain Alick and his pal Eric eventually found what they claimed was an even better place to swim, on the south of the harbour entrance. It had been a peace time Italian swimming and diving pool with steel ladders bolted to the rocks; natural caves even provided changing rooms. The clear, blue water of the Med was such a real antidote to the excessive heat, that a plunge in the sea was considered essential every time the men found themselves near the shore.

On the hillside opposite the billets, there were several cases of hand grenades plus boxes of fuses, just lying around, by the sound of it. With the help of an Irish ground-gunner, Eric and Iain Alick soon learned to fuse the bombs and to throw them accurately. After wasting a few in practice, they formed the idea of fishing with them. Several evenings were spent on the shore followed by suppers of fried fish. The sea dump, where all the empty tins were tipped, was alive with an unidentified species of fish which looked rather like a cross between a mackerel and a codling. The two had failed to catch anything with rod and line, but they soon demonstrated bombing to be a much more effective method. They would lob in grenades, wait for the explosions and then wade in to scoop stunned fish off the surface of the sea. They did, however, miss out on shark steak. South African soldiers on the other shore of the bay spotted a shark, but although they managed to shoot it, a very large fish supper drifted out to sea before it could be roped and dragged to shore.

Every now and again, in the close reading of my father's diary, I had to remind myself that I was reading the account of a man in his late twenties, not that of the father and rather strict headmaster I had known in my early boyhood. It was like meeting him again, but with roles reversed. The reader, father of three sons; the writer roughly the same age as these sons. There was no sadness in reading the detail of the diary, but rather an element of joy in recognising some shared traits and in coming to know my father a little better, albeit in retrospect. There was also some joy for me in recognising, in my own three sons, the 'have a go' spirit of their grandfather. In attempting to read the diary, these three young men found their grandfather's small, old fashioned script indecipherable. It is hoped that this account can open for them a 'window' through which to discover something of the man they never could have met.

In addition to swimming, fishing and scrounging parts, Iain Alick found the firing range to be an area of excellent entertainment. In the very early days in Tobruk, he and two others had spent several evenings gathering an arsenal of weapons comprising three Lee Enfield rifles, two Breda machine guns, a mark 1 Bren and one German rifle. There were, apparently, boxes of ammunition for the mere picking up.

The detail of this section of the diary demonstrates my dad's real enthusiasm for guns, as he writes that, of the Lee Enfields, the most accurate was the one that had been through a fire. Most of the wood had been burned and the men had to wrap the whole weapon in a field bandage, taking care to preserve the proper balance. Another had a bent barrel causing its bullets to veer two yards left for every hundred yards of flight. This needed too much patience to be fun and, what is more, the barrel heated up. The first Breda required a great deal of cleaning. They had to dismantle it completely and leave the parts soaking in oil and paraffin for several days. They had found the other Breda in an outlying wadi, looking in good order, but when Iain Alick took it for testing he found it unusable, describing how the bullet went off alright, but the cartridge also went off, only in small pieces and in the opposite direction! Iain Alick recorded only a slight gash in his left arm. No further comment on this weapon seems required.

Eric and my father decided to spend one evening on the firing range which the Italians had established before their departure. A machine gun and a couple of rifles were selected plus a variety of ammunition, including some tracer and explosive rounds, much of which was used to riddle a derelict tank. After that, as dusk fell, our policeman and future headmaster decided it would be fun to fire off some tracer ammunition out to sea into the darkness. Tracer fire was immediately returned in their general direction. Apparently, they had come close to hitting an Allied motor torpedo boat the crew of which were returning warning tracer shots. It worked. The suitably chastened two dived for cover.

Mention of this incident brought to mind a story told by Uncle Roddy, a real raconteur, about a fishing trip he had enjoyed on Loch Finsbay with Iain Alick sometime after the war. One misty evening, the pair of them were out in a rowing boat on the sea loch close to their homes. They took it in turns to row and fish. A second or two after swapping places in the boat, a bullet whistled right between them. Someone on the shore had decided it was a good idea to fire a rifle out to sea in the mist. Who knows the intended target back in those days…seals… seagulls? A second or two earlier and one or both of the cousins could have been dead. Yet another close shave. His son and grandsons wondered if Iain Alick recalled his own firing blind out to sea off Tobruk.

Perhaps it was the incident with the motor torpedo boat that cooled the enthusiasm for weaponry, as Iain Alick and Eric turned their focus towards trying to build a motorbike and began to devote all their free time to scrounging parts, of whatever make, in an attempt to build a 'mongrel machine.' This considerably safer choice of hobby took up the pair's spare time for the rest of their stay in Tobruk.

At this point in his diary, my father caused me a bit of a puzzle. He wrote that he had found an Italian 'Alci' in good condition and that he was to use it as the basis for the planned 'mongrel' motorbike. As I had done with the Breda machine gun, I wanted to investigate this make of motorbike, but I could find nothing relating to motorbikes with that name. A general search for an Italian WW2 motorbike immediately produced the Moto Guzzi Alce 500. My dad's 'i' for an 'e' error had hindered the earnest researcher!

There was a lucky find during the search for an Alce in the shape of a photograph of an Italian despatch rider, not only sitting on an Alce, but with a Breda machine gun set on a mount on the handlebars; a very cool, but perhaps unreliable, combination.

Eric and Iain Alick managed to commandeer the Alce despite their being discovered by an officer as they struggled uphill out of a wadi with their prized find. Eric's stripes and a cigarette appear to have helped the boys get official permission. With their Breda and Alce, the two mates clearly had an eye for Italian style. The suspicion is that what they were to endure in the months to come would do little to nourish their enthusiasm for things Italian.

The following passage from my dad's diary had a profound effect on me. Appreciation of my father's use of English, in what must have been extremely challenging circumstances, was mixed at this point with sadness for the father, for the mother and for the sons whose time all together had been cut so short. Playing golf, fishing and learning Gaelic properly are all on the list of things that I would have loved to have enjoyed with the father I lost, but this passage encapsulated for me the very essence of what had gone from our lives.

'In retrospect, I am convinced now, as I was then, that the weeks spent at Tobruk were the happiest weeks of my service, if fullness of living, freedom from care and the entire absence from boredom can be construed as a state of happiness. Through physical activity and the pursuit of engrossing hobbies I attained and maintained a state of mental and bodily health which refused to tolerate any thought of danger, but danger, although we would not admit it, was ever present. Nature, fortunately, has endowed the human being with a spirit of indomitable optimism which prevails over reason. The theory is generally accepted that man has transcended the lower animals in the struggle for existence by virtue of his reasoning powers, but it seems to me that the qualities of courage and bravery which are so essential to his survival are born of illogicality and are entirely divorced from reason. I can offer no other explanation for the attitude of contempt with which we came to regard the nocturnal, moonlight raids which often kept us awake until dawn. The heavier the raid, the more picturesque was the scene, with clusters of slowly descending flares turning the bright moonlight a sickly yellow hue which contrasted strongly with the incessant flashes from the ack-ack guns. Occasionally, a badly aimed stick of bombs would explode in the sand and, for a few minutes, the picture would be blurred by a cloud of dust and sand. Our billets suffered no direct damage, but a communicating door from our room into the cook's room was a nuisance. It used to fly open and keep banging to and fro in perfect time with the bombs. We finally had to nail it firmly to its post and keep it permanently sealed. Although there has been no land activity for several months, we know that the God of War has not yet been appeased in the desert and that one side or another would have to make the attack before the heat of summer reached its climax. We were not surprised when, towards the end of May, we learned that the enemy had opened an attack on the Knightsbridge Sector of the front, but none of us dreamt that Nemesis was so swiftly and inexorably moving down on us.'

It seems that my father made a point of visiting the ordnance yard every evening to see if he could gain first-hand information on the situation from the crews of tanks, which they had brought in for repair. He writes of one young sergeant who was very pleasant, but who came across as a little naïve. He was full of respect for his crew and they, absolutely, for him. They had been surprised at breakfast on the first morning of the attack and had to retire from the battlefield with engine trouble in their Grant. Regarding the outcome of the war in the desert, the young sergeant was in no doubt. He was confident in the new American and British tanks and in British strategy. In fact, Iain Alick wrote that his confidence was beyond measure and bade the young man farewell, at dusk, on his departure with crew and tank for the front line.

~·~ Siege ~·~

At this point in the diary, comes the reality of a garrison under siege, although Iain Alick warns his reader that, writing as a prisoner a year after Tobruk fell, the truth of events leading up to the defeat was still hidden from him and his fellows, 'whatever conclusions the outside world might have drawn.'

The contact with soldiers involved in the initial fight revealed nothing but a strong feeling of optimism with, perhaps, a tendency to underestimate the intention of the enemy and the scale on which he was prepared to attack. Word did, however, get to Iain Alick from a BBC commentator that the defence of Tobruk was not considered imperative. That must have sent a chill through him and through all his comrades. It certainly caused wild speculation as to the reasoning behind that apparent attitude.

Unit plans were drawn up for evacuation, should the order be given. As he knew the state of the transport, Iain Alick viewed these plans with some misgiving, but he set about giving the Crossley an overhaul.

On the 17th June, the noise of battle became much louder and, in the afternoon, it was officially announced that Tobruk had become a garrison, the Bardia road having been straddled by the enemy. Those who had been through the previous siege acted quickly and, within a few minutes, before rationing could be ordered, the canteen was sold out of cigarettes and large supplies of tinned food had been bought for hoarding. With the siege announcement, all evacuation work stopped and, incredibly, Eric and Iain Alick went back to motorbike building.

From the Tuesday evening to the Friday, shelling went on systematically. As usual, the ordnance yard was one of the main targets, so life in the billet became increasingly precarious with many and prolonged air raids being pressed home with fanatical determination.

The Bofors gunners on the hill behind the billet shot down a Junkers 88, the plane nose diving before bursting into flames and careering to a halt on the rocks by the shore. My father's description of this success is totally matter of fact even though his readers will appreciate that he and Eric had befriended the gun crew. There is neither drama nor triumphalism nor, for that matter, any mention of the fate of the German crew. He gives an insight into the strains of his situation, his attitude to life at the time and also the language of the day in his following paragraph, referring to the shooting down: 'Such incidents serve as a grim compensation for the strain of being bombed. Over Tobruk, with its terrific ack-ack barrage, a raider has only a fifty/fifty chance and, therefore, I considered an air raid as a fair fight, but not so with shells. They seemed like stabs in the back, hits below the belt when the referee wasn't looking. During these days, it often occurred to me that the continuous, even haphazard shelling would sooner break one's morale than the most intense aerial bombardment.'

The statement by Iain Alick to his young son that he had never fired a shot in anger may have been accurate, but it gave no hint of what he had experienced under fire. On a run to the rations dump with two others in the 'Jerry' Ford, which he described as being a dodgy vehicle, he came under direct threat of attack.

On the way to the dump, Corporal (Cpl) Fred Taylor shouted out and pointed to his left where three squadrons of enemy bombers were to be seen approaching at low altitude. Iain Alick and his two comrades were witnessing the vanguard of the most violent attack in the history of Tobruk, although they did not know it at the time.

The squadrons broke formation with the majority of planes heading for the outer defences. Some planes, however, much to the concern of Iain Alick and Cpls Fred and Jack in the 'Jerry' Ford, headed straight for them. While Iain Alick did not think they would waste bombs on a single truck, he did recognise the distinct possibility of machine gun fire. The stretch of road offered no chance of evasive action as the sides were steeply banked, providing no escape route to the wide-open spaces and pressing the throttle didn't help as the 'Jerry' Ford was playing up again, reaching only 20 mph instead of the earlier 45mph – a sitting duck. For some reason, the planes banked away from an easy, if minor, target.

The three reached the location of the ration dump only to be told it had been shifted. At that moment, three Italian planes appeared overhead. They, too, were looking for the dump and were dropping the occasional bomb while they were at it. Iain Alick, Fred and Jack jumped into the lorry, but the starter motor failed. For a few minutes, my dad struggled frantically with his vehicle while 'the roar of the planes multiplied a thousand times' in his ears. Eventually, the Ford was towed into life and the three of them made it to the new dump location to find that they were the first to arrive on what Iain Alick called 'that fateful Saturday morning'. On joining a group of soldiers, talk was that the situation was very serious indeed with a large-scale land and air attack under way. Bombs began to land on all sides, sending up fountains of sand. The men dived for cover, then tried to load the lorry between the waves of aerial attack. Suddenly, three planes swooped and released bombs which exploded very close by indeed. A second flight came in with their bombs overshooting by only 50 yards. There had been no time to get into the dug-out, but Iain Alick had made it under his lorry from where he watched with satisfaction as two of the planes were hit by ground fire.

The journey back was an anxious one, my dad having to coax the 'Jerry' Ford along at slow pace. Back at the unit, the sky was clear of aircraft, but the outer defences were taking a systematic pounding. The bombardment became ever more intense, the billet suffering some damage, but remaining intact.

The next section of the diary left me genuinely in awe of the spirit of these men.

Normally, the 'swimming liberty' lorry left at 2pm and the adjutant, determined to retain routine, decided not to cancel the run, provided a minimum of twelve made up the party. Leading Aircraftman Womack went looking for volunteers. Once again, Iain Alick broke his 'no volunteering' code of practice and joined the group. The run to the beach was perilous as an ammunition dump was being shelled, but the shells were whistling over and landing out to sea. Sadly, the enemy soon adjusted range and, shortly after getting into the water, the bold swimmers accepted that they were in what Iain Alick describes with masterful understatement as a 'hot spot.'

On his return, the billet remained intact and the C.O. was ordering an attempted break out with as much equipment as possible. At that point, however, the station itself was hit and totally destroyed.

Iain Alick's unit were ready and simply waiting for a final order, but what that might be, they could not guess, as they reckoned the perimeter defences had already been penetrated with Tobruk itself likely to be entered that evening. The suspense of the next half an hour was a terrible strain, my father realising that it was impossible for their luck to hold much longer in the face of such a rain of shells. Shortly after 6pm, the command to move came and the C.O. jumped into his staff car ordering the others to follow in the prearranged sequence.

At this precise point in the writing of the diary, something changes in my dad's circumstances. Over sixty diary pages of small, neat longhand in fountain pen come to a stop and the remaining pages are written in pencil with a much larger script, before they come to an abrupt halt. My feeling is that the changes were not for the better. I am convinced that the change from ink to pencil reflects more than a broken nib or lack of ink. His script alters markedly as does his 'voice'. What is more, there are plenty of blank pages left in the jotter.

The really frantic nature of the final hour of the Allies' hold on Tobruk is set out for Iain Alick's reader in the last few pages of his diary.

All gear that was not essential had been discarded. Iain Alick noticed a pair of Lewis guns standing against the wall, recently arrived, never fired. Eric remembered to pour a gallon of petrol on their precious motorbikes and set them alight. One of them had only needed a throttle cable to make it roadworthy.

While comrades piled into the back of his lorry, my dad remembered his wallet and dashed back in to look for it in his discarded kit bag. He picked up the wrong bag and, with his convoy starting to move, gave up on his search. They followed the C.O.'s lead down into the town and on to the main square where hundreds of soldiers had already concentrated. On the pavement at the main crossing lay the body of the military policeman who used to direct the traffic. Very recently, I read on the website, World War 11 Today, the words of a Clifford Spencer describing exactly the same scene. It was strange for me to read the description of someone who had, physically, been very close to my father while, no doubt, remaining a complete stranger.

Iain Alick's C.O. sought orders from above and returned with the instruction that the heavy lorries were to be parked at an angle across the narrowest points of the streets as tank obstructions. Having fulfilled that task, Iain Alick's unit were ordered by the adjutant to take up position with their rifles as some German tanks had broken through and were expected up the street at any moment. My dad glanced at the adjutant to see if he was serious, 'but no man was ever more so.' The adjutant had already armed himself with a rifle and was selecting a spot behind the remains of a wall. Father followed him in, but he had hardly taken position when a further order arrived… 'man the vehicles, drive them to the shore and push them into the sea.'

That further order from the C.O. undoubtedly saved lives including those of my dad and the adjutant, but the bravery needed to face German tanks armed only with a rifle gave rise to admiration and pride over seventy years later. Iain Alick, with equally admirable honesty, wrote that he followed the order to head for the sea with alacrity. Somehow, he got his lorry turned, while as many as possible jumped in the back, and headed for the shore. The whole city was under long-distance machine gun fire, but Iain Alick slowed his vehicle to let the C.O.'s staff car take the lead. It didn't appear. Any hope of defending Tobruk had been forsaken and the work of destruction had begun in earnest with a 'scorched earth' policy moving into full swing.

My dad pulled up near the shore, as he was anxious about the rest of the convoy. His own lorry was in good running order and he towed no trailer, but on the other hand, the C.O.'s staff car was much faster than his truck and the new 3-ton Ford had no faults. Eric Barrington caught up with father and the two of them smashed the petrol tanks of some good, but abandoned, vehicles before setting them alight. Then they heard a shout and found their mates from the Bofors gun crew waving from the rocks on the shoreline. They had abandoned their Bofors and headed for the shore under the protection of a single Bren gun.

From amongst the rocks, Iain Alick could see the cliff lying to the west of the bay and, before long, he saw some of his unit's vehicles being driven towards the edge, the drivers jumping out and the vehicles plunging into the sea below. He remembered his own lorry and was on his way back to it when he saw it going over the cliff edge. The rest of his convoy had caught up and completed its destruction for him. Often in the time to come, he thought of its precious cargo of bully beef and biscuits.

Shortly after that, the remainder of the men caught up. They had been forced to abandon their lorry and the staff car had been set alight by machine gun fire.

'June 21st. Captured on beach.' is the last entry in the diary.

At the point of initial drafting of this chapter, I knew only what was written in his diary plus the little information my dad had divulged to me in early childhood and the few comments made by our mother. I had also heard of his release through Odessa.

Capture at Tobruk, detention somewhere in Italy, detention in Germany or Poland, liberation by Russians, Odessa. That was it. My father's RAF records seemed to list a POW camp in Austria, but then put a line through it.

While the rest of my account was being drafted, some more information came to light through internet browsing. Comments and extracts from memoirs of other Tobruk POWs are readily available. They make for grim reading. There were, however, instances of mutual respect between Allied and German soldiers immediately after the fall of Tobruk and, indeed, mention of outright kindness by highly professional Germans. The conditions for the Tobruk POWs deteriorated when the Germans handed them over to their Italian allies, the compound at Tobruk being cramped and without sanitation. The conditions during transportation by ship from North Africa to Italy were atrocious.

The Odessa link led to some horrifying reading on the unforeseen implications of political agreement reached at the time. I also discovered that the 2600 Allied soldiers who were liberated by the Russians and repatriated through Odessa were those either held in outlying work camps in eastern Germany or Poland or were sick and left with medical staff in these areas, while the other POWs were marched westwards. This tied in with suggestions by both my mother and, more recently, Uncle Kenny MacKenzie that my dad had already taken ill whilst in captivity.

Further research suggested that the handwritten 'Laussa' on the RAF records which had appeared to be scored out was not a reference to Laussa in Austria, but rather to Laussig in the former

East Germany. I then traced my father to Camp 603 where 92 British POWs were held near Laussig. It was a local work camp to which father would have been sent after processing through Stalag IV-D Torgau (Elbe), Sachsen, Prussia.

John MacKenzie, Iain Alick, died on 22nd February 1966 aged 51. Like so many who suffered gross deprivation in POW camps, he died a relatively young man.

On a dark winter's morning, our mother tried to break the news gently to her young sons. She had obviously risen early, which was not a surprise to me, as I knew that a replacement teacher was due to arrive that day to cover our father's absence in hospital. My mother's choice of clothing did, however, surprise me; a black turtleneck sweater and black slacks did not look appropriate for the headmaster's teacher wife on a school day. My attempted joke about mother looking like a rocker was ignored, so I spoke instead about the get-well card my buddies and I had bought for my father, our teacher. It lay on top of the fridge awaiting signature.

Margaret told her elder son that his dad would not be needing the card now as he had 'gone to sleep.' The language used coupled with my boyish optimism led me to think that all would be fine, as my father must only be in a coma. My brother's six-year-old face turned red, starting from his chin and rising quickly to his hairline; then the tears came. At that instant, aged nine and for some reason knowing what a coma was, I knew I had got it completely wrong.

ITALY

~·~ Tregozzano, Tuscany ~·~

In this account of how the Scot came to meet the Italian and its celebration of the places which they subsequently grew to love as a couple, Italy, particularly Tuscany, is central. Italy was the scene of events which would have a massive influence on the lives of a young Harrisman and a teenager from Tuscany and, later, on the lives of their respective son and daughter.

Although Scots and Tuscans can have much in common, Scotland and Italy contrast each other in many ways. Most people would place the weather at the top of their list of contrasts. After thirty-five years of visiting each other's homeland and, in Ale's case, living in mine, I still find Tuscany too hot and she still finds Scottish weather...dire!

Ale's views on Scottish weather were further reinforced by her recent overhearing of advice on how to store an eighteen-foot boat for a Harris winter whereby the boat was to be kept on its trailer with both boat and trailer to be lashed tightly to iron rings set in the ground. These rings, in turn, were not simply pegged into the ground, but set in concrete blocks which, in turn, were not simply sitting on the ground, but dug deeply in. No, the boat was not to be covered. In case the wind got under it, the fitted cover was to be removed and stored in a shed, the boat being allowed to fill with rainwater and the sooner the better; the weight of the water would be extra insurance against the gales.

At the other end of the scale, in sunny Tuscany, I do not do sunbathing, at all. As with other foibles, I have an excuse from childhood, a very bad case of sunburn from the beach at Aberdeen being the reason for this aversion. The memories are of pain, Calamine lotion and flakes of skin falling to the floor from my back. I even remember being sorry for my mum, as I heard her say that it was all her fault.

The fact that I am not too keen on beaches either, presents a slight difficulty for someone who is married to an Italian many of whose relatives live by the sea and enjoy going to the beach on an almost daily basis. During the summer holidays, they encourage all the MacKenzies to join them.

In the earlier days, I would go along to the beaches, listen to the mums' chat, get very hot and sandy and then get into a car to go for lunch. This could be five minutes away or, if in Pisa, twenty-five minutes away, with a repeat performance in the afternoon. 'What's not to like?' you ask. Where to start would be my quandary.

First, even if a parking space in the shade had been found, the car, on re-entry, would still feel like an oven preheated to Gas Mark 6. Second, all the Italians would head home from the beach at the same time, both for lunch and in the evening…and then complain about the volume of traffic. That's before we get on to the trials of being, during July in Italy, a Scotsman with only the mildest of golfers' tan, the rest of him causing locals to reach for their shades, or worse still, simply to stare!

Salvation was found in the shape of the *scogli* at Marina di Pisa. They are massive boulders formed as sections of breakwater to protect the sand or pebble beaches and to provide lagoons for swimming, snorkelling etc. The *scogli* were, I noticed, also frequented by fishermen. There they were, only a few minutes on foot away from my sister-in-law's house. No four-wheeled ovens in traffic jams, no sand scalding the feet, tee shirt and camouflage shorts de rigeur – excellent.

I started taking a telescopic fishing rod with me to Italy. It was nothing fancy, but rather the kind of kit you would buy for a child or a complete beginner; rod, reel, line and lures all in the one package, cheap as chips it was. The lures were not satisfactory and were substituted immediately, but the rod had become a favourite and caught seven or eight different species of fish including, by accident, my one and only salmon to date.

I fished in the Marina di Pisa lagoons where the young Italian nephews introduced me to their favourite bait, Korean worms. These worms were nasty, hairy creatures with a desire to nip human fingers, but they did catch lots of little sea fish. I also went to the outer *scogli* to cast in the open sea. Ale would come along, sit on a flat rock and read a book while the local *orate* (golden sea bream) would ignore the Dexter Wedge with its fluttering action and treble hook, no matter how enthusiastically it was cast and retrieved. It wasn't the right gear for them; they knew it and I knew it. I hoped for something a little bigger and much more aggressive. It still hasn't come along.

~·~ A Fisherman's Tale ~·~

Ale's cousin, Maria Cecilia, in Tregozzano, Arezzo, invited the two of us to visit for a few days. There is a lake in front of her large, modern house and I would be very welcome to fish; I packed the telescopic spinner.

I did not know the full detail at the outset, but I was to be visiting what I would later come to view as the wartime 'crucible' of Tregozzano.

The grounds of Maria Cecilia's house form part of what had been a traditional Tuscan estate, hence the small lake. The house itself is on a slight rise above the lake. Surrounded by mature trees, the setting is sheltered and peaceful, the house modern, spacious and cool. The welcome was very warm with huge, heart-felt hugs all round.

The fish in the lake were mostly carp which is a species highly regarded by a vast body of the angling world, but far removed from what had become my usual quarry of trout, pollack and cuddies. I had seen carp fishing on television, but usually switched it off, as it seemed a slow business compared with my preferred moving amongst remote lochs or around equally remote points and bays. Agreed the fish were very strong and required a great deal of skill to catch, but it all seemed a bit static to me, between bites anyway. The sight of the anglers using seats and tents had done nothing to tempt me to try it out.

Ale's dad, Nazareno, was also visiting Tregozzano at the time, staying with his sister, Lucilla, in her house a couple of hundred yards away and only a short distance from their childhood home. He is a mechanical engineer, farmer, inventor and generally a genial genius. So, as usual, where anything remotely involves practical handiwork, Nazareno's help was sought to come up with bits and pieces to suit carp fishing. He provided and adapted a prosecco cork for a fishing float and sourced a nut from the garage to serve as a weight, a tin of sweetcorn from the little grocery shop down in the village completing preparations.

I felt it would be very fitting to have some joint activity in Tregozzano with my father-in-law and decided that I would make sure we had some time by the lakeside together. Thoughts of a circle being completed after seventy years were coming to mind. More on that will follow, but first, there is a fisherman's tale to tell.

The lake is about the same area as a full-sized football pitch and is surrounded by trees, bushes, reeds and bamboo, nothing of which makes casting a line easy, but there is a perfect shady corner with a bench under a large tree. I really was not expecting any success at all, as carp are much respected as suspicious fish, smart and difficult to catch. Into the greeny-brown, still water, a far cry indeed from a Harris loch, went a handful of sweetcorn, as seen on television, shortly followed by hook, line and sinker plus, of course, the large prosecco cork as the vital float. Perhaps it was time to sit back and enjoy the peace. Not a bit of it. In less than a minute, the cork went down, the rod went up and I felt the strength of a carp for the first time. At that point, I immediately understood the enthusiasm of carp fishers and the plethora of programmes featuring carp fishing. These are very powerful and hugely determined fish.

There was no question of eating the carp from Maria Cecilia's lake, although she did mention that a previous guest had unexpectedly gone off with ten. There is far too much involved in preparing them for cooking and, even then, some say there is more than a hint of mud in their flavour. In addition, there was a suspicion that the hostess considered them almost as pets.

Two strong carp caught and released in the first twenty minutes was a triumph in my eyes and I was all set to bask in it for a while when Ale and Maria Cecilia joined me from the house. After casting out another baited hook, I rested the rod between two rocks at my feet and sat back. All I had to do was lean forward and lift the rod as and when the prosecco cork dipped below the surface. The two Italian ladies were talking about translation work; I listened in until it started to sound a bit too intense. They were also both speaking at the same time and managing perfectly well, it seemed. I stopped trying to keep up and switched off.

I tried to switch back on in a hurry when, after a period of complete inactivity, the cork was pulled under the surface without any warning. As I leaned down towards the rod, it was dragged out of my reach and then off the bank and into the lake. A fish, having grabbed the bait, was heading off for the middle of the lake, pulling the entire fishing gear behind it. For a few seconds, the rod sped along the surface before its cork handle lost its battle to stay afloat and the whole lot disappeared from sight. Gone.

'How deep is your lake, Maria Cecilia?'

'About eight metres.'

'Ah.'

I was crestfallen.

The two ladies went back into the house, leaving me composing a text to Seumas back in Edinburgh. I wanted to tell my marine biologist son of my painful encounter with a huge carp and fully expected a richly deserved 'ROFL' (Rolling on Floor Laughing) in response, but I was interrupted by Ale's return with a glass of cold beer. She was full of commiseration and positive noises about making up another rod; there was a reserve spool of line with plenty hooks and her dad would be good for another weight and float from the workshop, after he had stopped laughing, of course.

Dejection was gathering fast, all the same, my favourite little rod, which had been all over the place with me, lying as it was at the bottom of a foreign water. Worse for me was the guilt of my laziness and, worst of all, my complete incompetence.

Ale thinks she was the first to see it when the cork bobbed up on to the surface of the water, right out in the middle of the lake. Presumably the line had been broken and the fish was happily free from its strange burden which now lay on the lakebed to be found, who knows when, or by whom. Although there was no breeze to speak of, we thought we could see movement and sure enough, the cork was slowly moving towards our left and heading for the bank below the house. The fish must have managed to break the line free from the reel and rod, but it had been left trailing the float. That was good news, as the fish could safely swim around the shallower areas of the lake without distress and the de-barbed hook would eventually drop out. I knew that the fish would still be able to feed despite the temporary presence of my hook and my conscience was partially salved by the thought.

The two of us continued to watch as the cork slowly, but surely, headed for the reeds at the edge of the lake. On its arrival, reeds began to shake. Was the fish trying to free itself fully? After a while, all went still, so we walked round for a closer look, finding the prosecco cork floating amongst the reeds. The fish had managed to get free.

There were some cut lengths of bamboo lying nearby on the bank, making it easy enough to select one of an appropriate length to set up a basic rod comprising a pole, a fixed length of line and a treble hooked sea lure. The aim was to recover the prosecco cork as it might well still have the weight and perhaps even the hook attached. If nothing else, that would save having to ask Nazareno for replacements. The embarrassing stuff would be easier to bear later in the evening, over dinner and a bottle of his wine.

Using the bamboo pole to cast a mini grappling hook towards the prosecco cork proved quite easy and I snared my target at the second attempt. I expected little resistance as I lifted the pole to bring my 'catch' to the shore, but something was stuck. The hook was probably still attached and caught in a clump of weed.

Much stronger upward pressure on the bamboo pole brought some release and, to my astonishment, I found myself looking at the tip of my precious little spinning rod. It wasn't the hook that was caught up in the vegetation, but rather the reel. More and more of the rod rose out of the water. The last pull released the reel from the weed on the lakebed, leaving me holding my complete fishing outfit.

The power of that fish had been enough to drag the rod and reel fifty yards to the middle of the lake and then another fifty to the reed bed. There, the fish had combined its own 'catch and release' with the return of the rod, reel, hook, line and sinker, the prosecco cork flagging it up on the surface.

Once it was cleaned up, the little rod caught another eight carp that day and managed to stay on dry land too.

ALE'S DAD'S WAR

~•~ War Zone Survival ~•~

Tregozzano is a tiny village about three miles from Arezzo in Tuscany. Many of its properties are scattered across the hills which rise, gently at first, from the broad basin of the River Arno as it makes its way south before looping round and heading for Florence, then Pisa and the coast.

Arezzo is a small, strategically important, historic city about fifty miles southeast of Florence. It and its surrounding villages witnessed an intense struggle during WW2 as the Allies were met with very fierce German resistance in June and July 1944 during their advance northwards through Italy.

Tregozzano played an essential part in the coming together of the families Gori and MacKenzie. Over the years, I had heard many different parts of the story from my father-in-law and eventually, during a series of most enjoyable dinners in Marina di Pisa, I captured Nazareno's recollections of events; only Nazareno, Ale and I were at the table, my mobile set to record.

Nazareno's story included reference to the brutal, complicated times in Italy during his mid teenage years, but his description of events concentrated on the battle for Arezzo and the subsequent period of occupation by Allied forces.

Ale's aunt, Lucilla, who still lives in Tregozzano with her daughters, Maria Cecilia and Maria Gaia, was fifteen at the time, is now in her eighties and, both elegant and extremely kind, is one of my all-time favourite ladies. As a girl, she witnessed unspeakable horror after Italy surrendered to the Allies and then, almost immediately, declared war on Nazi Germany, thereby becoming a country occupied by enemy soldiers. There was much activity by strong partisan groups in the Arezzo area, countered by Nazi troops and fascist bands. While the Italian people suffered great harshness indeed during a bitter and shocking period, it is remarkably fortunate that Nazareno, his brothers and sisters, and indeed their parents, all survived relatively unscathed.

From the perspective of the Allied armies, their campaign through Italy encountered both very difficult terrain and most resolute, skilful and ruthless German defence. Nazareno's story began in the summer of 1944 with the Allies slowly approaching from the south. During this period, there had been attacks by partisans on German soldiers in the area between Tregozzano and Arezzo which had prompted reprisals by the German forces. Some local people had been taken away and Nazareno suspected that they would have been shot. He spoke about this in a very calm, matter of fact manner as he recalled events that had taken place more that seventy years previously. Those taken away probably had little or nothing to do with the attacks on the Germans, but it was a practice employed by the occupying Germans with a view to suppressing the activity of the Italian Resistance. Some of this ghastly activity took place very close to the home Nazareno shared with his parents, brothers and sisters on the hill just above the centre of the village and from where his father practised as the local doctor.

One day, two German soldiers came to the family home shouting, '*Raus! Raus!*' The Gori family was being ordered to come out of the house. When Nazareno's mother approached the troops, it was clear that the family had to leave their home immediately, as they were being ordered up into the hills above Tregozzano. In fact, the family were being moved behind the German defensive positions, Nazareno's thinking being that this was to prevent the possibility of any information on these defensive positions being passed on by civilians to advancing Allied troops.

Nazareno's mother, Angelina, gave instructions to the young ones for the immediate preparation of bags of food, clothes and kitchenware. He recalled that his own load was a bag of bowls, cups, plates and the like.

In addition to the immediate family, there were some other relatives staying at the Gori house when this rough eviction took place. One was Zio (Uncle) Zanobi who, at seventy years of age, was a retired doctor and a great-uncle of Nazareno. A total of fourteen were in the family group which was marched away at gunpoint. Zio Zanobi was in the lead with a German soldier bringing up the rear. On reaching a fork in the road, Zanobi started to take the wrong direction by heading back towards Arezzo rather than higher up into the hills. This enraged the German soldier who started roaring at the family before firing off several shots into the air. Nazareno expected the next shots to be aimed at his family and steeled himself to smash into the German using his heavy bag of kitchen crockery as a weapon. Crisis was averted by Zio Zanobi's instant appreciation of the situation and immediate about turn.

The teenage Nazareno's preparation to take on a heavily armed German soldier with no more than a bag of dishes, heavy but cumbersome to wield as weapon, was every bit as brave as my father's preparation to face a Panzer while armed with only a rifle. It was not the only time that a similarity between those two was noted.

Later in the march, Zanobi attracted further unwelcome German attention. He was wearing brand new, light brown boots and, when the family passed a group of German soldiers, he was ordered by an officer to sit down and take them off. The officer in charge duly tried the boots for size, seemed satisfied and gave Zanobi in exchange his own army issue boots with holes in the soles. The incident had obviously left a lasting impression on Nazareno who shook his head slowly at the memory of Zio Zanobi wearing battered, Wehrmacht combat boots. The sight of the German officer in Zanobi's boots was not recalled with a smile by Nazareno, but rather with a grim-faced comment that he had noticed SS men amongst the group of Germans. Nazareno did not specify which branch of that Nazi paramilitary organisation was represented. He didn't have to. Those initials were enough to deliver his message to me.

Moving on, the Gori family saw that the Germans had ordered Italian civilians to prepare holes for the laying of landmines, so they had no hesitation whatsoever in going further into the hills before looking for a place to camp for the night. Their trigger-happy German had left them by this time and eventually, after moving at a pace of their own choosing, they came to a wood where some trees had been felled, trimmed and logged, others having been felled, but left with branches still intact. The Germans had used one pile of logs to build a sentry post, so the Gori womenfolk and younger children used that as a shelter for the night. The men and older boys slept, or tried to sleep, in the open with only the branches of felled trees to protect them.

In the morning, Nazareno recalled, the older boys wanted very much to contribute to the safety and welfare of the group and constantly pressed their elders for instructions on what to do. Their mother, Angelina, put together some food and Nazareno's father, Dr Gori, tended to those who were suffering from the forced evacuation and arduous walk. Nazareno and his cousin, Gigi, were seriously concerned that their group was exposed on a lightly wooded hillside. In particular, they were worried about the firing of the type of shell which exploded in the air above the target to shower the enemy below with lethal fragments and splinters. These air bursting shells were used mostly against infantry in the open, but would not, apparently, penetrate trenches or strongly protected areas. Mere branches, however, offered no cover worthy of the name.

At this particularly serious point in the recording, there is an element of light relief as Nazareno and I try to get around some of the large gaps in my Italian vocabulary. Nazareno uses the word *scopa* which I think is something to do with a brush, as in floor brush. We then start having a guessing game type of conversation discussing the flowers on bushes in the north of Scotland, the cleaning out of cow stalls and even the making of charcoal before a little lateral thinking by me finally works out that Nazareno is talking about broom, the hardy bush.

The next problem arises when Nazareno is talking about the group's lack of tools. The Italian for a 'tool' and a 'wood saw' I am familiar with, but *roncola* – not a clue. So off we go again with talk of a half-moon this time. We move on to the flag of the

Soviet Union and 'Eureka!' we have a sickle type of tool called a *roncola* in Italian.

It takes a little imagination on either side, but we always get there eventually. With my vocabulary extended, Nazareno continued.

The Gori family gathered together bundles of broom which had already been cut and tied up by woodsmen, Nazareno's plan being to build a lean-to with the hope that it would offer at least some shelter and protection. He wanted to use branches of oak as a frame to support the bundles of broom, but the lack of tools was a serious obstacle. He did, however, know that there were seventy or eighty other people who had also been sent from their homes to survive, as best they could, up in the hills and set off to see what he could find.

The young Nazareno was in luck. A woodsman with another group was prepared to lend him some tools including a *roncola*.

The construction of the very basic shelter took a little longer than he had anticipated, but once it was finished, Nazareno set off to return the tools. About halfway to where the woodsman's group was staying, he heard the whistle of a shell or bomb coming in, so immediately threw himself down, pressing his face into the earth, wishing he could burrow right into the ground. There was an explosion only a few metres down the slope from where he lay. The noise was incredible, but so was his luck, a minor cut being the only injury he could find on checking himself over.

He jumped up and ran off. Unfortunately, however, in the stress of his situation, he left the tools behind.

Nazareno's had been a very lucky escape. He managed to make it back to his family safely and, once the bombardment was over, he left again to pick up the tools, intending to return them to the woodsman, but he was in for nasty surprise. For the young man, the absence of any sign of the tools at the site of his bomb blast was devastating; he was utterly dismayed. No doubt they had been gleefully picked up by others who were desperate to make some shelter. Whatever had happened, they were gone.

The woodcutter was not a happy man when Nazareno confessed that he had lost the tools. He was not in the least interested in the circumstances and let loose a mouthful at Nazareno. Far worse for the young man than any swearing, was the name-calling of his parents. Times were desperate. The Gori family and their neighbours had been driven into the hills with little food and less shelter; bombs and shells were landing in their vicinity. Nazareno snapped and snarled, fear and anger combining. He said something which has troubled his conscience, from time to time, ever since. His retort to the raging woodsman was to the effect that he could take himself off and step on a mine.

After the eleven-day battle was over, Nazareno heard the terrible news that the angry woodcutter had, indeed, lost a leg to a land mine. There was no link whatsoever between the verbal exchange and the tragedy which befell the unfortunate man. It is to be hoped that, in the recounting of the event, over seventy years later, a very fine, elderly gentleman, great of both faith and intellect, will cease to suffer any pangs of conscience over a heated exchange in massively stressful circumstances.

After Nazareno's group had been in the hills for four or five days, their food supply was running critically low, with no meat left at all. He decided that he would head down into one of the valleys to see if he could catch some fish, by one means or another.

His initial thinking was that, where there were flat stones in the riverbed, he could lob in some large stones hoping to stun the fish and then scoop them up. This plan sounded broadly familiar. It would seem that my dad, Iain Alick, may have passed reasonably close to Nazareno, in very harsh circumstances, on his way from Italy, through Austria to Stalag IV-D. His advice to Nazareno would have been to forget the stones idea and to scout around for abandoned hand grenades, as they are a much more efficient method of fishing!

On his way down to the river, dressed, he recalled, in shorts and a red shirt, Nazareno encountered a young German soldier who was setting out a telephone cable. Neither of them could have been keeping a very good look out at the time, as each was as surprised as the other. Nazareno acted first by offering a cheery 'Guten Tag.' His use of German in his greeting seems to have gone down well, as it was reciprocated. With little apparent difference in their ages, there was a big grin from each of them before they simply carried on doing what they were doing. It could well have been so different between two young men whose countries, by then, were at war with each other.

Further down, closer to the river, Nazareno heard two voices speaking in German. On this occasion, he had the time and presence of mind to whip off his bright red shirt rendering himself much less obvious through the branches. Two older German soldiers were patrolling the riverbank on a cart drawn by a mule. Nazareno decided, wisely, not to test the war zone relationship any further and instead to lay low until the cart had moved slowly past his hiding place. Once the coast was clear, he scrambled right down the bank on to the bend in the river where he hoped to try for some fish. There, he made a very lucky find in the shape of a fish trap, a conical sort of creel. The creel itself was a wonderful discovery, but even better, there were five fish trapped inside it. Back the fish went to his family, securely wrapped in the red shirt and, with them, the means to catch some more. His afternoon had been very fruitful, if a little too tense for comfort.

He recalled again that his family were not alone in being turned out of their homes at gunpoint to fend for themselves as he described how the various groups were able to exchange resources and ideas. At one point, Nazareno was alerted to a cornfield which had not yet been harvested. As it was said to be in a safe area, he led a number of his band to harvest some corn with nothing more than knives. Once back at the camp, he tried to fashion a stone-age style hand grinder for the grain and did well enough for his mother to produce coarse flat scones from the rough flour. Without salt, neither the fish nor the camp-fire baking was very flavoursome, but of vital sustenance, nevertheless.

News reached the Gori family camp that a bomb had hit a cowshed not too far away, so Nazareno headed off with a leather bag on his back to see if there would be the chance of some fresh beef. Word had obviously spread quickly, as he arrived to find that the poor farmer had a queue at his steading, an impromptu farmer's market. As Nazareno waited his turn, a group of partisans took some meat from the farmer telling him he would be paid properly after the war. The farmer was not in a position to argue.

Nazareno Gori, a brave, resourceful young man did his family proud during that immensely difficult period.

~·~ The Allies Arrive ~·~

After many days of intense bombardment, it appeared that the Germans were retreating from their positions. Nazareno recalled seeing a German soldier help a wounded comrade leave the area, the comrade having suffered catastrophic damage to an arm.

Far below, the woods were on fire at a point where many had sought refuge from the bombardment and its dreaded shrapnel. Many civilians had been killed and wounded. At one stage, the river level being low, Nazareno crawled between two large rocks which would normally have been submerged. From there, he could see his father, Dr Gori, leaving his own cover to respond to the cries for help. He recalled seeing his father carrying a makeshift shield as he moved amongst the injured, a frame of canes and branches interwoven with vines. Normally used for setting out figs, grapes and tomatoes to dry in the sun, it afforded Dr Gori a little protection from flying debris.

As the Gori family group tried to move generally in the direction of home, they constantly had to seek shelter as shelling and bombing erupted. During a lull, Nazareno was called by a couple of men who were sheltering under a bank with an old mattress affording them some minimal additional protection. Nazareno could not guess their nationality. Much of what they said seemed to end in 'ov' or 'off'. Russian? They seemed to have been prisoners of war who had been used by the Germans to carry munitions. They were likely to have been Russians who had taken the chance to escape and mingle with Italian civilians. Nazareno chose not to stay long enough to establish their nationality.

There was still German presence in the area so, as much as possible, the Gori group lay down amongst the uncut broom which gave both some shelter and some comfort, presumably more psychological than physical. At one point, Nazareno heard orders being given in German only a few yards from where he lay. Once the voices had faded away, the Italians struck out for home again. Nazareno remarked that the woodcutter with whom he had had the very angry exchange had decided to take the most direct route. Nazareno and his sister, Lucilla, led their group on a different course. It was, however, on this last leg of the journey home that the young Lucilla came across the truly unspeakable sight of the effects of high explosive on a German soldier; a German helmet, which she thought might be useful as a container, turned out still to contain much of the owner's head. The resilience of the Gori children was sorely tested during these days.

Very close to their house, the family found that Allied soldiers had already checked the cart track for mines, red and white tape being set up to show the route of a safe corridor. It was at this spot that Nazareno remembered seeing an Indian soldier for the first time. The vivid memory has stuck with him; very tall, turban, huge beard. Goodness knows how many nationalities passed through the Arezzo area, between combatants and prisoners of war.

Around a corner, Nazareno, Lucilla and their brother Pierluigi came across a group of tanks which the youngsters were relieved to see bore British markings. Sweets and chocolate were offered to them by the crews. Nazareno had taken German at school, but Pierluigi was learning English as was Lucilla. The Italian youngsters combined quickly to work out that the British wanted to know if they had seen any Germans during their journey home. Nazareno borrowed binoculars from a tank commander and pointed out to him the location of the only defensive position they had seen which was still occupied by Germans. Nazareno did not know what resulted from the information he had provided to the tank crew and, in the recording, he and I can be heard agreeing that it was probably best not to dwell on the point.

As he reached his neighbour's house, Nazareno came across a British armoured car. The driver was at the wheel with a couple of soldiers standing with him. The young man chose not to attempt to speak to the British soldiers, thinking that his English was not good enough. As he turned away to carry on towards his own house, he heard the whistle of an incoming shell and threw himself to the ground. After the huge blast, Nazareno could see no sign of the British or of their vehicle. It seemed that there was still some German presence in the area and fire had been directed on to his neighbour's house. He hoped the British soldiers had survived the explosion, but he did not stay around to find out. He had had another very narrow escape.

As he checked out the vicinity of his own home, he soon found a large group of armoured vehicles and lorries which signalled a significant British Army presence in Tregozzano; that presence was to last over a year. The villa near the Gori house was empty at the time, the owners being in Florence, so it was immediately requisitioned for occupation by British officers.

Before the main battle, Nazareno had taken it upon himself to hide his father's precious car, the Fiat 'Topolino', but not before he had stripped it of its wheels and battery which were then hidden in a nearby ditch. The car itself was concealed in thick bushes in the woods. He would have to get it sorted out again, a task he would have enjoyed, then as now.

Some of the British soldiers had visited the Gori household as a gesture of goodwill and Nazareno was able to scrounge from them a litre of proper petrol which he knew would help in getting the 'Topolino' started. It would be much better than the 'green stuff' the Italians had been reduced to using since their surrender. Luckily, although the area where it had been hidden had seen intense fighting, the car was undamaged. Close by, amongst much discarded weaponry and ammunition, he found a submachine gun in very good condition and decided to hide it between the axle and floor pan of the 'Topolino'. Once the wheels and battery had been located and refitted, he treated the little car to some British Army petrol, directly into the carburettor, thereafter managing to coax the engine into life. The young man did after all, go on to study both aeronautical and mechanical engineering and remains greatly respected for his ingenuity and practical skills. The 'Topolino' was, of course, essential to Dr Gori for his patient rounds.

Some months after the main battle for Arezzo, fresh British soldiers were welcomed on their arrival in the village. The first of these soldiers befriended by the Gori family was a sergeant named Walter Firstbrook who latterly lived in Oldham. Recalled as a warm and friendly man, Walter even spoke a little Italian and was invited into the Gori home where he entertained them on the piano. It is not hard to imagine the benefit, both to the family and to Walter and his comrades, of a little conviviality after the great hardships and dangers they had all suffered.

The family also invited the officers from the neighbouring villa to join them. Nazareno remembered, in particular, coffee and wine being enjoyed after dinner. The captain was more reserved than the others and also drank more wine. The padre, John Fletcher, having been seconded to the London Scottish from an English infantry regiment instead of enjoying home leave, got on very well indeed with the family.

Nazareno saw the opportunity of exchanging Gori wine for British petrol…not with the officers, of course. The difference between the 'green stuff' and real petrol was well worth some wine and some risk.

Padre John Fletcher would sometimes accompany Dr Gori on his patient rounds, but it is not known whether he was aware that the 'Topolino', in which he was a passenger, was running on British Army fuel. He was, it seems, of huge help to Dr Gori as the local doctor made his way around what was, effectively, Allied occupied territory.

His dealings with other ranks did not always go smoothly for Nazareno, as his attempts to speak English occasionally resulted in the odd German word popping out, resulting in serious ribbing for the Italian teenager. On one occasion, the teasing got a little too boisterous with one of the squaddies punching him on the arm. Naturally enough, the young man yelled in Italian, '*Basta! Basta!*' which, as many will know, was to let the Englishman know he'd gone far enough. Unfortunately, the Italian sounds rather like an English term of abuse. Result? A torrent of swearing in English was directed at the bewildered youngster. He still remembers most of the words. There may have been some wine involved, but, in any event, the kindly and sensible Walter Firstbrook came to the rescue. His explanation turned the tables on the ranting soldier who took his subsequent rinsing in good part.

Nazareno broke off from his recollections to explain his reference to the petrol substitute which compared so poorly to the British Army petrol. Warming to his subject, he explained that the Germans had been producing synthetic petrol on a large scale. In Italy, the 'green petrol' could be produced from potatoes and cereals, amongst other things. It was nothing like as good as proper 'red petrol' access to which on a regular basis would be of huge benefit to Nazareno's father and his little Fiat. The young man saw the chance of expanding on his earlier exchanges of a bottle of wine for a few litres as his rapport with the British troops increased. A two-litre bottle of Gori wine would be exchanged for the filling of a twenty-litre canister with British petrol. The benefit to his father, of course, was enormous. The benefit to the soldiers was pretty good too.

During their period of being stationed at Tregozzano, the officers became regular visitors to the Gori family home. They would come over from their villa after dinner, have coffee, listen to the radio and generally enjoy company. The young Nazareno was particularly comfortable in the presence of an army doctor, Kinsella and of John Fletcher, the Scottish padre. The fact that the captain tended to prefer Gori wine to conversation clearly made a lasting impression on the young Nazareno, as he mentioned it more than once. John Fletcher's willingness to accompany Dr Gori on his rounds made a great and lasting impression on the whole Gori family.

Like many a good storyteller, Nazareno is not averse to going off on a tangent. Just as he was about to reach a critical point in his recollections, he decided to break off in the direction of a motorbike. Having impressed with his description of looking after the 'Topolino' while the battle front passed through, he wanted to reminisce about his efforts to build himself a motorbike. If for no other reason than a sense of familiarity, his interviewer encouraged him to go ahead.

Nazareno explained that there were lots of bits and pieces of machinery lying about, so he focussed first on trying to build an engine. He found many of the components he needed, but he was lacking a piston. During one hunt for parts, a neighbouring farmer, Enzo, asked Nazareno what he was after.

'A piston.'

'What's that? What does it look like?'

Nazareno told Enzo that it looked a bit like a cup, but Enzo moved away, seemingly not really any the wiser. A few days later, Enzo called over to Nazareno that he had found his cup for him. True enough, there it was, exactly the part the teenager was looking for.

He spoke of how he had to be careful about the 'Red Caps' or military police. Surely, they would be more interested in the wine for petrol exchanges than his scrounging for motorbike parts. His efforts appeared to grind to a halt and it was only once the British Army was preparing to leave that he managed to obtain the rest of the parts he needed from the surplus stores to complete his bike. He did not mention whether barter was involved or not.

Returning to his main theme, Nazareno prepared to explain how his enthusiasm for British Army petrol nearly cost him his life.

~•~ The Fire ~•~

One evening, while the officers were socialising with his parents, Nazareno reckoned it would be a good time to do some bartering with the ordinary soldiers. It was dusk and therefore pretty dark in the garage which had no artificial light. The garage, integral to the family house, was quite spacious and he recalled that it had sufficient room for it to be used for the storing of lemon trees to protect them from frost during the winter. Nazareno mentioned that there were some drainage channels across the floor, reference to which did not appear immediately relevant.

Only one vehicle was parked in the garage that evening, the 'Topolino', on account of a problem with its differential, being parked outside. Bicycles were also stored in the garage so Nazareno had to be careful in the near darkness. Having entered the garage through the connecting door from his father's office, he did not even have the benefit of the main garage door being open, so decided to light a match. With movement awkward in amongst the parked bikes, the match touched some paper which, of course, immediately caught fire. The young Nazareno appeared to discount the risk, as the paper allowed him to see much better while it burned brightly on the floor where it had fallen. He may even have considered it a stroke of luck.

In order to empty one canister completely for use in his intended trade, he tried to pour its dregs of petrol into another canister without realising that the second one was partly squashed. Some petrol spilled and was gathered in a drainage channel along which it flowed straight to the burning paper. Up went the petrol.

Nazareno's first instinct was to run and that's exactly what he did, straight out of the main door of the garage, before pausing to consider that the remains of one canister plus two full canisters of petrol were still in there. Fifty litres of precious fuel or a bomb with the fuse activated? He did not divulge which thought was uppermost in his mind initially, but he realised very quickly that his parents and the officers would be unaware of the grave danger. Wearing only a shirt and shorts, back in he went, three times, to remove the canisters.

Whether on account of adrenaline or focus, he does not know, but he saw that he was on fire before he actually felt the excruciating pain.

As Nazareno made his way towards the front door of the house after depositing a canister of petrol in the safety of the woods, his father called out to him to get water from the well. Dr Gori could not have realised, at that point, that his son was badly injured. Nazareno tried to do as he had been told, but he could not draw up any water at all, his hands being too badly burned to allow him to grasp the chain for the bucket.

Very quickly indeed, the battalion fire crew was summoned and began to deal with the fire which, fortunately, remained within the confines of the garage.

In the chaos, Nazareno decided to go into his home, intending to lie down until his father could come and help him. The house was deserted due to the ongoing drama, so he headed instead for the farmhouse next door. The evening was still, leaving the area round the house heavy with smoke from the midst of which he heard an elderly neighbour screaming in fear. Diverting to help her, he bent to pick her up, but as he did so, her rough clothing pulled the skin from his chest and arms. The pain was intense and had the young man struggling to stay on his feet.

After he had calmed the little old lady, young Gori set off again, this time heading straight for the farmhouse. It too was deserted, but he spotted some olive oil on the kitchen table and smothered himself in it before collapsing on a bed.

Having been both unwise and unlucky in the first place, there had been a turn in Nazareno's fortunes which he only discovered later. The loud bangs of the bicycle tyres as they exploded in the heat alerted both his parents and the British officers, so the battalion fire crew attended quickly, ensuring that the damage to the building and contents was not nearly as catastrophic as it might have been. The damage to Nazareno, however, was worse than he knew.

He recalled waking up with one of his sisters leaning over him asking him how he was. Her enquiry of, '*Come stai? Come stai?*' was met with a less than gracious, '*Vai via!!*' as he ordered her away from him. His description of how Lucilla's long hair was brushing against his burns, as she bent over him in her concern, explained his reaction eloquently enough. He had suffered extensive first and second-degree burns.

The local pharmacy was closed due to the chaos of the times, so Dr Gori had no access to the medical supplies he needed to help him treat his son properly. It was at this point that the friendship which had formed between the family and the British soldiers played a vital and unforgettable part in Nazareno's life.

In the recordings, Nazareno declares more than once of the army doctor, Dr Kinsella, '*Mi ha salvato la vita.*' 'He saved my life.'

With the young Italian being in great pain, Dr Kinsella was in a position to administer morphine which would otherwise simply have been unavailable, even to Dr Gori. Nazareno's clothes, or rather, what was left of them, were cut from him, revealing the full damage to his arms, upper body and legs. The burns to his face had been obvious. The army doctor insisted that he learn to drink while lying down and to drink copiously in that position. Looking back, Nazareno reckoned that he had benefited from the doctor's experience in dealing with the burns suffered by tank crews. Glycerine gauze bandaging and constant visiting to tend to him, saw Nazareno make steady progress. Rosa, from a neighbouring farm, visited him and pronounced that, as he had been burned while the moon was waning, he would make a full recovery. Even country superstition was trying to work in his favour!

Whether Dr Kinsella knew it or not, the recordings do not reveal, but Nazareno fixed the differential problem in his dad's little Fiat before he was even fully out of bandaging. I had not heard that previously, but somehow it didn't surprise me. I chose not to ask if the hidden weapon had contributed to the problem in the car's axle.

The impression made on the young Nazareno by the British officers, particularly Padre John Fletcher and Dr Kinsella, and by Sergeant Walter Firstbrook went far beyond his gratitude for the provision of medical care which, without doubt, was lifesaving. His emotion as he gave his recollection of these men, over seventy years later, was indeed touching to hear.

That fire was nearly the end of Nazareno, but it became, instead, the start of our beginning.

REV JOHN FLETCHER

~·~ The Highland Padre ~·~

*'I would as soon think of going into battle without my artillery
as without my chaplains'.*
Field Marshal Bernard Montgomery.

My late stepfather, John Fletcher (John F), the British Army
padre or chaplain who features so prominently in Nazareno's
story, was born and brought up on the Isle of Skye, the son of
a Merchant Navy officer. Like Iain Alick, he was a native Gaelic
speaker.

He was ordained at Trinity Church, Lockerbie in
Dumfriesshire in September 1939 and was, apart from his war
service as a padre mostly with the London Scottish, minister
there for the rest of his working life. As a padre and as a minister,
he was greatly respected by and immensely popular with both
troops and parishioners.

I had seen and heard for myself both in his church and around
Lockerbie how popular my stepfather was with his parishioners
and the townsfolk in general. Being driven around the town by
him was never dull. He had a very distinctive way of gripping his
steering wheel at least on straight stretches of road, my recollection
being that he leaned his right forearm across it and held the rim

pencil style almost at ten o'clock. The left hand was in reserve around seven o'clock. This style was the subject of banter at least once, with a suggestion from someone that driving a tractor might have encouraged it. He certainly looked relaxed and confident at the wheel, somehow more gentleman farmer than minister with his little West Highland Terrier, Cindy, often perched between his shoulder and the back rest of the driver's seat. Even the shortest car journey would see him return many waved greetings, each time with a broad, occasionally mischievous smile.

I was also aware of the respect and affection in which he had been held by the officers and men in what all came to regard as the regiment to which he truly belonged, the London Scottish. Their gift to him of a superb, suitably engraved sgian dubh (traditional dirk) was rightly cherished.

John F's stay at Battalion HQ in Tregozzano was, of course, known to me, but my knowledge of how he came to be there was scant. Happily, some information came to me, by complete surprise, just in time to help me with my final draft of this account. I am grateful to The Trustees of the London Scottish Regiment for material willingly given and to Andrew Parsons, Curator and Archivist, London Scottish Regiment for the manner in which he assisted me.

John Fletcher served in action in Italy with the Royal Wiltshire Yeomanry for six months and was actually on a boat on his way back to Scotland on leave when he was told to disembark and report to the London Scottish. He joined the 1st Battalion while they were engaged in the Gothic Line battles, a baptism of serious fire for any serviceman, never mind for one who had thought he was on his way home on leave.

Rev John Fletcher

According to an article in the The London Scottish Regimental Gazette of August 1945, Padre John Macrae Fletcher did not have an easy job ahead of him on joining 1st Battalion, as he was replacing the very well-liked Padre Bobbie Macpherson who had been killed in one of the Gothic Line actions.

'One of Padre Fletcher's first tasks was to win the affection which the Battalion had felt towards his predecessor. This he has done through his blunt, honest Highland manner. He will stand no nonsense from anybody and his "talks" to us are straight and to the point.'

The article is a full front-page feature on John F headed, "Captain John Macrae Fletcher, M.A., C.F." with a sizeable photograph showing him at a Regimental Aid Post at Cassanego near Sant' Andrea. He is commended for taking in his stride a posting which had him one minute on a boat heading for Scotland and the next heading for the front line.

During a rest period at Porto San Giorgio after the Gothic Line battles, Padre Fletcher was asked whether he would like to return to his old unit, but nothing would separate him from the Battalion in which he had already made so many friends. The thought offered by the author of the article on my stepfather was that John F's affection for the London Scottish began on his very first evening when, sitting on a biscuit tin by the cookhouse fire, he found that his companion, a private soldier, could converse with him in Gaelic.

After the rest period, it was back to work with his London Scots for the River Senio battle, the crossing of the Reno and all the actions in which the 1st Battalion took part until they reached the river Po. At that point the article tells us that John F was very badly burned and had to spend some months in hospital. I had heard mention of these burn injuries from my stepbrother, Allan and his sisters, but it seemed that the immediate family did not know very much about the circumstances. Strangely, the article gave no background information saying only that John F had succumbed to them in an accident.

There are clear indications from both before and after his time in hospital that my stepfather was close by his fighting Battalion comrades when they were in action and that a strong bond developed. In their words, 'During our periods in action, Padre Fletcher was always at the regimental Aid Post bringing comfort…and making himself useful in many different ways.' In his, 'No man could have received more friendship and co-operation than I did whilst serving with the Regiment.' (Note from Trinity Manse, Lockerbie, March 1947.)

Much as our father's war diary with its scope and detail came as a surprise to my brother and me, so did the excerpts from The London Scottish Regimental Gazette when they were made available to John F's son and daughters in the autumn of 2019. Allan was provided with the relevant section of any issue of the gazette where mention was made of his father and amongst the paperwork he then copied on to me was an extensive article entitled 'I Was There' by L.W.G. (Topper) Brown. I knew that somewhere in the article, John F would appear, but decided to resist the temptation to scan through looking for the name Fletcher. I would read the full article.

Topper Brown's story started with his volunteering for 1st Battalion the London Scottish at Folkstone. I liked Topper's style of writing immediately and checked the index of excerpts to see that it was from a 1991 issue of the Regimental Gazette. After two years in Kent and East Anglia, Topper saw Cape Town,

Bombay, Basra and Kirkuk before, as he put it, being deposited on the beach at Salerno, south of Naples.

From Salerno, I willingly followed Topper as he made light of twice being wounded and hospitalised before returning to join in an attack on what he called the inevitable objective – the dominating position in the vicinity – a group of farmhouses situated atop a hill. This resulted in his unit being surrounded, eventually withdrawing with their weapons to a quarry, honeycombed with caves.

Once in the cave system, Topper found civilians in a pretty desperate state, huddled together with meagre possessions and then describes being kissed 'principally by male inhabitants, alas, as a liberator' but he did not add to their worries by contradiction just then. Of course, my mind was immediately taken to Nazareno's description of his own family group in the hills above Tregozzano.

Topper's unit eventually made it back to their group to be welcomed by the Major's assertion that he had witnessed the return of ghosts from the unknown.

Topper then records the death of John F's predecessor, Padre Bobbie Macpherson, who appears to have been killed while conducting the laying to rest of fallen comrades. Up to that point, I had been enjoying Topper's 'voice', his surviving of wounds and his condensed description of action. The circumstances of Padre Macpherson's death drew me up.

When I reached the last page of Topper Brown's article, the London Scottish were at the River Senio and in the left-hand column of the page, with the name Fletcher prominent at the top of the right-hand column. Topper is the right man to take us from one to the other.

'The platoon area was comfortably fortified, and the sentries on post had the outside area covered from the slits left in the sand-bagged outer reinforcing, whilst within, those off-duty were able to smoke and play a quiet game of all-absorbing rummy. But that was before the platoon commander, Lieut. Gordon Clilverd asked for volunteers to dismantle a troublesome enemy O.P. on the floodbank of the river. Volunteers were quickly forthcoming as the patrol was scheduled to take place at dusk, and the game was the all-important immediate happening. We had been briefed as to procedure and as to where our mines were planted.

A mist developed, and it was decided that the patrol would go out at once, and – echoes of Sir Francis Drake – we'll carry on with the game afterwards. We got to the foot of the floodbank, and whilst some members were detailed to deliver to the German "Peeping Toms" with love, their 'coup de grace' by way of grenades, I was to go to the top of the bank and give cover to the assault body. I went about half-way up the bank when Whoosh! I had been thrust upwards with a bang and, accompanied by showers of mud, landed on my back, looking at once for cover. I rolled down into a sunken fold of ground and looked around for comrades. It was very misty and very still, not a sound, and not a sight of friend... or foe!

My legs felt very cold, and the left one, at the middle of the shin, complete with boot, sock and foot, was absent. In place of the necessary portion, it appeared that lots of spaghetti in tomato sauce had been substituted.

Curiously, I looked around for my boot, and so on, but not a sight or sign of it was to be seen.

Rev John Fletcher

Then, from the bushes and from the ground itself emerged the rest of the patrol, and they converged on me, disregarding possible disaster to themselves, had me on a stretcher and carried me back to a Bren-Gun carrier which in turn got me back to the R.A.P. Here I was tidied up by the Medical Officer. The Padre, John Fletcher, took the practical step of supplying and holding in position, cigarettes, in company with two American Red Cross volunteers who laced me with delightful soup.'

Topper Brown then writes that he was soon on his way to a Casualty Clearing Station and the end of his active service.

Had that been the end of Topper's reference to my stepfather, I would already have been indebted to him. His story, written in a tone which I found first engaging and then remarkable, had vividly described life in the war zone which was effectively my stepfather's moving parish. In addition, I had quickly grown to admire Topper, even to like him. If this was a typical London Scot, it is no wonder that John F held the Regiment in the highest of regard. Once again, as when reading my father's diary, I felt in awe of the spirit and sheer courage of these men, in Topper's particular case, not only at the front, but also at the time of submission of his article.

But L.W.G. (Topper) Brown was not quite finished. This indomitable fighter left a gem to be unearthed for John Fletcher's family many years later. Topper's final paragraph reads:

'*Anyway, I give thanks to all of those with whom I served, for they taught me to be a man. And to Padre John Fletcher, for teaching me to live as one.*'

~•~ The Silent Toast ~•~

For me there is a certain challenge in following Topper Brown's beautifully succinct, yet arrestingly powerful expression of thanks. An address by John Fletcher to his former comrades, perhaps to them reminiscent of one of his 'talks', shows that he, himself, is up to the task. Through his words at a London Scottish dinner in March 1971, John F can again stand shoulder to shoulder with Topper Brown, just as they once stood shoulder to shoulder in war.

'It is my privilege and honour to propose the Silent Toast. Tonight, we of the London Scottish remember with gratitude those of our number who – in two World Wars – paid the supreme sacrifice.

Anyone who served with the Scottish in either of the two wars must have been struck with one supreme and outstanding fact – that he had joined a great comradeship. It was not something I or anyone else can explain, it was one of the finest things in life to be experienced. There it was, all the petty and trivial distinctions and snobbishness of civil life were forgotten and men of all classes rubbed shoulders together and were brothers, animated by one great uniting purpose, to do their best for their country and win the war. The thought that they were doing anything heroic and exceptional never entered their heads, and despite the dangers and hardships, the hunger, discomfort and fatigue, the hours of overtime they put in for nothing at all, they were happier – I believe – than most of us have been since.

Rev John Fletcher

101

All this urge to make money, all this selfish materialism which is out to look after 'Number One', the whole trend and spirit of our nation is not the one which animated those whom we remember tonight.

For what did those whom we remember tonight sacrifice their lives? I do not think any more demoralising thought could enter our minds or any more destroying notion could empty our hearts of any hope for a better world than just this – that all our comrades died in vain, that they sacrificed their lives for just nothing. If we believe that, we defame our dead and break faith with those who with their dying hands handed on a heritage for us to cherish.

Let our remembrance this evening stiffen our resolve to work to bring our country back to discipline and a simpler, sterner morality. As trustees of the fallen, it is our duty to carry on their struggle.

Gentlemen, I give you the "Silent Toast."

~·~ Nazareno's Hunt for John F ~·~

In 1966, John F lost his wife, Beth. In the same year, my mother, brother and I lost husband and father.

First, our mother replaced our father as our primary headteacher in Dumfriesshire. Then, in 1968, we moved to Corstorphine in Edinburgh and she reverted to teaching Modern Languages at secondary level.

John Fletcher and Margaret MacKenzie, who had met through John F's involvement with the Board of Education in

Dumfriesshire, were married in the groom's own church on 2nd April 1971, but less than a year later, illness forced him to retire prematurely from the ministry. Having had two homes for a while, Edinburgh became the couple's home. It was to that Edinburgh home that Nazareno, the former Tregozzano teenager, managed to track down the former padre.

Nazareno's quest in his epic journey in 1974, was to find and renew his friendship with the former British soldiers who had been so kind to him in his youth during their war service in Tregozzano. The Italian had set off for Britain with his wife and four young children in his massive, yet beautifully aerodynamic, Citroen DS Estate. His Alfas, his sprinters, were for shorter journeys. The Citroen remains his treasured, principal car to this day, Rovers being his 'workhorses'.

The Gori initial enquiries at the Lockerbie Post Office, about John F's whereabouts, were in some difficulty as redirection of mail had long since lapsed and the staff were unable to help. As Nazareno was leaving the building, a retired 'postie' happened to look in and his former colleagues asked if he could be of help to the Italians. This was a very lucky break for all concerned and the Citroen was soon pointed in the direction of Edinburgh... to a house in Caroline Terrace, Corstorphine to be precise.

John F wasn't actually in Edinburgh on that day. He was at Mains of Balavil near Kingussie, Balavil being a gem of a traditional Highland estate, owned in those days by John F's sister, Peggy, and later transferred to his son, Allan.

With my mother and brother out at a supermarket, I was alone in Caroline Terrace. What is more, I was on the point of showering and dressing for my 'end of school' dance and was not really in a position, or in the frame of mind, to entertain visitors. At the door appeared Nazareno with what looked like the road vehicle equivalent of Concorde parked at the end of the garden path. English was not going very far as a medium for our attempted conversation, so we tried German. The gist was clearly that this Italian, who seemed to be a decent fellow, was looking for John F.

I could see a pile of kids in the car, so I thought it best to explain John F's absence and invite the Italians to go and have a look at Edinburgh, in order to give my mum time to get home and take responsibility for dealing with them. (I was to find out many years later that my politely received suggestion was the last thing family Gori wanted, as they had been 'doing' Edinburgh all day and were exhausted.)

By this stage, fortunately, Cipriana had come to her husband's aid. A teacher of Latin and Italian, she also spoke excellent French. I knew my mum would have no difficulty at all in offering directions to Kingussie in French and that the Italian lady would have no difficulty in understanding her. Feeling I'd sorted things reasonably, I waved the Italians off, left for my girlfriend's house and on to the dance, thinking no more about the surprise visitors.

Arriving home late, I was surprised to see 'Concorde' berthed at the side of the house. I was equally surprised to encounter four young Italians camped out in various parts of the house. Eugenio, Alessandra, Eleonora and Elysabetta were their names, not that I paid much attention.

The Italians left for Balavil the next morning. I have heard both John F's version and Nazareno's version of what happened after the Italian had managed to negotiate the notorious old A9.

John F clearly had no idea who Nazareno was on the latter's arrival in the courtyard at Mains of Balavil. This was no wonder. The seventeen-year-old Italian boy with curly hair had become rather like a shorter version of Eric Morecambe, slightly receding dark hair and heavy rimmed glasses. Morecambe and Wise, the English comic double act, were at their peak on British television in those days.

While John F's mind went absolutely blank as to who this Italian visitor might be, it was far easier for Nazareno to be sure he had found the right man, as John F had retained all his hair and even wore it in the same swept-back style. Admittedly, it had become a most distinguished silver, rather than black.

Nazareno was getting nowhere until he played his trump card, mimicking his mother's call to bring him in from out of doors at mealtime.

'NazaRAYno!!!'

John F wept.

Nazareno's account of the meeting was given softly and very movingly. Goodness knows what memories he had brought back to John F. Of course, the kindness and camaraderie would have been evoked, but so too the hardship, the suffering, the death. I recalled John F once speaking to me of the impact on him of seeing a lorry heavily loaded with the bodies of British soldiers, his message, at the time, being that there is no shame in a man shedding tears.

We knew that John F was injured at one point and I recall my mother saying that she had heard, from one of his former comrades, that the padre had jumped into a tank to replace the wounded driver, presumably to drive the wounded man and the rest of the tank crew to safety. A padre or chaplain would be a minister, a priest or a rabbi, a man of faith; in fact, a man both of great faith and great bravery, unarmed save for his belief and courage, protected by the 'flock' he sought to tend. The British Army lost ninety-six such men, killed in World War 2. I remember a feeling of great pride when listening to the story of my stepdad's actions, partly because of what he had done and partly because he had never mentioned the event himself.

The desire and determination of Nazareno had succeeded.

Margaret and Cipriana kept the two couples in touch over subsequent years with Christmas cards and the occasional letter; there was a standing invitation to visit Pisa.

ALE AND I MEET AGAIN.

~•~ My Positive Premonition ~•~

At this juncture, I recall two points from my formative years. Firstly, at primary school age, I had an appetite for the stories of the Greeks and Trojans and of Scotland's William Wallace. What the Greeks did to Hector was bad enough, but what the English did to William Wallace had me, aged not very much at all, making a solemn vow that I would never marry an English girl. Secondly, I had a distinct and recurring premonition that a tall, blonde girl was going to appear in my life and that would then be that.

Back in the eighties and I cannot explain why, it appears that I was guilty of having in my mind an ignorantly held stereotypical image of Italian girls as being short, dark haired and deeply tanned in appearance. There is no more validity in this than there is in believing that Scottish men all resemble the bearded, kilted piper of cartoon caricature, keen on whisky and on observing what a lovely, bright, moonlit night he was enjoying. To my eternal shame, this did not prevent me from picturing a short, dark bob-cut, deeply tanned, apprentice '*mamma Italiana*' figure, with arms akimbo when, in 1983, I was invited to take a week off work to accompany my mother and John F to Garden Cottage, Balavil with a young Gori daughter in tow. The idea was sold to me by the offer of the use of my mother's car (new, reliable, petrol paid by her) to get to a few golf courses and perhaps to Loch Ness and Skye to show them to the imagined 'short, dark schoolgirl' Italian guest. She was not English, obviously, but otherwise she was still most unlikely to fit the premonition description, according to my subconscious.

It nearly didn't happen at all. Alessandra's letter to Margaret, written at the suggestion of Cipriana, looked for help in finding a job as an au pair/babysitter/nanny for the summer holidays with the practice of English in mind. Ale was at university, majoring in German coupled with English as her secondary subject.

Margaret and her friends were all beyond the stage of needing the kind of help Ale was offering, but she responded with the offer of a two week visit with plenty of English practice available. Ale very nearly graciously declined, as she doubted that the length of stay would provide her with the volume of practice in conversational English that she thought she needed that summer. Fortunately, she decided to accept and booked her flight.

By this stage, both my brother and I had left home, had bought our own flats and my brother was engaged. Dinner was arranged chez Margaret and John F, with my brother and his fiancée forming the reception party at the airport, in the company of Margaret. I would arrive in time for the evening meal once I had played for the Court of Session football team against one of the big law firms in Edinburgh. It was an enjoyable time of the year for me with plenty daylight for evening golf; the rugby season was over, so click into football mode. Some of the opponents didn't seem to have a switch to click nor anything other than long, metal studs. So, for me, it was a case of, 'Hello. Welcome to Scotland. Excuse me while I patch up this gouge out of my leg.'

There was no ice to be broken by the time I reached my mother's house. The 'short, dark schoolgirl' of my caricature turned out to be twenty years of age, tall, cascading blonde waves, brown eyes often widened in animated conversation, tanned only to the shade of honey and all hand gestures, loads of hand gestures. She would struggle for an English word, but only for an instant before her hand would be raised as if directing traffic to come to an immediate halt, then, 'Wait!' in a distinctly north German accent, followed by the furious turning of pages in a tiny dictionary. She was quite something, but it was Scottish eyes which met Scottish eyes across the dinner table and almost imperceptibly widened at the sight of Ale reaching confidently out to the wine bottle in the centre of the table and helping herself. It didn't register with the MacKenzie boys that the wine was from Nazareno's vineyard, sent over with his daughter in gift. Wine at our mother's table was novel enough for the brothers without the sight of a young guest diving in and helping herself – utterly unthinkable for either son.

The teasing must have started almost immediately, as my brother has been quoted often since as having assured Alessandra that Scots only tease people they like. No doubt Rev and Mrs Fletcher's eyes met and perceptibly widened when I was found to be helping to dry the dishes after dinner. I am sure that within three hours of our meeting my brother nudged me in the ribs and urged me to befriend the young Italian lady or, at least, something along those lines.

In the days that followed, I am told that I suddenly found time to drive from my office to my mother's house for lunch and then to reappear for dinner in the evening. Mother, apparently, told the family later that Ale would not eat until I arrived, no matter if work, football or golf kept me very late.

On one of my journeys in for dinner, I was nearly delayed on a long-term basis. I had been cruising along quite happily in my old mini, when a black car came right out in front of me from a side road on my left. It felt like the wee mini's nearside wheels left the ground as it got itself round the black car before making it back on to its own side of the road – no anti-lock braking systems in those days, at least not in old minis. Looking back to see if the other car was ok, I saw it had stopped so I did the same. The driver came forward to thank me and congratulate me, in colourful terms, for my evasive action. We parted as new best buddies. Alessandra's reaction, on hearing of the incident after dinner, was (wide-eyed of course) to take my hand in both of hers – nice. I was really getting to like this very foreign girl.

As to the week which followed, there is an unusual source of information. On 14th December 1996 Ale, John, Seumas and I were surprised to find ourselves in colour on the cover of the weekend section of one of Scotland's national newspapers with the words 'The Europeans' emblazoned below. The four of us, pre-Finlay, were surrounded by cartoon Santas in the traditional styles of half a dozen European countries. The Glasgow Herald was running a feature on how Europeans had made Scotland their own. What had the Europeans found in Scotland? What did they miss? What part did they see Scotland playing in Europe?

In addition to the group photo on the front, inside there was a close-up of Ale, taken at her desk, the caption reading, 'The Gaelic *Dolce Vita*.

Ale had clearly spoken freely to the writer of the article, Jane Scott. There are one or two quotes which, on re-reading the piece for the first time in many years, I found touching. In addition, there was a paragraph on Ale which remains pertinent, namely, 'Her first foreign language was German. When she first came here, she had a German accent, but she has a superb ear. When she speaks now it is pure Edinburgh. After holidays on Harris, the island of Duncan's father, her accent is often mistaken for Hebridean. She is proud of that.' Ale still comes back from Harris sounding like Auntie Mary Ann in Quidinish.

The article did carry one serious error slap bang in the middle of the headline which read, 'A first kiss upon the moor.'

No.

On the absolute authority of one of the parties to that first kiss, it is confirmed that it did not occur up on the moor. It happened a good two or three hundred yards below the edge of the Balavil moor, on the track, in the woods. Alessandra leaned forward, she still insists, to brush away a beastie which had landed on my collar. I misinterpreted the approach and there we had 'the first kiss upon the track, two or three hundred yards down from the moor and thanks, in part at least, to a visiting insect.'

The suggested trip to Loch Ness did not happen, but the two of us did take off for a day trip to the Isle of Skye which is only about two hours away from Balavil.

Scotland, it must be admitted, had a very good summer in 1983, good enough to amount to a clear case of innocent misrepresentation to a visiting Italian. We stopped off at Invergarry where Ale took a photo from the riverbank. An enlarged version of that photo has hung above our open fireplace for over thirty years and it shows that the day must have been quite hot.

While we were walking in single file along a narrow path in the glen, I realised that things had gone quiet. There was no sound at all from the enthusiastic conversationalist behind me. I turned around to find Ale looking like a feeding duck, head in the river, both cooling off and controlling the former cascading waves, which had first become slightly unruly curls and which then became, instead, cascading ringlets; so, cooled and controlled, the operation worked on both counts. The feeding duck reference is perhaps best consigned to history; she probably didn't find it funny, even then.

Over on Skye, on Broadford pier to be precise, I heard a burst of Italian (no German accent) which rang a few bells from early Latin classes, *Amo, amas, amat* and all that. By the time the week was nearing its end, we had talked about Protestant/Catholic and Scottish/Italian marriage and even the raising of children. Discounting the 1974 discovery of bivouacked children in my home, I had known Alessandra for all of two weeks.

Other people noticed what was going on. Allan and Marjorie invited, what they clearly already considered, the new couple to join them at a picnic with friends on the shores of Loch Insh. About twenty-five years later, again at a Loch Insh picnic, another couple, who had been in the company that evening, spoke of having noticed the 'rapport'. It seems to have been pretty obvious to most.

There were a couple of minor hiccups that second week. An undercooked burger at the picnic had me distinctly unwell during the night and when Alessandra found me in the morning, feeling very sorry for myself, sitting in the sun at the front of Garden Cottage, something based on pure lemon juice was put together and offered with great sympathy. It worked.

Slightly awkward moments came on the delightful golf course at Boat of Garten. I felt I had enough difficulty controlling my golf swing, which I described back then as being like an octopus caught in a whirlpool, but that may have been an exaggeration. I have admitted that, yes, I could belt the ball a long way, into the next county at times, but it was entirely in the lap of the gods as to whether that county was to the east or to the west. What I really didn't need was my brand new, utterly gorgeous, Mediterranean girlfriend seeking to remove her blouse and stroll down the fairway at my side, clad only in bikini top and denim shorts. Having regularly enjoyed a warm welcome at Boat of Garten, I had an emergency word in her ear about golfing dress code.

Alessandra herself recently recalled choosing, yes choosing, to blow her nose right at the top of my backswing. She thought I'd be so focussed on the ball at that point that I would not notice. I wish! Her golf course etiquette has, long since, become absolutely impeccable; my swing has become short and horribly cautious, but I am working on it.

As her departure from Scotland grew near, the two of us acknowledged that our relationship, which had developed so quickly, should be given a chance despite the obvious difficulty of distance. She was setting off for the north of Germany to practise that accent before returning to Pisa for the new academic year at university. We came to an agreement, nowadays apparently referred to as 'going exclusive'. Neither would date anyone else until we met up again in Italy; a visit to Pisa was planned for October.

We arranged to celebrate our decision at a restaurant in Queen Street on Ale's last evening in Edinburgh. I was pretty taken by the transformation in the girl I already thought was quite something. 'Stunning' is a much over played word, but the combined effect of make-up and that dress was exactly that…even before she smiled. The only description I have ever given anyone of that dress was that it was in the colours of the Wallabies, gold with green trim. Even if I couldn't describe it properly, I know I won't forget.

At the restaurant, there was another 'golf course moment', this time with a distinct whiff of holier-than-thou, when Ale was caught out by the waiter offering pre-dinner drinks. 'Oh, WE only drink when we are eating.'

Awkward pause.

She relented. Dry martini – straight, no ice.

~•~ Christmas Eve 1983 ~•~

During the weeks between her departure from Scotland and my arrival in Italy, Ale and I kept in touch by handwritten letters sent by express airmail and the occasional phone call. This was well before Skype, WhatsApp, Facetime, email or text. It was a world still without mobile phones or laptops. The time passed remarkably quickly.

I felt a little trepidation prior to my departure for Italy and what was to be only my second trip abroad. British Columbia, on tour with Stewart's Melville Rugby Club, had not involved a foreign language and the Canadian dollar didn't frazzle the brain like I expected the Lira would. I was also going to have to call on long-forgotten school French and German. Nine years had passed since I had used both, with Ale's parents in Edinburgh, without any need for recourse to either.

At the Arrivals gate in Pisa, the colour scheme was not Wallabies or Springboks, but Manchester City – sky blue for Ale and way over-dressed for me. My choice of Levi cord jeans and leather boots was fine for Edinburgh, but far too heavy for Tuscany in the autumn.

Had I wondered if she would still be as lovely as I remembered? Yes, I had and yes, she was.

Ale's brother's English was good, but it was an American accent for him rather than German. Whether that was down to his teachers or rock albums, the two brothers-in-law have never since remembered to discuss. Nazareno's English was locked away at the back of that busy brain of his, so it was mostly German with him. Cipriana's French was very clear and correct. While my level of comprehension could cope with both, my problem was that I had been doing Gaelic at night classes for four years, French and German having really been left unused. That all combined to leave me tongue tied in anything but English with French, German and Gaelic words popping into my head at random as soon as I tried to speak in anything else.

At the first Italian lunch, the second helping of pasta was gratefully accepted, only for me to find that the pasta dish was just the starter. I regretted having eaten on the plane as a platter of sliced roast beef arrived next, but my appetite returned in time for spit-roasted quail in the evening.

Of course, the Leaning Tower of Pisa was climbed, an experience I have blamed as being responsible for a long running discomfort in high places. The problem with the tower was a combination of my leather soled boots, well-worn stonework underfoot and an absence of railings at any storey save the very top, and it did lean over, quite a lot. The urge to jump from the top, in the belief that flight to the roof of the cathedral was possible, was overcome.

With Ale's brother, a man with many friends in high places, we visited a beach normally reserved for off-duty members of the *Carabinieri*. It was deserted. Ale's brother wind-surfed to leave us in peace.

Discreetly chaperoned by Ale's mum, we left Pisa for a while to stay in her little flat in the square of Scarperia, a small village in the mountains above Florence. From there, we visited Siena and San Gimignano, just to look around from the streets and squares, it being quickly recognised that I preferred to appreciate famous Tuscan towns from the fresh air and pleasant warmth of my first Italian autumn, rather than from the interior of cathedrals, churches and galleries. If Cipriana was a little disappointed with my desire to stay outside as much as I could, she hid it well and accepted my excuse that I was, after all, a barbarian from ancient Caledonia. 'Sono barbaro' became a catchphrase in a warm friendship with our dinner table conversations over the years, often about language, being a particularly fond memory.

By the time Ale and I had spent only three weeks in each other's company, getting married was being discussed, initially in a light, flirtatious way and then more seriously, with obstacles being imagined and promptly swatted away. I even phoned home from the public telephone in the little bar in Scarperia's square and heard myself say to my mother 'I think this is it.' If there was an element of surprise at the far end of the line back in Edinburgh, it was only at my happy candour.

On the evening I arrived back in Edinburgh, I phoned Ale, possibly starting the call as if I were sounding her out on how serious she had been in our talk of engagement. As I was sitting on the floor at the time, I eased myself onto one knee and proposed to her. She accepted. It had been two weeks in Scotland, two weeks in Italy, engaged by telephone.

I wrote to Nazareno and Cipriana seeking their approval. My letter was in English, of course, so Ale did the translating for them. Despite the fact that their daughter would be heading for distant Scotland, they gave their blessing. In true Nazareno style, Ale and I exchanged ring finger sizes by swapping circles of chicken wire by air mail. Cipriana then accompanied Alessandra over to Scotland for the Christmas holidays, the engagement being officially celebrated on Christmas Eve 1983.

I had been clear on my wish to wear an engagement ring and it came from Certaldo where Nazareno has his farm. With three types of gold and tiny diamonds, I liked it so much that it was later to be blessed as my wedding ring.

~•~ The Italian Wedding ~•~

The wedding was set for 20th July 1985 at San Paolo, on the banks of the river Arno. It was the Gori family church, less than three hundred yards from their Pisa home. There were seventeen Scots at the wedding.

On the evening before the wedding, the arrival of two or three from the Scottish contingent caused a slight stir in the centre of Pisa.

As his father John F had done before him, my stepbrother, Allan, had married a widow, Marjorie, who had three sons. Two of Marjorie's boys, Antony and Michael, were on holiday in France and able to drive down for the wedding, arriving in Pisa in some style. The Gori family was having a gathering in their house to welcome guests who were coming from some distance away, so Ale and I decided to go out for a stroll in the general direction of the hotel where the Scots had rooms booked. It was located in the centre of Pisa, not far from Corso Italia, the pedestrianised central street which runs from the River Arno towards the main square and the station. Around Corso Italia, the streets are narrow and the buildings tall, a bit of a maze with one-way streets all over the place and certainly not the easiest to negotiate when arriving from Scotland by car.

Most guests had arrived safely and could begin their short walk to Ale's home, but there was no sign of Antony and Michael, so we set off to check the rabbit warren of little streets around the hotel.

We heard the boys long before we saw them. Just at whom they were tooting was never established, but the sound of an old-fashioned car horn was getting closer until, around a corner they came, the wrong way up a one-way street.

The cream coloured Morris Minor convertible that is 'Snowberry' had made it all the way from Balavil, Kingussie. She was a fine sight as she rolled gently to a halt, defiantly facing the wrong way, at the hotel's front door. The Balavil boys had arrived and Pisa had noticed. In a part of the city where looking your best is mandatory before you step out, 'Snowberry' and her crew turned heads.

Her arrival in Pisa was, however, surpassed the following day when 'Snowberry', trailing a cloud of dust, swung into the grounds of the reception venue, high in the Tuscan hills, with a kilted Michael in the back belting out 'Highland Laddie' on his pipes. It was a sight never to be forgotten by the groom.

Throughout the wedding day, the Highland garb did run into a difficulty or two. We MacKenzie brothers, in our wisdom, having chosen to wear the Montrose jacket with jabot and cuffs, had noticed the jacket's tendency to ride up at the back. We had no desire to present glimpses of pale Scottish skin between black and tartan, so decided to wear a shirt of some sort underneath the Montrose. I went for a thin, white tee shirt, but my brother felt dark blue was what he wanted. The only dark blue shirt he had in his case was a heavy London Scottish rugby jersey. During the wedding ceremony, guests were at liberty to walk around San Paolo and take photographs as they pleased; that produced a series of shots where my dear bro can be seen trying to ease the jabot away from his neck in the hope of allowing heat out and a little cool air in. He is then pictured dropping his head lower and lower as heat took its toll. His nose never quite reaches the order of service on the pew in front of him, but it becomes a close-run thing. Overheating was deemed the principal cause, but over thirty years later, Eugenio wistfully recalled sitting outside, until very late in the night before the wedding, enjoying chilled German beer with the groom and, in particular, his best man.

The other Highland dress problem was, more specifically, a sporran problem. As the church congregation plus a squad of curious passers-by stood in Piazza San Paolo immediately after the service, Antony developed his wardrobe malfunction. His vintage sporran, which involved some deceased Scottish wildlife, started to come apart, the noon sun having softened the glue. Now, if kilts attract attention, sporrans seem to inspire fascination, especially if they are falling apart.

It is said that the kilts stopped the traffic on the road between the church and the River Arno. Certainly, two *Carabinieri* vehicles parked up for a look. Far more impressive, however, was the sight of Cipriana directing traffic on the way out of Pisa to the reception. Tradition has it that a wedding convoy should not be interrupted by other vehicles.

Nazareno's Citroen DS led the convoy, as he knew the way, with the bride and groom being driven immediately behind. At a major intersection, Cipriana jumped out of the Citroen and strode, in her wedding finery, to the centre of the crossroads to countermand the traffic lights. Once the whole convoy passed through, mostly on the red light, she jumped back in the Citroen which then overtook the lot to take up its lead position again. It was taken in the best of spirits by other drivers and was saluted with much enthusiastic sounding of horns.

Other than the name of the red wine, *Rocca delle Macie*, the multistorey fresh fruit wedding cake and the intertwining of arms as we toasted each other with champagne, I have remembered nothing of the meal. That I hardly ate was a pity, as it was a veritable feast. I do, however, recall two tables of guests starting to throw corks at each other. The new Mrs MacKenzie contributed to this unscheduled entertainment by standing up and telling off her siblings, her cousins and her recently acquired brother-in-law. Quite authoritarian about it, she was.

Ale's cousin, Francesca and her then fiancé, Francesco, drove us away from the reception towards Florence, Ale's veil streaming from her window as we cruised along the autostrada to the sound of Simon and Garfunkel and, of course, many, many car horns. When Francesco stopped for fuel, service station staff gathered round the car to wish us well, offering handshakes through the open windows.

Cipriana, Eleonora and Elysabetta had prepared the little flat in Scarperia for the newly-weds. Prepared it was, right down to the stocking of the fridge with Parma ham, dolcelatte, bottles of spumante and the provision of that wonderful rustic Tuscan bread.

In the morning, we made our way by local bus to Santa Maria Novella, the main station in Florence, the bride's flowers prompting congratulations from the driver and the other passengers. Cipriana had gifted her daughter and new son-in-law first class tickets on the Rome to Vienna sleeper. The arrangements were not a secret and one or two guests even looked in for a chat and a plastic cup of spumante as we sat in our carriage awaiting departure.

The first half of the honeymoon was in Sierning, Austria and the second in Quidinish, in the Bays of Harris. While Tuscany and Balavil had been fundamental both to our meeting and falling in love, each of us was now taking the other, for the first time, to a place they held very dear. From this point on, Harris and Austria would be shared. A shared love of Balavil and Tuscany was already well established.

August Dobringer:
~·~ The Austrian Connection ~·~

On the way to Austria, I heard something of the Gori family connection with Sierning which is a small market town near Steyr and how it had come about, namely the rescue, soon after the war, by Nazareno of a young Austrian who had been pressed into service in the German army.

Many years later, as we neared the end of recording his account of the war and meeting John F, I asked Nazareno to tell me the story himself. The recording turns into a three-way conversation. Nazareno hesitates and Ale starts to tell the story instead, relating that the young Austrian, August, was on a train between Florence and Arezzo, intending to visit the graves of his brothers, both of whom had died as they served in the German army during the aggressive retreat northwards in the face of Allied advances through Italy. When asking if the train was about to reach Arezzo, August's Austrian accent was close enough to German to be picked up by some young Italians whose partisan comrades had suffered at the hands of the SS.

August was a mild-mannered, gentle man who had been a radio operator. Conscripted, he was about as far from a battle-hardened warrior as you could imagine, but the three young Italians, forearms like whipcord, were looking to make trouble. One started slapping August around the head, goading him to stand up.

Nazareno is a highly principled man of genial disposition, but you cross him at your peril. In those days, he was a boxer and very fit indeed. Not the tallest, he was apparently blessed with quick hands and a long reach. Nazareno was on that train, travelling home from university.

By the time he heard an Italian hissing about a blade, Nazareno was already on his feet. His request that the foreigner be left alone was ignored, so with a vicious combination of punches and a highly un-Queensberry elbow to the point of a chin, he flattened two of the Italians. The third suffered an overwhelming attack of common sense and backed off out of the carriage.

At the station, exit Nazareno and his newly found friend. Nobody had the stomach to follow. Thus, apparently, began the friendship with August Dobringer of Sierning.

Well, not exactly it seems.

The incident Ale had recounted was entirely family folklore, at least according to Nazareno. Stories had been mixed up and exaggerated by Ale, her brother and sisters to such an extent that they had themselves convinced. Her father's first meeting with August was nothing of such drama at all. In the recording, you can almost feel Ale's surprise as her father insists that he simply gave August directions and, as the young Austrian had some time to wait, he invited him home to Tregozzano for a meal.

The last voice on the recording is Scottish and sounds rather deflated.

'Nazareno, you've just spoiled a whole chapter.'

Wherever the exact truth lies, the train journey was the start of a connection with families in the Sierning area which in at least one case is now into the fourth generation. The second generation of one of the families, *Familie* Baumschlager, hosted us during our first week of honeymoon at their wonderful hotel, Gasthof Forsthof – their very kind wedding gift.

Later, in the 1990s, Nazareno and Cipriana inherited a house in Austria. Their dear friend, August Dobringer, was due to be left the property in terms of a will. A very interesting man whose great loves were nature and travel, he asked the granter of the will to leave her summer house to his Italian friends, whom she knew well, rather than to him, as he wished them to benefit instead so that their children, to whom he was as an uncle, could enjoy the wonderful Austrian countryside whenever they wished.

August would be delighted to know how much joy that lovely little house has given and continues to give to the Gori children and their families.

~·~ Iain Alick Helps Nazareno ~·~

Central to this account of the coming together of two families or more accurately, three, is the connection between Nazareno Gori and John Fletcher. My dad, Iain Alick, is bound to have passed fairly close to Nazareno at one time, but that and a shared desire to build a motor bike would hardly qualify as connections between my father-in-law and my father.

In the late 1980s, Iain Alick's Harris links did, however, play a part in Nazareno's ambition to locate Dr Kinsella who had done so much to save the Italian's life. The doctor had not been found during the original trip in 1974.

Amongst the Scottish guests at the wedding were four natives of South Harris. Two were cousins of Iain Alick from Quidinish, Roddy and Mary. Roddy's wife, also Mary, originally from Northton was a third. The fourth was Anne whose father had run the post office in Finsbay, only a few hundred yards from Iain Alick's home.

As a very young teacher, arriving to begin a new post at Currie High School, Anne's accent had been immediately spotted by my mother. On being asked where she was from, Anne replied in general terms such as up north, west coast, Outer Hebrides before appreciating that my mother's growing frustration arose from her knowing fine and well that the accent was from Harris and that the question was intended to establish which village. On finally revealing that she came from Finsbay, Anne was recognised as 'little Anne Campbell with the pigtails from the post office.' Anne turned out to be related to me albeit distantly by mainland standards. We are third or fourth cousins, depending on the route you take.

Anne and her husband, Malcolm, became close friends of Margaret and John F and of the two of us. Malcolm was also at our wedding in Pisa, where Anne was a witness, and they later became godparents to young John.

A couple of years after the wedding, Ale and I, with Nazareno and Cipriana, were at dinner with Malcolm and Anne. Nazareno's failure to locate Dr Kinsella had been mentioned while he was telling Malcolm and Anne about his original quest in 1974 to find the soldiers who had looked after him so well. Malcolm immediately recognised the name, saying that his uncle had at one time been in partnership with a Dr Kinsella in the Midlands of England. Seeing the light of hope in Nazareno's eyes prompted Malcolm, probably a little rashly, to offer to see if he could help locate Dr Kinsella. Given the passage of time since he had heard talk of the name and, with his uncle long retired, he didn't really know where to start. He thought of the British Medical Association (BMA), but assumed they would be bound by confidentiality and, anyway, the doctor himself would be long retired. Fortunately, the BMA did feel that they could help, having heard the circumstances, and Dr Kinsella was located.

Nazareno and Cipriana detoured on their return journey to Italy to meet with Dr Kinsella and his wife plus their daughter who joined the two couples for afternoon tea. Yes, indeed, Dr Kinsella remembered his time in Tregozzano, the friendship with Dr Gori and his family and of course, the young Nazareno with his extensive burn injuries. Contact was maintained and Dr Kinsella's daughter later visited the Gori family in Pisa.

Had it not been for his wife's connection with Iain Alick, Malcolm would never have met Ale's dad. Having found the kind Sergeant Walter Firstbrook in Oldham in 1974, Nazareno finally found the last of the British Army soldiers who had befriended his family, the one whose medical skill and dedication had saved his life.

BALAVIL, KINGUSSIE

~•~ 'Finlay's Pool' ~•~

The link among the families MacKenzie, Gori and Fletcher, with its roots in the war, has given members of each family the opportunity to enjoy the areas associated with the other two; MacKenzies to Balavil, Tuscany and Austria; Fletchers to Tuscany; Gori family to Edinburgh, Harris and Balavil.

My brother and I were fortunate to enjoy visits to Balavil from 1971, our first being with our stepsister, Liz, during that summer. Following John F's suffering of a stroke only a few months after his marriage to our mother, Liz volunteered to host her new, teenage stepbrothers first at her home in Devon and then at Balavil. An unforgettable summer it was for the two of us, Devon countryside being followed by a sporting estate in the Highlands.

After Balavil was transferred to Allan, John F changed from Mains of Balavil, where he had welcomed Nazareno and his family, to the lovely Garden Cottage. Following our loss of John F in 1990, Allan very kindly allowed relatives to use the cottage when it was not required for skiers or shooting season staff. My brother and I, together with our families, have enjoyed many happy holidays and weekends on the estate, Balavil playing a very significant part in our lives for over forty years.

Balavil had been in Allan's family since 1790, but it was finally sold when he and Marjorie retired from the very demanding work of running a Highland estate, both as a family home and as a business concern. The estate is roughly triangular in shape and extends to approx. 6,800 acres, most of which was sold with Allan and Marjorie retaining Croftcarnoch, a former farmhouse and steading with surrounding woodland, where they have built a new home.

Garden Cottage lies just off one of the main estate roadways and is reached by a short track which crosses a little stone bridge over Raitt's Burn. The burn can be a gentle brook or a raging torrent, depending on rainfall and snow melt up on the moor. It was a very useful cooling off and play area for the family dogs while, for the family, it provided an emergency source of water on the odd occasion that the private supply failed. The water source was a spring, in a wood, on the hillside far behind the cottage. On one occasion, a sudden loss of water signalled a serious problem in the system which was traced right the way back to the spring in the wood. A recklessly curious mallard had somehow got his head stuck in the intake pipe. This proved to be utterly catastrophic for the water supply and utterly fatal for the duck.

Balavil has been seen regularly on television, as it hosted a series in 2009 of 'Kill it, cook it, eat it' with Allan and his gamekeeper, Arthur, proving to be comfortable in front of camera and microphone. Earlier it was 'Kilwillie Castle' in the British television drama series 'Monarch of the Glen'. Both the estate and Balavil House were well worthy of the favourable comments they received following television exposure.

Raitt's Burn flows down to the Spey, which famous river effectively forms the base of the triangular shape of the estate. The burn enters the river at the Laird's Pool, which local fishermen have been heard to refer to as Harry's Pool, very probably named after Harry Brewster-MacPherson who was a well known photographer and naturalist. The Laird's Pool has a pebble beach and was a favoured spot for picnics as well as for fishing. It was here that I discovered the fun of fly fishing, albeit rather late. I would visit the Laird's Pool occasionally with my spinning rod, without ever being tempted to try fly fishing properly. Allan had given me casting lessons in the courtyard at Mains of Balavil with a double handed salmon rod in the early days, but although I liked the act of casting, I had never taken it to the water.

Anne Easton, my secretary of many years who became a family friend, had passed to me, from her husband, a fly rod he was retiring from his own use plus its reel, line and some flies. The idea was that the young boys, John and Seumas, might like to try fly fishing. One Saturday, down at the Laird's Pool, Seumas gave the fly rod a go while I was using the spinner. Frustration set in almost immediately for the youngster and Seumas soon proposed an exchange of rods. Two casts of the fly rod later, I had caught both two brown trout and the extraordinary passion of the recently converted; another novice had been hatched to thrash the water and create birds' nests out of tangled line.

Fishing inexperience played havoc, within a matter of weeks, at the top end of the Laird's Pool. The rest of the family had gone ahead to Italy as soon as school finished for the summer and I had driven to Garden Cottage to join up with my brother, a proper fisherman, for the weekend. There had been word of pike at the Laird's Pool with my nephew, Sean, having caught one which he had dispatched and taken back to Garden Cottage. Said 'dispatched' pike woke up, with a sore head and in a foul mood, on the draining board of the cottage kitchen sink. Startling for all, it was. One could understand how the local trout population was under some pressure with these hard, killing machines as near neighbours. I thought I would try to match Sean's effort, if only to assist the trout.

When I got down to the river, I could see that the pike were not alone in challenging trout numbers as I watched an otter slipping off the opposite bank and into the water. The Dexter Wedge lure I fired out into the river was grabbed and released a couple of times, persuading this enthusiastic novice that the pike were there, but just weren't biting at the business end of my lure. When pike take the lure properly, it can feel like you have snagged a sunken branch; you feel completely stuck. You then manage to pull the 'branch' towards you just a little and then the 'branch' pulls you right back again.

One pike was caught before all went quiet, so I moved upstream to a broad slow bend in the Spey. The beginner had read somewhere that pike prefer slow water.

I cast the little rod and the Dexter Wedge plopped down into a calm stretch of water close to a thick forest of reeds. As soon as the lure hit the water, it was grabbed; it must have landed virtually on the nose of whatever had got a hold of it. Whatever it was took off upstream, my little reel having little or no say in the matter at all. It didn't feel like a pike at all. It occurred to me that an otter might have taken off with my lure. Well, if a seagull could grab my Dexter Wedge at Cnoc Eisgean, Quidinish, then why not an otter on the Spey? Had I not just seen one slipping quietly off the far bank and into the water? This Spey creature was like nothing I had hooked before. (This incident happened a good while before the carp experience of Tregozzano.) I told myself, out loud, to be patient and to stay calm. I already had a pike on the bank, so if this got away, at least my afternoon would not be a total blank. There was to be no self-imposed pressure.

It took an age, but once the fish came up to the surface, the tail and fins looked familiar from the occasional game fishing programme I had seen on television. This was either a salmon or a big sea trout. Had the fishing programmes not suggested that sea trout are usually caught at night?

Very slowly, the fish was brought on to the shingle beach. It was silvery, by some way the biggest fish I had ever brought to shore and it was very firmly caught on the treble hook of the Dexter Wedge. Nowadays, I would have squashed any barbs on the hooks before starting to fish and would also have a pair of forceps in my pocket – rookie errors both on that day.

I dispatched the fish with a heavy stone and, years later, still regret my action.

I phoned up to the Garden Cottage, told my brother of the pike and confirmed that it had already been knocked on the head. On being asked if I had caught anything else, I said that I had, but needed advice on whether it was a salmon or a big sea trout. The response was that it was highly likely to be a salmon rather than a sea trout and to ask what had been done with it. The matter-of-fact response that I had already knocked it on the head and placed it on the bank was met by a mild expletive and a reference to a 'catch and release' policy on the River Spey. Elation became deflation in an instant. I really do like to stick to the rules… all rules.

There was nothing for it, according to my fisherman brother, but to take the fish back to the cottage and have it for dinner, but there was little enthusiasm for the meal on his plate on the part of the successful angler. I thought it might have been proper to offer the fish to the laird, but Allan and Marjorie were away for the weekend. My conscience did insist that, at the first opportunity, I should admit my error to Allan.

At the mention of an 'error of judgment down at the river', the look on Allan's face was not good. Had a neighbour been peppered by shotgun pellets? There may well have been relief spreading across Allan's face as the explanation unfolded. Certainly, the landowner's response was gracious. There was no need to worry about it and I was absolutely to enjoy having caught my first ever salmon.

The salmon, incidentally, was astonishingly unlucky. The novice knot on the Dexter Wedge gave way on my very next cast, releasing the lure to fly free to the middle of the Spey and plop out of sight for good.

A few hundred yards upstream from the Laird's Pool lies 'Finlay's Pool', which name you will find neither on any map of the estate nor of the river. Duncan, Alessandra & Co christened the pool, there being no highly revered ancestor of Allan's nor any other famous figure involved, just a young Finlay MacKenzie.

We MacKenzie brothers were having a joint weekend at the cottage with some family and a couple of guests. An afternoon's fishing had been arranged with spinning rods for the youngsters who were to fish together, their mums in charge, while Uncle John and I moved further upstream onto a wooded island. Uncle John was going to show me some places where he had caught good fish in the past. The two of us cast into the shallow run opposite the island, allowing our flies to tumble down into the deep pool below. A couple of nice brown trout were caught before our relaxed concentration was broken by a commotion from the riverbank adjacent to the deep pool.

Trees obscured my view.

'Did you see that?' asked my brother.

'Nope.'

'Just as well, maybe.'

The youngest guest had snagged his lure on an overhanging branch when casting towards the pool. Finlay, being a kind, helpful, young boy, saw that his mum was struggling to free the lure and stepped further down the bank to offer his help. As he did so, the heel of his wellie boot landed squarely on a big brown slug which, up to that point, had been enjoying a reasonable afternoon. No banana skin has ever been as slippery as that slug proved to be for Finlay, who tumbled straight into the Spey. The ultimate fate of the slippery slug was not investigated.

Fortunately, the downstream end of the island was very close to the bank at that point and this created quite a large pool with little current. It was deep all the same, but with plenty of lessons plus swimming in the sea off Marina di Pisa in his locker, Finlay responded strongly to his mother's terse instruction of 'Swim, Finlay! Swim!'

As he neared the bank, he stopped in mid-stroke. Consternation in the gallery! The panic was mercifully brief, Finlay explaining later that one of his wellies had come off as he tumbled into the water and that, as he swam, he felt that he was losing the other one, so interrupted his stroke to pull it back on. Then, he had an urgently needed lightbulb moment. His dad, he said, had always told him that if he ever fell in with wellies on, he had to ditch them straight away. He did so and made the bank confidently.

The rumour that her young son's response to Ale's persistent and anxious encouragement to swim was totally unprintable, is simply false. Now, had it been Uncle John who had fallen in….

The total bag that afternoon from what became "Finlay's Pool" amounted to: totally average brown trout-2; bedraggled youngster-1; submarine-sized brown trout, promised by Uncle John-0.

~·~ 'The Tromie' ~·~

Around the corner, upstream from 'Finlay's Pool' is my favourite area of the whole estate, a place where, in recent years, I have spent countless contented hours. Apart from Balavil House and Garden Cottage, this spot will be the part of the estate I will miss most. We MacKenzies simply call it 'the Tromie' but, in fact, it is a section of the River Spey where it flows straight for over a hundred yards through a sheltered corridor beginning at the point where the River Tromie joins its big brother.

On the Balavil side the bank is initially flat before it rises in what must have been part of an historic flood prevention embankment, beyond which are trees and bushes. There is ample shelter, but still room for a full back cast with no need to attempt any tricky casting techniques. On the opposite bank, lies a mature wood. If luck is out with its direction, the corridor can be a bit of a wind tunnel, but most of the time it is a peaceful, secluded retreat where man and dog can concentrate on fishing and nature watching. It is also an ideal spot for newcomers to fly fishing and was always enjoyed most when the MacKenzies had company.

When the river was at normal level and running gently, it was an ideal section for casting very slightly upstream, right across to the shallower water under the trees on the far bank. The flies would then drift down a little before coming into the deeper water in the middle and finally reaching the deepest water at the near bank. Fish could take at any point of the wide arc the flies travelled. Uncle John had advised very early on in my new pursuit that it was important to prevent the flies moving in what looked like a totally unnatural manner. If it's supposed to look like an aquatic insect larva, don't suddenly have it skiting off at ninety degrees to the flow of the stream and so on. My combination of flies, Hare's Ear gold-head nymph and Greenwell's Glory, was supposed to look as natural as possible on its downstream journey and not suddenly to accelerate off-piste. This is easier said than done. Even a short cast that landed in a crumpled heap, however, had the chance to catch a fish as the floating line gradually unravelled itself downstream.

Scudo had learned correct fishing form quickly. Sit to my left to minimise the risk of being foul hooked by my flies; I cast right-handed. Ale, wouldn't you know it, does everything right-handed apart for casting. The dog had to keep his wits about him when he was out with the pair of us and also developed the endearing practice of lowering his head while the false casting backwards and forwards was swishing the air above him, looking up only when the fly line landed on the water. Thereafter, he would focus intently on the line for any signs of a fish taking before getting overly excited when a fish was hooked. He lost his four-paw grip only once, while trying to reach a nice trout, and did a 'Finlay' into the Spey. Nobody was fooled by his, admittedly impressive, attempt to make it all look absolutely intentional.

Often, I would let the dog select the fishing spot and once Scudo felt his master was getting restless, he would consider it his duty to stand up and head for another natural casting platform. The man with the rod would follow and would only rarely disagree with his canine ghillie's unspoken advice.

It is such a secluded stretch of river, up there by the Tromie, that I have enjoyed watching deer come out of the wood on the opposite bank and cross over to Balavil. I must have been well down wind. I have also watched an osprey swoop down and take a fish only a few yards from where I was sitting, leaving me to shrug in the face of superstar competition.

One memorable weekend, Ale and I managed to get all five of the family fishing together at the Tromie. Scudo felt obliged to attempt to keep an eye on Ale, John, Seumas, Finlay and me as we fished about twenty-five yards apart along the Balavil bank. John had been in the habit of teasing me over my new-found enthusiasm for fly fishing, but he was caught punching the air with delight when he eventually got past hooking himself in the backside and landed his first trout on the fly. Twenty-eight trout were caught that day, but the 'catch and release' lesson had long since been learned. Four were kept for the table with the others being carefully returned to the water.

Nazareno, himself, has had the pleasure of fishing at the Tromie while enjoying a weekend at Garden Cottage. Finlay and I fully expected him to emulate the feat he performed at Geocrab on Harris. Having reached Harris with a heavy cold, Nazareno had put himself in solitary confinement for a couple of days. Finlay and I had gone off on the third morning of the visit to fish off the rocks in the bay at Geocrab. Out of the blue, appeared a much happier Nazareno who took over my rod, caught two fish and sauntered back up the road for his breakfast, all in the space of about five minutes. Alas, his debut at the Tromie did not go as well as his cameo appearance on the Harris rocks. Fly fishing is one fishing technique which had passed him by. Spinning with lures and bait fishing, both fresh and saltwater, spear gun, snorkelling for mussels, he had done the lot.

At the Tromie, to move things forward more quickly, Finlay and I cast out for Nazareno, then handed the rod back for him to deal with the downstream drift and retrieve. Once Nazareno had seen it done a few times, he took over and did his own casting. He was up and running.

To minimise the risk of time-wasting tangles there was only one fly on Nazareno's line, a Pheasant Tail Nymph. It had just been eulogised in an edition of 'Trout Fisherman' as the essential pattern for the river fisherman's fly box and had seen regular success at the Tromie. It clearly imitated quite well what the local trout liked to eat.

After a little, I noticed that Nazareno was in a major tangle, so I moved over, sorted out the line and offered to send the fly back out for him. During my false casting, the fly didn't look right or sound right as it sailed above my head. My Pheasant Tail Nymphs are copper not white.

There was a daisy impaled on the fly. How?

Nazareno confessed immediately to attaching the head of a

daisy to the world-famous fly which imitates so well a variety of natural trout snacks. Why? To make the fly look more attractive to fish, of course.

Taxing my Italian vocabulary to its limit, I suggested that I was going to offer Nazareno a plate of lasagne that evening, but then stick a freshly cut tree branch in the middle of it. Appetising thought Nazareno? Point made and accepted with laughter all round.

The joy of that day at the Tromie was that Nazareno had made it over some difficult terrain to the family's favourite fishing spot on Balavil, once again demonstrating his fitness and great spirit, well past his eightieth birthday.

~·~ Lessons Learned and a Rare Sight ~·~

Turning away from the Spey, the Balavil marshes are crossed using one of the raised embankment paths and then it is over the railway, the old A9 and the new A9, to get back to the main part of the estate. At this level of the Balavil 'triangle', are to be found three farm steadings, lying about half a mile apart, starting in the village of Lynchat and ending beside the Highland Wildlife Park. In that order, they are Chapel Park, Mains of Balavil and Croftcarnoch. In the MacKenzies' time, Chapel Park was the main working steading, but all three have been places of interest and enjoyment for the family.

In the early days, while John F had the use of the farmhouse at Mains of Balavil, I stayed there while helping on the farm during both school and university summer holidays. Farm work during the day and rabbit shooting in the evening was the perfect combination for me. This was long before fishing and golf started to compete for my time. My shooting only scratched the surface of the significant Balavil rabbit problem back then. One half of Scudo would have been in his element. By way of dogs, Margaret and John F had a shih tzu and a westie respectively, the former was a bold wee boy, but we are hardly talking proper country dogs. I would have welcomed something more in the springer line at the time.

Forking loads of cut grass in the silage pit or, with the little Massey Ferguson 35 shuttling to and fro, swapping trailers with what then seemed like a huge, modern tractor in the shape of the 135 with forage harvester in tow; stacking and carting hay bales; the work was all enjoyed immensely. I am referring, of course, to the old-fashioned hay bales, brick shaped, not huge cylindrical things. It was labour intensive, a bit of hard, outdoor exercise between exam time and the start of pre-season training. It was just perfect.

I still hanker after a wee tractor, but I am seriously shocked at the prices for old Massey Fergusons. They seem to be highly sought after. For now, I will make do with the occasional shot on Nazareno's little old SAME tractor on his farm at Certaldo in central Tuscany.

As can happen with youngsters, the enthusiasm for tractors, trailers and the rest resulted in a couple of painful lessons. When helping to cart hay bales in for storage in the buildings between the Mains and Garden Cottage, I was invited to hitch a lift back out the hayfield by riding on the 12-tine buck rake which was coupled to the back of one of the tractors. Fully loaded with bales on the way into the shed, it was empty on the way back out.

I was holding on to the rim of the cab roof which was just as well. The trip mechanism on the buck rake had not engaged fully, so when we drove over a bump on the track, the catch disengaged and the tines beneath my feet dropped like a trap door. My grip on the cab roof saved me from more serious injury. No stitches were needed when we reached the doctor's house, but I did have two parallel lines down my tummy for years thereafter.

On another occasion, I was riding on the draw bar of a trailer which was being towed out of a field at Lynchat on to the A9. A new estate employee was at the wheel of the tractor. Being temporary and by far the youngest on the staff, I did not get to drive when working alongside any of the others. The manoeuvre may have been carried out a little too sharply given the slope at the field gate. Whatever the reason, the trailer started to topple. It was one of these slow-motion events, allowing me time to step forward on to the back of the tractor itself when I realised what was happening.

Had the force of the falling load been sufficient to spring the draw bar free from the tractor altogether, the accident would again have been much worse. Perhaps this thought was going through my mind when I accepted, for the first and only time in my life, a shakily offered cigarette which made it as far as my lips before being hastily returned. That focussed my mind and I went off for immediate help, as the overturned trailer was blocking one of Scotland's busiest roads.

These incidents, coupled with brother's having to be rescued by a neighbouring farmer after he bellied Uncle Roy's tractor off the end of the silage pit at Grange in Banffshire, meant that while my three boys were given the chance to learn to drive at an early age, it was in cars, on the estate tracks, rather than on a tractor. Our mother never did get to hear about her younger son's silage pit adventure and his age at the time is not being revealed even now.

The highlight of the working summer at Balavil was the clipping, a kind of industrial strength version of the Harris 'fank'. There were hundreds of sheep on Balavil.

The shepherd doubled up as farm manager and called on all his colleagues in the valley firstly to help gather the sheep off the moor into the fields around the steading and then, providing it had stayed dry overnight, to shear the lot in one day.

There would be those who were experts at shearing, others who would keep the pens full by bringing batches of sheep in and those who dragged the sheep from the pens to their appointment with the barber. This last job I enjoyed hugely.

The sheep were blackfaces, curly of horn and slightly manic of eye in what were, for them, exacting circumstances. They were forced to leave the open hillsides for a busy field, then a crowded pen, before getting caught by the horns and being dragged into a hot, noisy building. The final ignominy was being flipped over and parked on their backsides, their horns being passed to the shearer. Things improved greatly for the sheep after the overly warm fleece was off. Once shorn, some would take the opportunity to butt any unwary human tail during their exuberant exit back to fresh air.

Harry, the tractor-man, revelled in having the worst job at the clipping. Most of his long day was spent in huge sacks, suspended from the rafters. He would be passed a rolled-up fleece which he would slide past his chin, past his chest and down below his feet, so he could stamp on it to produce a tightly packed sack for transportation. Think heat, think smell, think dirty tails, think ticks; Harry was, nevertheless, the cheeriest guy throughout.

On the subject of Balavil characters, mention has to be made of Angie (short for Angus not Angela), the gamekeeper back in my early days. I am no longer sure how much is my own recollection and how much has been gleaned from Allan, a great storyteller and another big Angie Bain fan. Angie was a living portrait of the old-school Highland gamekeeper.

From the top Angie was, Harris Tweed Deerstalker casually adorned with a selection of salmon flies, dancing eyes as alert as those of any creature in his domain, a well-maintained bristle of a moustache with pipe below, tweed jacket with plus twos, colour co-ordinated socks and garters, stout brogues. Over the shoulder would be a leather cartridge bag.

In my mind's eye, I will always have a picture of Angie leaning on a long crook. Although he covered the ground quickly, there was the hint of a limp from being gored by horns or antlers. His shotgun was usually in the crook of his arm and was of vintage design. Does the mind's eye recall his gun having external hammers? One thing I do remember from Allan is that Angie was reputed to wait until he could line up two rabbits to take them out with only one cartridge – keeping a careful eye on the estate overheads!

Croftcarnoch holds a couple of vivid memories which tend to pop up when Scottish wildlife is the topic of a conversation. I proffer the view that if you walk stealthily around the woods with a gun (but without a dog) hoping to bag a rabbit or two and you make as little noise as possible, you can, with a little luck and a favourable wind direction, surprise even the wariest of creatures.

As I rounded a very large rhododendron bush between Croftcarnoch and Balavil House, I came face to face with a Scottish wildcat. This was in the late seventies, but even then, they were very scarce. This animal was the real MacKay, no hybrid he. He was sitting on a large tree stump and met my startled stare with one of his own, before recovering his machismo and slinking off into cover with a most baleful backward glance. It was an extraordinary meeting, at least for one of us, the breadth of the animal's face leaving an indelible impression.

Imagine Gilbert, The Famous Grouse, a television whisky advertising star for over twenty years; give him a broader tail and some more black in his plumage. Now imagine him four times bigger or even five and the result would be close to a capercaillie. They are huge, woodland grouse. To come across a large male capercaillie in his natural habitat was another privilege enjoyed by me in the woods at Croftcarnoch. Having had to be reintroduced in Scotland, they are at risk of extinction here for the second time. They have a problem with flying into deer fences and this often proves fatal, especially for younger birds. Their favourite habitat of native pinewood is also shrinking. Capercaillie are a fine sight though... if you are very lucky.

~·~ Highland Retreat ~·~

Over a period of many years, for Ale, the boys and me, Balavil's Garden Cottage was like a weekend home from the beginning of May until the middle of July. Our favourite visit of all was when Ale's sister, Eleonora, came over from Marina di Pisa with her husband, Riccardo, it being his first visit to Scotland. Eleonora had left her busy household the previous year to come over to help while Ale underwent one of her operations. My stepsister, Joan, did the same from Portsoy at the time of other surgery during that most difficult of years. It was a real pleasure for us, and for me in particular to see Eleonora being able to enjoy a visit to Scotland in much happier circumstances.

The Garden Cottage always felt at its best when there was company. It might have been a family of friends visiting for the weekend, Allan and Marjorie coming down from Balavil House for supper or Antony, he of the melting sporran, looking in for a warming dram after a late evening on the river. The visit of Eleonora and Riccardo was, however, special.

After being picked up from Prestwick Airport and driven to Craiglockhart, they were happy to jump back in the Land Rover and head up the A9 to the cottage. While there was still light they were taken in the 4x4 to all the favourite parts of the estate. Despite Riccardo's instant great faith in the car's 'terrain response special programmes' dial there was, sadly, no chance of driving to the Tromie, but we did go through the woods, across the ford and up to the moor. The off-road tour was conducted before showing the Italian guests around the cottage, so that their first view of the living room would not be until after dark and there had been the chance to prepare it properly.

The word 'atavistic' is relatively new to me. I came across this English word from my Italian wife when she used it of me; it does come from Latin, after all. We have had a bit of fun with it. My hunter-gatherer enjoyment of catching or shooting food for the table was the start of it, especially as I leave my womenfolk, Ale, to do the gutting, skinning or plucking. Equally ancestral (much nicer than 'primitive') is my love of chopping wood and getting a log fire going. I do, however, have a nagging doubt that Ale's application to me of the adjective 'atavistic' may not be entirely benign.

We managed to keep Eleonora and Riccardo out of the living room until my fire had taken well, the lamps were switched on and the curtains closed. The two Italian guests were already smitten by the cottage by the time they settled in front of the roaring log fire. Riccardo, the master of *grigliata* in Marina di Pisa, set up an impromptu grill in the fireplace; Kingussie steaks grilled Italian style by a Highland log fire, red wine, homemade oatcakes, strong cheddar. We enjoyed being together for the first time in Scotland and we toasted in celebration of that and of things being so much better than they had been. It was an evening which will long remain in my memory.

Eleonora and Riccardo were not the first of their household to visit the MacKenzies and be taken to Balavil, having sent their elder daughters over in previous years. One of those daughters had an adventure just up the hill from Garden Cottage, very near the second bridge over Raitt's Burn. The bridge was already infamous as being the site of the jump in despair of a maid from Balavil House, more of which later. The section of track up to the bridge is steep. Allan taught me how to hill start there and I, in turn, taught John and Seumas. If you can hill start there, you're fine anywhere.

Balavil, Kingussie

As John and Seumas had done so well in Defender, Alfa 164 and Citroen BX on the Balavil private tracks, I thought I would give our Italian niece a head-start for her driving lessons which were due to start soon, back in Italy.

She had done very well in the family's Sharan over a couple of weekends so, on the way back from Chapel Park, I thought it would be fine for her to turn right at the bridge, take the car down the 'hill start' slope and drive all the way back to her aunt at Garden Cottage. She had done reversing, emergency stop, turning in the road. All had gone perfectly well.

The Sharan was brought to a halt on the bridge; niece selected first gear and the right turn started… but, sadly, never stopped. Perhaps the sight of the incline caused a freeze of confidence. The right turn continued until the Sharan's bonnet was hard up against the wire fence separating the roadway from the steep bank down to the burn. A combination of me on the handbrake and niece on the brake pedal had brought the vehicle to a halt in time. Then, it started going forward again. Before I could think of knocking the car out of first gear, we were off. Slowly, but inexorably, the Sharan nosed its way through the post and wire fence and started its descent of the steep bank, with me almost on my feet, hauling on the hand brake.

The vehicle was moving slowly, staying upright. I could see flat rocks down in the burn, but immediately dismissed them as our likely destination. The Sharan was never going to reach the burn, as it would be stopped by a scattering of young trees whose trunks would certainly be strong enough to arrest our slow descent. That thought brought relief before, happily, the car came to an even earlier halt. Out of gear by now, it had bellied itself in soft earth which eventually was found to be wedged fast between the fuel tank and the floor-pan.

The scene must have looked dramatic from the roadway above. First and foremost a rather quiet niece was passed into the care of her aunt, before I set off for assistance. The Sharan was supposed to get us all back to Edinburgh the following day and to leave for Italy within the week. Arthur, the gamekeeper, was immediately recognised as the man to provide rescue services. He had taken over on Angie's retirement many years before and knew Balavil inside out and upside down. Tractors happened to be his hobby and, in particular, he restored vintage Nuffield tractors of which he had built up a collection. Several had been restored to complete and pristine condition, but I knew that Arthur also had a much more modern tractor, a direct descendent, a big Marshall. The bigger would certainly be the better for this task.

Arthur must have known there was a problem when he saw me approaching the Keeper's Cottage on foot, but on first listening to the story with a smile, he cheerily suggested that his Land Rover would be sufficient to tow the Sharan back on to the road. On visiting the scene, Arthur did an about turn and immediately drove off for the Marshall, his biggest tractor!

Fortunately, the Sharan had a tow bar which easily accepted the hook of Arthur's towing chain. He proposed that, while he drove the big, white Marshall on the driveway above, I would steer the Sharan's wheels to assist the manoeuvre. Having just been relieved to exit the Sharan, I chose not to get back in and steered, instead, through the open window. I needn't have been concerned. That one of the tractor's wheels initially struggled for grip on the dust and stones of the driveway showed how

Balavil, Kingussie

firmly embedded the Sharan had become. Very carefully, Arthur inched the tractor forward until the Sharan was free and then accelerated very gradually, keeping full tension on the chain, until the people carrier was back on the roadway and secured.

The Sharan left for Italy within five days with Ale, sons and niece on board. Kwik Fit near Craiglockhart had checked the exhaust, repairing minor bracket damage free of charge. A garage in Penicuik had been approached for help by a work colleague of mine and had beaten out the slight dent in the wing, had ensured all was well with the fuel tank and, importantly, had allowed the Sharan to jump their queue of work. Allan's fence was repaired at very reasonable cost, it coming to light that the fence had been repaired at least twice before on account of vehicles ending up down that slope.

As for our niece, she recovered the desire to speak, a long four hours after the mishap. A game of rugby ball Piggy in the Middle with uncle and cousins did the trick and only a year later, the same niece confidently drove me from Marina to Pisa having passed her driving test first time. We enjoyed a smile together but said not a word about 'off-roading' at Balavil.

~·~ Short and Sharp ~·~

A while back, there was, for the extended family, a large weekend gathering at Balavil with all of John F's children, their families, Iain Alick's sons and their families. One of many varied activities was a group visit, led by Allan, to Raitt's Cave which is on the hill behind Chapel Park Farm steading. Although it is called a cave, it is believed to be an Iron Age souterrain, an underground earth dwelling, built into the hillside, with some massive stones having been used in its horseshoe shaped structure.

Allan's gift for story telling came into its own before his audience of relatives. The local folklore on Raitt's Cave was his subject.

The cave had been 'converted' by a band of robbers, McNivens allegedly, who had clearly been given a very good start by their Iron Age ancestors. Above the cave, these McNivens had constructed an innocent looking peasant type dwelling. It sounded as if they must have ended up with a 'Tardis' affair with room for far more people inside than the external appearance would suggest.

The occupiers of the peasant dwelling looked poor and innocent enough, but in reality, they were sharing in the spoils of the marauding McNivens who had set up base in the large cave below.

The local Macphersons were the ones who suffered the brunt of the skilful banditry which was perpetrated on the residents of the area for years. Thanks to the pretence of the conniving family on the ground floor, their downstairs neighbours seemed to vanish into thin air following their raids.

Eventually, however, McNiven success seems to have gone to their heads. They became careless and Macpherson suspicion started to home in on the 'Tardis' dwelling. A particularly cunning Macpherson came up with a plan, a particularly cunning plan which involved his disappearing from public sight for quite a time. He feigned serious illness to allow his hair and beard to grow long and unkempt, then disguised himself as a beggar and called at the door of the dwelling, above the McNiven hideout, asking for both food and shelter.

The womenfolk were happy to give him some food, but absolutely refused his plea for shelter. This was not in Macpherson's script. Thinking quickly, he reverted to his initial idea of feigning illness, the old tales suggesting that he faked an extremely painful bout of kidney stones.

The McNiven 'front' women relented and let him fall asleep by the fire…only he didn't. While pretending to be deeply asleep with his long, matted hair over his eyes, he was able to watch as a large flagstone was shifted to one side and food for about a dozen men was passed down below.

In the morning, his hosts were relieved to find that the 'beggar' had recovered sufficiently to be able to move on. After offering his sincere thanks, Macpherson did exactly that and straight back to his clansmen he went. After his wife had been to work on his hair and beard with sheep shears, he returned to Raitt's Cave, only this time with thirty of his kinsmen at his back. The McNivens were trapped in their underground den and easily overpowered.

There was no trial before a judge and jury, nor even any plea in mitigation, just the roughest of justice in the shape of a grim-faced Macpherson clansman with a big axe, a nearby tree stump serving as the executioner's block.

~•~ MacKenzie's Farewell to Balavil House ~•~

A couple of hundred yards up from the bridge is Balavil House itself, a substantial mansion, designed by Robert Adam, but to the MacKenzie family, it was a place of warm welcome, much conviviality, generous hospitality and great fun. Whether it be family weddings, lunches or dinners in the grand dining room, informal dinners at the round table in the kitchen, or a glass or two of wine with Allan and Marjorie in their family sitting room, it was a joy.

When Balavil came on the market, there was some publicity given to its friendly ghost, Sarah. There had been word of a 'grey lady' for many years. Furthermore, strange happenings had begun when the basement area below the kitchen was opened up and developed. A kettle switched on; a fire set and lit; a guest's clothes folded; hot taps turned on in bathrooms, all without explanation. Happenings such as these had been going on for some time, but Allan was at pains to make it clear that there was never any sense of threat or feeling of fear. It was all very positive. Well, he does tell a very good story and the property was for sale.

Sarah, a maid, had apparently fallen for the butler of Balavil House, but in his view at least, he was too far above her in social standing, so love could be in one direction only. Devastated, the maid had thrown herself off the bridge and down into Raitt's Burn, or more accurately, on to its rocks. Obviously a decent and kindly soul, she was found stone dead...or so the story goes.

I had occasionally enjoyed playing a few tunes on the grand piano in the main reception hall of Balavil House, but always felt I was under the fixed stare of the many wall mounted stags' heads, interspersed with some more exotic trophies from a bygone era, notably a particularly angry-looking African buffalo. It had been a notion of mine to play a couple of tunes on the accordion from the balcony above the buffalo's disapproving glare. In truth, reference to a disapproving glare does not begin to give the full flavour of the picture of incandescent rage that adorned the wall. Like the idea of trophy heads or not, one would have to concede that the taxidermist had brought this big fellow back to life, the beast looking like he had just rammed his head and horns right through the wall, his malevolent stare challenging anyone to say a word in rebuke.

About a week before Allan and Marjorie moved out to Croftcarnoch, I asked if I could wander about the big house with the accordion. With permission willingly granted, I played my usual melancholic stuff. It was, after all, 'MacKenzie's Farewell to Balavil House' and my habit of slowing all tunes down seemed quite appropriate for the occasion. Lentissimo feels like a race to me most of the time, but I managed to brighten a tune or two up a bit when I ventured on to the second floor and propped up some sheet music on the windowsill of one of the bedrooms overlooking the Spey valley. I could never visit the second floor of the big house without remembering that it was the location where a 'grey lady' had most often put in an appearance and where Sarah, the friendly and helpful ghost, had done some of her good deeds. There was a distinct feeling to the second-floor corridor.

The view from the window was magnificent. A large field below the big house bordered the new A9 which, at that point, runs close beside the old road. Then there was another narrow field adjacent to the railway line, across which lay the marshland down to the Spey itself with woods and hills beyond.

It was a sunny day, providing a glorious panorama. I was also feeling quite sentimental, feeling that it was the end of an era and a private moment to remember. I don't play much without needing the music in front of me, so I was busy dividing attention between the view and the notes when I began to feel a presence, not really spooky, just a presence; hairs on the back of the neck stuff, all the same.

Second floor. Grey lady? Helpful ghost? The Scottish Paranormal Association had told Allan that the place was full of spirits, mostly 'friendly'. That little letter 'r' makes all the difference.

The last time I had been alone on the second floor was years back. I had been volunteered to collect a spare chair from an empty bedroom up there. In fact, none of the rooms on the second floor had been occupied at the time and there had been an undeniable chill about the long corridor with its occasional creaking floorboard. It had not been an entirely pleasant experience!

Concentrating on the sunny view, I dismissed memories of that last visit and played a little louder. The feeling passed.

I eventually turned around from the window and, of course, there was nothing there but the open bedroom door. Packing away accordion and music, I went down to join Ale, Allan and Marjorie who were drinking mugs of coffee together in Allan's office.

'I did come up to offer you one,' said Ale, 'but you were concentrating so hard, I thought I'd leave you to it.' Benevolent spirit, right enough.

With a last look up at the glowering African buffalo, I bade farewell to Balavil House with its tales of ghosts and its many memories. From there, my 'tour' of the estate follows Raitt's Burn upstream through the woods and across the moor. There are happy times to recall on the way to the scene of real tragedy.

When you continue up the main driveway from Garden Cottage to the bridge where our niece and I went rather more off road than we intended, you turn right for Balavil House or left for Chapel Park Farm. On foot, or in a 4x4, you can also opt to go straight on through a gateway. The track becomes steep and rough at this point, but once you go past what was, long ago, a little golf course, you meet the deer fence, where the road is much better again and not so much of an enjoyable challenge. Once through the high gate at the deer fence, you are in native Scottish pine wood through which almost every trip offers something of interest. Osprey, red squirrel, roe deer, red deer and, right at the top, even blackcock can be seen. The last named provide a sight to quicken the pulse of anyone with a love of Scotland's high moorland, whether their bag be grouse or Munro.

Half-way through the wood, a very sharp turn to the left and down takes you across a ford in Raitt's Burn to 'Marjorie's folly'. This was a rather grand fishing hut, used in the 2000-05 'Monarch of the Glen' television series, relocated to a perfect picnic area, down by the burn and far enough into the woods to be sheltered and peaceful. If it started to rain, the table and chairs would be moved inside the hut and, almost seamlessly, the picnic could continue.

Most importantly, 'Marjorie's folly' had a barbecue grill and, with there being a fine, traditional butcher shop in Kingussie, the coming together of location, grill and quality Highland produce regularly proved idyllic. Even my penchant for an open fire was very well served by a huge brazier, made by a friend of Allan's, modelled on an idea he had seen in Africa. A lorry wheel, no less, formed the base, minus its tyre, of course. Iron bars rose perhaps three feet from the base with a metal band forming a rim at the top. It was a solid piece of metal work, very simple, yet brilliant. Once lit, it would accept substantial branches from fallen timber, the circumference being tight enough to hold them in place with the gaps between the bars being sufficient to allow plenty air to reach the base of the fire.

It was always worth coming to a halt as the top of the wood was reached. A pause there would often allow a herd of deer to be sighted, usually only if they moved. They seemed to be more comfortable if the engine was kept running, probably because nobody had ever shot at them from a moving vehicle. They would be difficult to distinguish lying down by the burn to the left. It was easier to spot them on the higher ground on the right, as moving deer would often break the skyline.

After dinner in the Garden Cottage, either by ourselves or with visiting friends, Ale and I would regularly come up to this point in the Land Rover. We would wait until darkness had just about fallen before setting off and it was often a source of amazement to our guests how close we could get to a herd of deer, the animals hardly heeding the headlights. Our visitors were always well taken with the nocturnal safaris to seek deer up on the moor; high up above the Spey valley, dozens of pairs of eyes shining out at us from the blackness.

A long, long way up the track and not too far from the apex of the estate's rough triangle, is 'the bothy'. It used to be solely a shelter for walkers and climbers and that function continues, constant access being available for the public to one section where there is a supply of candles, matches and fuel for the fire.

A large extension has been added to the original bothy, the new section being locked and shuttered when not in use. It comprises a large dining area with French doors facing back down to the Spey valley. At one end is a huge open fireplace where logs, peat or a combination of both, could generate all the heat needed for a 'function suite', miles up on a moor.

The bothy was the scene of many celebrations. In the MacKenzie family, Ale's 40th was enjoyed there as were other birthdays. One fiftieth birthday-boy opted to walk all the way up to the bothy for a celebration lunch, choosing to join the empty picnic hamper in the back of the Defender on the way back down again; a wise decision by our good friend, Bruno. Happy times indeed.

Not very far from the bothy, however, is the scene of a WW2 tragedy. Although the estate track ends just beyond the bothy, the extent of Balavil reaches up to the valley of the River Dulnain. I believe that I am the only MacKenzie who has reached that point on the estate and that only on one occasion when I stood in, on a grouse shoot, for a delayed guest.

Seumas tried to reach the end of the estate a few years ago on an end-of-season weekend away with some rugby teammates. It was June, but they were beaten back by snow! White out conditions without warning could have proved very nasty for these young rugby players in t-shirts and tracksuit trousers, no matter how fit they were. They had taken a wrong turn, but common sense kicked in, Raitt's Burn being located and followed downstream as quickly as possible. Seumas and his mates had set out to find the wreck of the crashed bomber.

On the night of 31 August 1944, a Lancaster bomber with a Royal Australian Air Force crew of six, plus a flight engineer from Glasgow, crashed, killing all on board. An article originally published by the Badenoch and Strathspey Herald in July 2009, updated in November 2011, provided some background as it spoke of the two theories on the cause of the crash viz: a lightning strike or ultimately fatal damage suffered on a bombing mission the night before. The crew were newly qualified.

The article indicated that a veteran, who had flown in that very plane on a bombing mission over Germany the night before it crashed, had visited Balavil in his eighties. He had told Allan that, on their return flight from their German raid, his crew had had to shut down one of the engines. The plane had then been repaired before setting off, the very next day, on its doomed training flight over the Highlands of Scotland.

Of particular interest to me in the article, was a quote to the effect that the Royal Air Force (RAF) were especially pleased to have recovered, in 2009, one of the plane's landing wheels, as it was fitted with a smooth tyre. It was the only original in existence, as all other surviving Lancaster tyres were of the treaded style. Strangely, that smooth tyre is the strongest visual image in my memory of my visit to the wreckage in the early eighties. I did, however, also remember noticing the lack of guns amongst the wreckage. That was explained to me many years later....at a local shinty match.

The family have been to a few shinty cup finals over the years. A young Seumas has even sipped whisky from the Camanachd Cup after one of Kingussie's victories. I did not regularly go to Saturday league matches but one Saturday afternoon, there was an irritating wind direction at the Tromie and the fish were not playing at all, so I decided to catch the second half at the Dell shinty ground where I got into conversation with an old fellow,

Kingussie born and bred. Fishing at Balavil was mentioned as was a WW2 gun emplacement which had recently been pointed out to me, not far from the Balavil boundary at the Tromie end of the estate. The shinty fan then asked me if I knew about the bomber. Of course, I did. The old fellow went on to tell me that the guns had been taken off the plane very quickly after the crash site was located. They had been brought down from the moor on ponies and it had been decided that the marshes near the river would be a good place for them, the reason why not being offered. Whether that was to be a temporary arrangement only, was not clear either. Sadly, the location chosen was so boggy that one of the ponies disappeared along with the guns. That discovery will cause a puzzle for someone in the future, because as far as is known, the guns are still in there.

Recalling that conversation, I researched further and found an excerpt from the RAF Operations Record Book, RAF Station Longman, Inverness for the morning of 1st September 1944 showing that a Royal Observer Corps post had reported the crash. An RAF crash party was out for 19 hours 'in very wild, hilly country' and reported that they reckoned that the bomber had exploded at 10,000 feet, as the debris was spread over two square miles.

The initial remarks of the aircraft's home station commander had also been abstracted, with the despatch of the training flight being considered justified given the weather forecast for the area. The veteran's comments to Allan about the damage suffered by the plane, on its bombing mission the night before it crashed, came to mind.

I have since found out that the veteran was bomb aimer Bill Jackson from Queensland, Australia who had flown several successful missions in the plane and having visited the crash site with his wife, Daphne, remained in contact with Allan and Marjorie until he died at the age of ninety-three.

It was Flight Officer Bill Purdy from Sydney, Australia who took delivery of the brand-new Lancaster on 6th August 1944 at RAF Waddington in Lincolnshire. At the age of ninety, Bill flew to London and took a train to Inverness to be met by Allan. Once his guest had recovered from the marathon journey, Allan drove him in an amphibious all-terrain vehicle six miles over the Balavil moor to the wreckage of the crashed plane. The two are still in touch, having met for dinner in Sydney as recently as December 2018.

On board the Lancaster, the six Australians, known affectionately as a 'sprog' crew due to their being newly qualified, were Flying Officer Robert Beddoe (21), the pilot; Flight Sergeant Frederic Walker (32), the navigator; Flight Sergeant Stanley Abbott (21), the mid-upper gunner; Flight Sergeant Terrence Dent (21), the wireless operator; Flight Sergeant Bevil Glover (23), the rear gunner; David Ryan (30), the bomb aimer whose rank was not given. They were laid to rest in the Commonwealth War Graves Commission Cemetery in Cambridge.

The sole RAF airman on board was the flight engineer, Warrant Officer George Middleton (37). Some believe that George managed to bale out and land safely only to die in a fall from a rock face as he tried to reach help. He is buried in Rutherglen Cemetery in his native Glasgow.

In 2008, on the sixty-fourth anniversary of the tragedy, a memorial to the crew, incorporating a single blade of one of the plane's propellers, was unveiled in Balavil's own private graveyard.

Balavil, Kingussie

It is perhaps fitting, that even this short description of very happy times spent at Balavil includes reference to a wartime event, albeit a tragic one.

These young men who died on Balavil's moorland in 1944 have not been forgotten.

THE LANDS OF OUR FATHERS

~·~ A New Chapter in Harris ~·~

During the first nine years of my life, there had grown in me a very strong attachment to Harris – the island, its people and their way of life. I just loved everything about it. While my real home will now always unquestionably be wherever Ale is, I have long described Harris as my 'spiritual home'. I had, after all, heard my father refer to Harris only as 'home' during my early childhood.

Some fifty years after my father's death, a new Harris chapter opened for me during my initial absence from work. As with Colinton Dell, it was hoped that Harris, the township of Quidinish in particular, could be a place to aid recovery.

The look on Scudo's face on the morning of my early departure was both incredulous and accusatorial. Leaving without my wife was bad enough, but to leave without my dog was inexcusable. The facial expressions spoke volumes.

The dog did have a point.

After a mildly vexing session of canine mind reading and the quelling of second thoughts, I set off at 6.30 on a lovely June morning for the five-and-a-half-hour drive to the ferry terminal at Uig on Skye. My destination was croft number 7, down at the far end of Quidinish in the Bays of Harris, virtually next door to Auntie Mary Ann and her three sons, Norman, John and, when not down in Edinburgh, Donald Iain, known as DI at number 8. At least I would have local expertise on hand.

The crofters at no 7 are good friends of the MacKenzies, both parents and sons. Annick was taking herself off for a couple of weeks to her native Belgium, leaving her husband, Chris, to concentrate on his order book as a noted craftsman of exhausts in the world of racing karts. I was to look after their small herd of Highland cattle and their poultry on the happy understanding that I would still have plenty time to spend with my relatives and to fish. The herd was nineteen strong that June, ranging from the bull, Uist Boy, down to the youngest calf, Wee Dunc, named two months previously after me. The fact that Wee Dunc was a difficult little so and so, was entirely coincidental, allegedly.

The friends have a double croft in Quidinish with permission to graze on a third and, in addition, have a further croft up the coast in Flodabay. These crofts include some very difficult underfoot conditions and all have headlands sticking out into sea lochs or into the Minch itself. There is much bog, rock and heather with some dramatic drops down to the shoreline. There are also sharp precipices inland. All of this means that it is essential to check on the stock every day as, even though Highland cattle have the reputation of fending for themselves, beasts have been known to get stuck in peat bogs and to topple over edges.

The hen and duck runs are on the top of the hill behind the Quidinish croft house and within easy reach of two lochs for the entertainment of the ducks. Not long into my tour of duty, I went to feed the poultry and shut them away for the night. There was no sign of three of the ducks and patient scanning of the vast area visible to me revealed nothing. As usual, I was fearing the worst. Mink? Eagle? Otter? I certainly didn't want anything going missing on my watch. Finally, movement on the calm surface of the loch far below betrayed their position as the three youngest ducks gracefully enjoyed an evening swim in perfect 'V' formation. Incredibly, given the distance involved, a few shouts of 'C'mon the ducks!' and enthusiastic rattling of the grain box brought the ducks to the shore whereupon any sense of grace evaporated in a frantic uphill waddle at impressive speed. They were lost to my sight a few times, but the fervent quacking never wavered. They were in a hurry, which was just as well, as I wanted back to my cousins' house for an Italian football match live on television.

I formed a perfectly enjoyable relationship with the hens. One of them, but only one, would peck grain from the palm of my hand. The relationship I formed with the ducks was a little more complex. From them to me it was entirely based on cupboard love, the same as the hens. The sound of my voice meant food was on the way. From my side, however, there was an undeniable element of affection with the ducks always able to raise a smile. In my eyes, they were a team of stand-up comedians who thought they could double up as a commando unit. In the mornings, I had to ensure that the hens ate their fill before the ducks were released, otherwise there was an immediate raid on the forecourt of the henhouse. At the outset, the ducks would feign disinterest to lull me into a false sense of security, but once their tactics dawned on me, a strict routine was put in place.

The cupboard love approach to all in my care was adopted right at the start of the three-week stay. It has its uses, but also some risks.

My tour of duty had started with a handover period with Annick. Obviously, I was keen to meet my wee namesake, but held off entering the enclosure until Annick appeared with a bucket of sugar beet shreds and bruised barley for the little chap's mum, Toutou, a cow sizeable for her breed and boasting a vast pair of horns. There was no way I was coming between mother and calf before formal introductions had been made and Toutou's nose was wedged in a bucket and that was even before I read that 74 people had been killed by cows in the UK in the previous 15 years.

Wee Dunc was absolutely immaculate. In his first photo, he is lying on short, clean, dry grass with a few clumps of heather around him, looking straight at the lens of my mobile. One pristine, white hoof is just visible, testament to the dry weather. His coat is short and bushy on his forehead, nothing like the long, thick, forelock of his mother, his eyes clearly visible. With her eyes, you need to be well close and hoping for a breeze to catch a glimpse! The big surprise was that Wee Dunc was red, despite both his parents having black coats. Very sadly, he mysteriously dropped dead at the age of one, lending a distinct quality of sentimentality to that first photo.

Within twenty-four hours, Wee Dunc's mum was accepting freshly plucked grass from my hand. She did not appear to have done this with anyone before and the operation was a bit awkward to begin with. It was easiest for her if the plucked grass was offered protruding horizontally from either side of my clenched fist. The highlight for this apprentice stockman came when the mother and calf both took grass, sharing the same handful; a simple, little pleasure enjoyed at first through the strands of a fence. It was particularly rewarding, as the calf had just had his ears tagged and had not, when I first arrived, been at all happy at the sight of any approaching human.

Soon enough, the mother would come to me when called; she would hesitate, lick her lips like a big puppy, then amble her way over to accept a treat of long grass. She ended up expecting fresh grass as a dessert after her bucket of shreds. By that stage, the feeding was done without the hindrance of a fence, but care was taken not to stand anywhere between Toutou and her food bucket, as her acceleration was noticeably better than her braking. In addition, feeding by hand always involved the planting of my duck-head staff to be held between her horns. An inadvertent sideward turn of that shaggy head could lead to a horn heading for the ribs which the staff was poised to parry. It never happened, but the staff was always planted, just in case.

No real liberties were taken because, earlier in the year, when helping with winter feeding, I had seen how quickly the bull could cover even the most difficult ground as he aimed for his breakfast. Respect had to be maintained, but even the bull followed a bucket of feed when he was being moved, as it seems that Highland cattle respond better to being led than to being driven. Getting Wee Dunc happier with human contact after his painful ear marking was the start of trying to raise him to be reasonably trusting and therefore more manageable.

~·~ The 'Flodabay Five' ~·~

It was decided on day two of my stay, that I would try to engage the 'Flodabay Five' up close. They were bullocks, between one and two years old; I had already met them in March/April.

There was a domino effect in operation in Flodabay at feeding time. Their clear group pecking order manifested itself in a cascade of bullying from the strongest down to little black Eddie who had nobody to bully. At least seven piles of cattle nuts had to be set out for the five, so there was always alternative food for the beast that had been knocked away from his first course. Nobody ever finished what they started, their buddy's feed lying a few feet away always being more appealing. Horns were employed with some force, but only to intimidate rather than to injure.

It was clear that little Eddie had not flourished at all between April and June. Winter feeding had stopped by the time of my June arrival, there being plenty of grass, but the bullying had continued. The other four were visibly thriving. The intention was that I supplemented the grazing with beef cattle nuts and, after a few days of rattling the feed bucket and delivering seven piles of cattle 'treats' over the fence at Flodabay, I started going over the style to join the beasts on their side of the fence. I would lead them a little way with the bucket and then dish out portions of nuts aplenty.

The young cattle were quickly getting used to me; the heads would lift up immediately at the sound of the Land Rover stopping at the gate. One morning, all five were out of sight over a rise, so I rattled the bucket loudly and called for them. If it works with ducks…….

Over the brow came four of them at a trot and accelerated downhill towards me. They may well have been licking their lips, but I was more taken by the impression that I was facing a bovine charge. OK, it wasn't Waterloo or Balaclava and the bucket was the target, but it did concentrate the mind. It was time for respect to be shown…by the beasts.

Instead of dropping the bucket and stepping smartly back over the style, I bellowed at the bullocks and raised my staff. Foolish it may have been, but my confidence was high. It brought the four of them to an immediate halt. In a cartoon, there would have been skidding and screeching with smoke coming up from the hooves. There was not much chance of that on heather and moss, but the thought gave me a smile.

The four bullies were left to dunt each other in their game of musical chairs while I went to Eddie and let him fill his boots from the bucket in peace. As I left, however, I saw Eddie being knocked away from the water supply out of sheer spite, the aggressor not even bothering to take a drink from the vacated trough. Eddie has since been brought back to the main herd to escape the bullying that was holding him back.

While I loved every minute of working with them, I did think it was very likely that the presence of an unfamiliar dog might have caused the cattle to have been less amenable. Scudo would certainly have been kept well out of the way if I was going anywhere near the new calf and his mum. The vicinity of the bull would have been strictly off limits too, but part of my daily routine would have been tailor made for my dog's company.

The routine started with breakfast for Toutou as she was suckling Wee Dunc. She would come looking for me at the gate behind the bothy and, if I didn't appear by 8.45am, her impatient bawling would start – quite the demanding customer.

After that, it was a sweep of Quidinish Point to check on the various cattle grazing out on that large headland with its small lochs, slopes, rocks and steep drops down to the sea. The weather had been unusually dry, so light boots were enough rather than the standard Landmaster wellies; certain marshy areas were still to be avoided.

I started out up the hill behind the bothy. From the top, you can look across Loch Finsbay, Finsbay itself and right up to Roneval, the highest hill in South Harris. That hill is a grand sight in its own right, but it doubles up as a weather forecaster; a cap of cloud on Roneval means you can expect rain and, if you can't see Roneval at all, the rain has already arrived. It can be worse. If there is no sign of Finsbay, an unpleasant morning awaits. Worst of all is when the Minch is crashing waves on to the shore of Quidinish Island and the white spray is nearing the height of its central hillock; that is a clear signal to turn back and give it half an hour to improve.

On the southern shore of the headland is Loch Finsbay which is popular with pleasure boat crews on the lookout for a sheltered mooring for the night. Finsbay and Quidinish Islands are obvious hazards to avoid and MacAskill's reef is easily spotted too, but there are loads of other rocks around there some of which are visible at low tide from the shore. The way the boats would come confidently sailing in suggested they all had the best of up-to-date navigation equipment.

If I was not in a rush, I would stop and admire the gannets fishing off the two islands, turning themselves into armour piercing arrows as they plummeted from height. They must have reinforced foreheads, throats and chests plus some way of protecting their nostrils. It makes for quite a sight.

Further out, I would pass along the slopes leading down to Leac a' Bhodaich – the Old Man's Rock – which is one of the family's favourite locations for rock fishing. In good weather it is a magical place. If the fish are not taking, you can always enjoy the view straight across to Skye and the mainland.

High above Leac a' Bhodaich, turning my back on the sea, I would be able to see halfway across South Harris. Up there at the Ordnance Survey trig point on a quiet day, the view is breath taking, but on a rough day, it is difficult to breathe!

Having moved north over the slopes and gullies, I would find myself close to Cnoc Eisgean, considered to be the east wing of Quidinish, blessed with sheltered and productive fishing rocks. I would be looking down on the sea loch at Flodabay and on over to Manish, Geocrab and Stockinish.

In that area of the Point, the heather is deep and more than once I have had narrow escapes with hidden holes. A broken leg out there would be a very serious business. If I were lucky enough to have mobile network, help would be quick enough and maybe even on a quadbike. Otherwise, I would not have been noticed missing until I was perhaps an hour or so late for a meal with my relatives.

The slopes down to Loch Flodabay seem dramatically steep, but there is a tricky little path down through the heather to the spot called Leana Caor. There is an area at the foot of the slope about the size of a football pitch with rocks, grass and rock pools. Once you are down there, it is easy to move about for a variety of casting points and the climb back up is not as difficult as it looks. Leana Caor has a second, important role to play. When all else fails and the whole headland has been scanned, that is where you will find the cattle!

Late one morning, the cattle were well ahead on points in my daily game of hide and seek; they had to be, as my score was nil. As I got to the ridge above Leana Caor, I noticed a small, open fishing boat, with a crew of one, cruising gently amongst a series of buoys not very far from the shore. My thoughts turned back to the previous day when I had enjoyed a meal of fried herring and boiled new potatoes. The herring were early season and just landed in Stornoway. No vegetable was served with them, that being the Harris way. What is more, my cousins recommended a glass of milk rather than my usual water. Despite thinking that milk would be a strange accompaniment, I took the advice and was easily convinced that no other drink could complement the dish as well, subject always to the proviso that Sauvignon Blanc was out of consideration, at least at lunchtime.

There was talk over the meal of the practice of eating herring and potatoes with the fingers and I recalled my late stepfather delighting in telling of the fingers then being run through the hair. I had enjoyed taking that as gospel especially from the Rev John Fletcher who had sported a shock of black and then silver hair all his days.

Leana Caor does have its difficulties, although the natural fishing platforms are excellent, with many having a ledge just below, right at the water surface, as a bit of 'Health and Safety'. The path down requires proper care and much respect is due to the cattle that make it down and up, albeit with the advantage of four hoof drive.

As I stood above Leana Caor that fine morning and watched the boat in the bay below, I was breaking the skyline and wearing a bright yellow shirt at that. I must have been visible, but no wave was forthcoming from the lone fisherman and none was offered by me. For the fisherman, it was either Hebridean reserve, poor eyesight or both! For me, it was evidence of being lost in the moment of my being happy to be out, looking after animals, in the land of my father and countless generations before him, even though (1) I couldn't actually find the cattle, (2) I was missing my wife and (3) I was feeling guilty about not taking my dog up there with me.

On that day especially, it was as well that Scudo wasn't with me as I finally found the cattle perched precariously on the edge of steep cliffs above the Minch. Had they had finger-nails they would have been holding on by them and the sudden arrival of a strange dog might have startled them, triggering a horrible disaster.

My morning routine was that, once the beasts on Quidinish Point had been checked, the next stop was to visit the 'Flodabay Five'. They were on a much smaller headland which was divided into inner and outer sections by a fence. The outer section was only a short walk across the poorer ground of the roadside section. Usually the five beasts would be waiting by the fence having heard the engine, but occasionally there was the chance to go looking for them further out. That doubled up as a seal spotting tour.

Now, I am not a great seal enthusiast, but I was pleased for the crofters that there was a healthy seal population around the furthest point of their Flodabay croft. There would be between ten and twenty of them basking on the shore or on the reefs just off it and my arrival would usually cause all the seals to take to the water and disappear. Curiosity would then get the better of them and one black head after another would pop up to see what the visitor, with his duck's head staff and red bucket, was up to.

The answer was simple. Check the five cattle were there, that the four bullies hadn't run Eddie into the sea and then give them all a treat of cattle nuts, the staff being to encourage reasonable manners; nothing serious, just a tap on a horn when absolutely needed.

Next on the standard route would be a short drive back down the road to Quidinish to make sure the bull and his Tracy were safe and well. They grazed on the Craobhag, yet another headland, this time opposite the croft house. It is named after a little tree that must, at one time, have tried to survive on it, but didn't manage. With the prevailing west wind, the bull and Tracy spent much of their time on the sheltered side and therefore in easy view from the house and its bothy. Those two could often be checked by binoculars from the breakfast table, but the checking was never taken lightly, even so close to home. There are dangers galore out on the Craobhag.

~·~ Poultry Problems ~·~

The route just described would form my regular morning tour of the cattle, but at some stage along the way, I would also feed and water the hens and ducks.

Despite the fact that I was missing Scudo, I was glad I did not subject the Quidinish ducks to the unsettling company of an unfamiliar dog, as I had really quite taken to them. Some evenings, I would find that they had come to meet me, registering first mild complaint at the lateness of my arrival followed by enthusiastic celebration. They would then turn around and waddle ahead of me to their enclosure where the quacking would build to a crescendo and then stop the instant the first handful of grain hit the ground. Frantic eating would be interspersed with equally frantic waddling to the water bucket, all in a silence of concentration.

I reported back to Ale early on during that first solo stint that, after 35 years in law, I had perhaps found my true place in life – losing games of hide and seek with cleverly camouflaged Highland cattle and getting henpecked into the bargain. It was not, of course, all sweetness and long hours of daylight through my entire three weeks.

The hens had the sole use of the substantial ruins of what had been a black house on the hill behind the main croft dwelling. The thick stone walls remained almost wholly intact and one of the two rooms still had a roof on it, although certainly not the original thatched style. Inside were two wooden hen coops plus small tables for water and grain dispensers. The other room, which formed a retreat and feeding area, had a net over it to discourage wild birds from stealing food and to keep out real nasties like crows and buzzards. The view from the front door looked over other crofts, a loch and a sea loch. Beyond those were the moors and hills of South Harris. It was a fine outlook.

Just about fifty yards away was Loch an Nighe, but there are loads of those. The name just means it was the loch where the womenfolk would do the washing, but it is now a water supply for ducks and hens. It is particularly important for ducks to keep their nostrils clear of mud, apparently. The ducks, of course, also use the loch for whatever ducks do during the day. Their separate enclosure does have a little artificial pond in it for emergencies, plus a duck house with two nesting boxes.

The very pleasant location did not mitigate much when it came to the duty of scraping hen droppings from the two tables into a barrel (daily) or changing the newspaper floor covering of the coops (weekly), but I got used to the chores and was always cheered when eggs were produced.

One hen did grow weaker during my stay and I reported to Chris her absolute refusal to move from her straw bed. The advice was to check her breastbone. If she was plump, there was no real worry, but if the breastbone was prominent, things were not good. It was so prominent it was almost sharp to the touch. She had to be put out of her misery, a duty I was happy to leave to Chris.

One of the ducks also developed a problem. She limped noticeably and fell well behind the others as they made their way back from Loch an Nighe when dinner was announced. Within a couple of days, her comical gait became a pitiful sight. In her haste not to miss out on her share, she would use her wings like walking poles to improve her balance and pace. Chris, who had kept some rarer breeds of duck when he farmed in England, was called to come and check on her. I was glad to listen and learn; I even learned about circulation in the legs of ducks from my zoology graduate cousin on the croft next door. Every day is a school day on Harris.

The duck's difficulty was a badly swollen joint. There was even word of the ankle having to be opened and drained, not by a vet, you appreciate, but by Chris and me. South Harris is the sort of place where it pays to be a first responder in veterinary science, first aid, plumbing and car mechanics. Fortunately for all concerned, Chris decided to see if nature would do the healing and it did, after a week or so.

The only really embarrassing incident in the three-week stay was duck related. Having been told during the handover that the ducks had gone off laying, my checking of the duck nesting box was rather cursory. I would slide the window to one side and pat my hand quickly on the nest. I found nothing for the first four or five days, but I saw no problem with that; I had been warned that they were not laying. How wrong I was. When Chris came up to check on the lame bird, he got down on his knees and pretty much got his upper half right into the nesting area, before reversing out having located about a dozen eggs. Unbeknown to me, there was a second nest of volcanic proportions behind the easily visible nest I had been checking up to that point; not only that, but on leaving the nest for the day, the ducks were burying their eggs into the walls of their straw volcano. It was excruciating for this enthusiastic, trying as hard as possible, no mistakes allowed, croft-carer, but the eggs were still fresh enough and no harm had been done.

The end of term report card indicated that I was the first provider of holiday cover who had not suffered a catastrophic decline in hen and duck egg production.

~·~ Quidinish, Isle of Harris: Early Memories ~·~

In the summer of 2015, Ale and I were celebrating our thirtieth wedding anniversary. As it had become very clear that I was to be off work on a mid to long-term basis, Ale suggested an extra visit to Harris in addition to our usual weeks in April and October. To make it a little different, she also booked the smaller ferry from Leverburgh to Berneray, so we could have a look at the Uists for the first time. It turned out to be memorable.

The extra Hebridean visit developed into something rather more than just a holiday. Oddly, perhaps, the real recognition of what the whole trip eventually came to mean for me dawned on the Skye ferry during the journey back to Edinburgh.

The ferry was not far out of Uig Bay, when I came out with a heartfelt 'Bloody Hell!' While it was said with a tone of awe, it was utterly devoid of information for the listening Ale who had to wait to learn that what I had seen was a major disturbance on the surface of the flat calm sea, not far off the starboard side of the boat.

My first instinct was that a jet skier had come out from Uig to meet the ferry and to show off, doing whatever the jet ski version of handbrake turns and donuts might be, but there was no noise and no trail leading away from the large patch of frothing Minch. Then up it came, massive and astonishingly close to the boat. Not unlike a rocket launch, was my afterthought. My first thought was dolphin, but it kept on coming. There was soon far too much of it to be a dolphin as it kept rising and rising before slamming back down on the surface, creating huge displacement. It jumped a total of four times without fully clearing the surface, but the disturbance of each landing was enormous. The display seemed to be for pure enjoyment.

Sadly, Ale's phone was out of charge. Even worse, I couldn't possibly have worked out how to use my new one before the acrobatic display ended. A member of the ship's crew confirmed the large, marine gymnast to be a minke whale which finally gave me the proper answer to a question I had asked well over fifty years before.

I can only remember my mother and Uncle Johnnie being in his large, black rowing boat. My father and little brother must have stayed back at the house. The family were up in Harris for our usual summer holiday at Sruthmor, overlooking the sea loch at Finsbay. Uncle Johnnie was taking his sister-in-law and young nephew out sea fishing with the possibility of landing on one of the islands for a picnic. His choice of drink was not a flask of tea, but a can of Sweetheart Stout. It had fallen out of the picnic bag and was rolling around at his feet as he rowed. I thought it odd that a can of beer had a picture of a lady's face on it, a strange memory to have retained so long.

I cannot remember whether we actually landed on either Finsbay Island or Quidinish Island. I do remember though that it was my mother who was doing better at the fishing. She was using a hand line set-up with a series of feathered hooks and working the lures up and down, while Uncle Johnnie held station over a good mark. The tactic was doing very well for her. She was catching lythe and saithe (pollack and coley) regularly, much to the envy of her little boy. That might well have been why I turned my back on the fishing and, instead, sat on the narrow bench in the bow of the boat, looking out to sea, waiting for my turn.

Out in the open Minch, well beyond MacAskill's reef and Quidinish Island, I watched as a couple of very large shapes came straight up out of the sea and crashed back down, landing almost horizontally. The activity was a long way out. When I asked the grown-ups what these creatures would have been, I got no more than a verbal pat on the head. The two adults weren't quite suggesting that I was imagining what I described, because there was mention of basking sharks, but in truth my question was not being taken seriously. Between that and all the fish my mum was catching, a wee black cloud settled firmly around my head.

Over fifty years later, on the ferry, I finally got my answer. It was a brilliant sight which stirred very deep memory.

I was told that I was only a few months old when I was first taken, by plane, to Harris. Ale, on the other hand, first went to Harris on our honeymoon and received a very warm welcome indeed, a welcome which has now been extended to her another fifty or so times, she reckons. It always raises a smile when someone over there, meeting her for the first time, politely enquires if it is her first visit.

In recent times, the strength of my bond with my father's island and my father's people and the depth of my love for both were highlighted to me when I called in to visit Uncle Kenny MacKenzie, who was enjoying the hospitality of Pitlochry Community Hospital, following a hip replacement. I was on my way to Harris and was welcomed in despite my early morning arrival with a kindly warning that I might find that Kenny had become a little confused in the year since our last meeting.

Sure enough, the announcement of another Mr MacKenzie to see him didn't register immediately with Kenny. Mention of the

Christian name fared no better. From the doorway of his room, I offered a '*Donnchadh mac Iain Alick*' in the hope that the Gaelic patronymic, Duncan, son of Iain Alick, would help. Were it not for his recent hip operation and the Hebridean view that man hugs should be left to European footballers, Kenny looked as if he would have jumped up and opened his arms. He then told the surprised nurse that I must just have celebrated my sixtieth birthday, because he, Kenny, had been best man at the wedding in 1955 of my parents and I had been born in early April '56. He then recounted how I had greeted him from a highchair in a schoolhouse in deepest Banffshire a year later, rather rudely as it turned out. Not much confusion there and a very happy half an hour of trading Harris thoughts followed.

Kenny's parting words on the pride Iain Alick would feel if he knew of his son's love of Harris will be treasured, as will the memory of what proved to be my final time alone in the company of my dad's best man, a very fine man indeed.

My earliest memory of Harris is of crossing the Minch on the 'Lochmor' or the 'Loch Seaforth'. I cannot remember if it was the short, stubby one or the longer slim one. For some reason, I had ended up sharing a hand towel with a member of the crew, much to the amusement of my dad and the MacBraynes' sailor. Less pleasant, on arrival, was having to press my face into Uncle Johnnie's wet sou'wester during a piggy-back from the end of the Finsbay bridge up to the house at Sruthmor. It was dark, wet and windy, so it must have been very late at night, probably early in July. Summer shorts didn't make the piggy-back over the rough track any more comfortable, but there was a peat fire at the end of it and a collie to pet. A very wee boy immediately felt at home.

The early Harris memories are a bit jumbled up with the chronological order definitely suspect. Some are like short videos, others probably just imagined, fuelled by small black and white photos.

One Sunday, most of the Sruthmor household had gone to church. It must have been Communion, because the young MacKenzie brothers and their mum were left at home, Auntie Maggie's own mother being the only other person in the house. This great-aunt was probably the oldest person I had ever met at that stage in my life. The official line was that she couldn't speak English, but there was a suspicion that she could at least understand a little.

Although we were under strict instructions not to leave the house and absolutely not to make any noise on the Sabbath, my little brother and I may have been responsible for the back door of the croft-house being ajar. It was a sunny day, but any playing outside would not have been on the agenda at all, even though almost every other living soul would have been in the church and well out of earshot.

A large blackface sheep managed to get into the kitchen. It may have been a former pet lamb, hand reared and on the look-out for a piece of oatcake. Its response to a horrified greeting from our mother was to panic and duck under the kitchen table into a complete tangle of clattering horns and chair legs.

Our mum was city born and bred, music her greatest love. She did, however, have a very heavy first serve at tennis and could crack a golf ball well down the fairway. Her tall, athletic frame had been commented on favourably to Iain Alick when he brought home his newly wed wife. 'Good for carrying the peats,

Iain!' Our father should have kept comments like that from her hearing, as she did not think that they were entirely in jest and they did not go down too well. She could silence a classroom with a stare and sing solo contralto to a full concert hall, but her Glasgow upbringing, even followed by a few years in rural Banffshire and the Borders, had not prepared her very well to repel an invading sheep. She was not about to reach confidently under the table and disentangle the panicking ewe.

Enter Great-Aunt Catherine, alerted by the commotion, still in her night-gown. She would bring some native experience to the problem. Back she went to her bedroom to return with two walking sticks, whereupon our mother and great-aunt overcame the language barrier and dovetailed beautifully in freeing the poor sheep, eventually hooking one horn each and marching her out of the back door. Not a single word of English was spoken by Great-Aunt Catherine during the entire operation, nor indeed anything from 'Gaelic without Groans' by our mother.

Mother's encounters with Harris livestock feature elsewhere in my mental video library. The effect of her encounter with the MacKenzie family cow was more psychological than physical. When she heard from her boys that their Aunt Maggie had not only shown them how to milk the cow, but had also squirted warm milk from the gentle beast's teat all over their faces, but mostly up their noses and into their gaping mouths, the notion visibly brought on for Margaret a feeling of utter revulsion.

Being handed a live hen as a parting gift on a visit to 'central' Quidinish was another testing moment for our mum. The bird's legs were bound together, but its beak and wings were unfettered. I think it might have been wrapped in a towel for the very short car journey back to the Sruthmor path end. The gift was, of course, the height of generosity and kindness, the hen intended for the table rather than for egg laying. A hot potato for her in the car, Margaret, no doubt, handed it over for despatch to a native, just as soon as she could.

A much easier gift to handle was the bar of Fry's Chocolate Cream given to me. Apparently, it was the first mass-produced bar of chocolate in Britain – famous, but not to the taste of a little boy who found the dark chocolate bitter and the fondant centre a waste of space which could have been better occupied by chocolate, bitter or not. That adult bar of chocolate has remained in the memory as vividly as the rolling can of Sweetheart Stout.

The generous donors of the hen and the grown-up chocolate lived in a house which is now, sadly, falling into ruin. It is in a very sheltered, but likely very damp, location by a small bay amongst the Quidinish crofts and is Category B Listed. It is described as a three-bay, rectangular plan blackhouse which had been altered to accommodate 1960s style corrugated roofing. Whether it was still thatched on my first visit, I cannot recall, but I did find it very cosy. One aspect of the listing detail struck a chord with me in that it referred to thick rubble walls with rounded angles and very deeply set small window openings. It remains the darkest house I have ever visited. It would cost a fortune to restore it plus a great deal of skill and time, but the finished article would be a picture and would stand anything the weather could throw at it.

Johnnie and Maggie MacKenzie's house at Sruthmor, now the home of their daughter, Cathy Ann and her son, John, stands above a tidal pool which is fed at one end by a river and at the other, as the tide rises, by the sea as it flows in under Finsbay bridge. Ale and I are in agreement that this must be one of the best locations for a house on Harris. The view to the front is over the tidal loch. There is, in the back garden, a hillock from where the view takes in Loch Finsbay and out towards the Minch. From the kitchen window, you can look across the moor to Roneval. Behind the house, is the old grass road from Finsbay to the Quidinish road end, passing between Lochs Holmsaig and Dempster on its way. Not far from the grass road you might find the ruins of the old MacKenzie house where Iain Alick and his brothers Duncan, Murdo and Johnnie were born. Life was made much easier when a vehicle access was formed up to Sruthmor from the end of the Finsbay bridge. No more piggy backs.

It is still a lovely place to visit now. Back then, for the two young MacKenzie brothers, it was an absolute adventure playground, although Iain Alick's warning tale about seeing a cow stuck in marshy ground on his way to school and then seeing only the horns sticking out of the ground, on his way back home, gave us a very healthy respect for peat bogs. A swimming lesson in the icy pools of the river served the same purpose for both river and tidal pool. Otherwise, we were free to roam and climb.

Uncle Johnnie had his defunct motorbike parked at one end of the bridge and many happy times were enjoyed on that with never a thought that it might topple and injure the 'rider' or spectator. At the other end of the bridge was John Norman's little shop. Penny Dainties and McCowan's Highland Toffee are the only items I can recall from the shelves. They were much preferred to the type of biscuits (too many wafers, not enough chocolate) our granny kept in a tin on her windowsill, but we didn't like to disappoint her when she knocked on her window and beckoned us in.

Margaret Morrison was the only near neighbour, as far as we two little boys were concerned, with Finsbay seeming quite far away. She went one stage further than our granny and beckoned us in for a second sit down lunch! This Margaret was reputed to be a very good angler. She must have been exceptional, as her skill at fishing is still talked about, many years after her passing. Did I not hear recently that her nickname was the Gaelic for that most patient of fishers, the heron?

As very small boys, my brother and I slept in the upstairs front bedroom at Sruthmor. The room had a skylight and we would take it in turns, long after we were sent to bed, to look out at the view. Usually it would be the splash of a fish in the tidal pool that would attract our attention – salmon or big sea trout. There would be broad daylight for hours after our bedtime and the fish were obviously more plentiful then than they are now. Quite a few sea trout still make it in from Loch Finsbay, but the catch record for Finsbay Fishing boasts only three salmon caught in the last five seasons. In addition to all other difficulties which a salmon must encounter, a Finsbay fish has to run the gauntlet of a large colony of very well-fed seals parked on the rocks, only a hundred yards away, on the seaward side of the bridge. Ale has been heard to count up to thirty on the way past and that's without getting me to stop the car. Yes, they are very popular with the tourists, but at least one family thinks that it would be good if they could spread themselves out a little more, up and down the coastline. Perhaps they could consider concentrating on pollack, or even better, coley. It would give the salmon and sea trout a break, allowing the angler a little more opportunity to practise 'catch and release'... maybe.

Another of my video memories is vivid, albeit in black and white, or rather, mostly grey. Sure enough, on a rough day Loch Langabhat is a grey and surly expanse of water lying beside the 'peat road' between Finsbay and Leverburgh. Iain Alick had been given permission by Rodel Hotel to fish for salmon and had taken me with him. Along the shore of Loch Langabhat, the road has several blind corners and a surface only a 4x4 could love. Heading towards Finsbay, at the relevant spot, you can see well ahead, so I rarely pass without a glance down at the rock formation which was our fishing platform that afternoon. I believe my father may have gone out earlier to 'bait a few rocks' with crushed mussels before returning with his little son to start fishing with the worm. Whatever the detail, Iain Alick hooked a large fish which, when it was eventually brought to the shore, I reckoned was as long as I was tall. What the young boy couldn't understand was the disappointment of his father and the sage nodding of another angler who came for a quick look.

The fish was declared to be a kelt and looked huge to me, but as a fish which had been worn out and starved while going through the spawning process, it may well have been long, but was very thin. Certainly not for the dinner table, it would have been lucky to have had the strength to make it back to sea. A confused young son could only share in his dad's patent disappointment.

I would inevitably have been disappointed, this time on my own behalf, during my first recorded attempt to catch a fish on Harris. This episode does not form part of the video library, monochrome or colour. There is instead, a small photograph in an album showing a tiny fellow, probably no older than three. His shorts are so baggy that they look like a skirt, especially above those white ankle socks and the open sandals. Is that a hopeless grimace on the wee face? He has been set up to fail. In the background, is the tidal pool and beyond that Loch Finsbay, confirming the location as right in front of the house at Sruthmor. Despite the proximity of real fishing waters, he has been set up with a stick from which a thick, dark line dangles into a zinc bathtub. No wonder the urge to fish thereafter lay dormant in me for years.

While I have a laugh at my own predicament, I nevertheless treasure that photograph as, behind me, my mother stands smiling, hair slightly blown by the breeze, young and happy. Beside her is Great-uncle, Seocan MacKenzie, who has taken his flat tweed cap off for the photo and it is held before him, sporran-like. Although he is without a tie, indeed his shirt is minus its collar, there is a handkerchief appearing immaculately from the breast pocket of his suit jacket. It gave me huge pleasure to show that photograph to Uncle Kenny MacKenzie during my early morning Pitlochry visit for Kenny to reach out a finger and say, 'That's my father.'

Although I have no recollection of fishing in the bathtub, I do remember being taken to see Seocan on a subsequent Harris visit. The grand old fellow must have failed, as he was bed-bound and I vividly remember being invited to his side to speak into an ear trumpet so that Seocan could make me out. One hundred years on from the Battle of the Somme, I realised that I appear in a photo with a former soldier whose regiment certainly had one battalion at that battle. That was thought provoking two generations down the line.

Great-uncle Seocan was a career soldier, a sergeant serving both with 5th Cameron Highlanders and 8th Seaforth Highlanders. His granddaughter, Gina, told me recently that he was badly wounded in the lower leg in 1917 or 1918 and that, had it not been for a medical orderly, she would never have been born. After receiving first aid, Seocan was lying on a stretcher awaiting further attention when an orderly noticed profuse bleeding. Without that medical orderly's intervention, Gina's grandfather would have died.

~·~ Quidinish: A Continuing Legacy ~·~

The Harris holidays came to a complete halt for the young MacKenzie boys and their mother on the death of Iain Alick.

A devastated young mother may have found the prospect of further visits too painful, or she may never truly have fully taken to the island and its way of life, or both. Whatever the reason, Margaret nevertheless did help to maintain the link with Harris while she met, head on, the challenge of replacing her husband as head teacher and of raising their young sons single handed. Of particular help to our mother in maintaining the link, at that time, were two of Iain Alick's cousins, Morag and Mary Macleod, from Quidinish, and their husbands.

Auntie Mary and her husband, Roy, hosted my brother and me and, in the early days, our mum too, on their dairy farm at Grange in Banffshire. More than once, tears could not be held back in the car as we young boys started the journey home again.

At one stage, a possible return to teaching in Banffshire was briefly considered by Margaret who knew how much her sons enjoyed their holidays on the farm. I like to demonstrate the immediate depth of my attachment to Mary and Roy and their farm with my claim that, as a football daft ten-year-old, I chose to help wash Roy's cows for milking rather than stay indoors and watch all of England's World Cup win. I did see the extra time.

Then Inverness based, Morag and her husband Callum, himself a Harris MacLeod, were, along with their four children, a strong Harris connection. Whether it was they who encouraged Margaret to arrange the return to the island is not known, but they were in Tarbert to meet her and her boys from the ferry in July 1975. Callum led the way down the east side of South Harris. Where the road branches off towards Geocrab, I, at nineteen, was hard pressed at the wheel of my mother's Renault 12 to keep Callum in view. My wounded pride on the narrow, twisting switchback between rocks and lochs was soothed by my mother's observation that Callum was, after all, a native.

Whatever prompted the return to Harris after a gap of ten years matters not now, but that return visit fully re-established my bond with the island which my father's Macleod cousins had helped keep within touching distance. I remain grateful that my mother helped make the initial return possible that year and that she loaned me her brand-new car to go back the following summer.

It was not an easy return to Sruthmor for Margaret. Uncle Johnnie had died not long after my dad and, on our arrival, their two widows wept in each other's arms.

It happened that a law lecturer from Paisley College, Bill Lawson, was staying as a Bed & Breakfast guest at Sruthmor on his way to, or back from, St Kilda. He was completely unfazed at being reduced from guest bedroom to parking his sleeping bag on the living room floor. Strangely for us all, he knew infinitely more about the background of the MacKenzies than we knew ourselves. Bill had started coming to the islands when he was at Glasgow University and, in short, he became an authority on the social history of the Hebrides, first relocating to Lewis and then opening the Genealogy Centre at Northton in South Harris. He has written many books and has lectured extensively abroad.

While still at the hobby stage of what was to become his career, Bill took out his notes and produced for me a hand-written family tree which, over forty years later, remains a valued source of information, going back, as it does, six generations through Iain Alick's father and eight on his mother's side. Finlay MacKenzie (Scarista); Donald Morrison (Taransay); Neil MacLeod (Taransay); Dugald MacAulay (Cliasmol) and many, many more. Those early generations are mostly shown as being from settlements or islands on the west side of Harris: Nisabost; Crago; Killigray; Berneray; Pabbay.

Generally, the west side of South Harris is machair and sand. The east side is rock, bog, heather and loch with a shoreline of rocky inlets looking out on to islands. The later generations on the family tree are on the east side. A favoured topic of debate with my Quidinish cousins, in recent times, is 'east side or west side?' if you were to buy or build a house. From a crofting point of view, the answer is west side, but you then have to factor in the additional cost of a tractor!

Why did the MacKenzies' forebears leave the more fertile west side to attempt to carve out an existence on the east where 'lazy bed' methods of cultivation had to be used? Why give up good machair to spend time and effort in creating countless narrow banks of soil separated by drainage channels? Seaweed had to be gathered and applied to the soil in an attempt to improve it. Did they have a choice? Were they evicted by landowners looking to cash in on sheep or had they gone across to harvest kelp only to find the bottom falling out of that market, to disastrous financial effect? Eviction to make way for sheep is what I was told as a youngster.

Another of my dad's first cousins was Murdo Macleod, again of Quidinish. He had been at sea for many years, but returned to Harris full time, taking on the crofting at No 8 to help his parents, along with other work. He also married the girl next door at croft No 9, Auntie Mary Ann. His cousins must have held Iain Alick in high regard and with great affection. Uncle Murdo had heard that Iain Alick's sons were, as he would put it, 'coming home' and he appeared at Sruthmor in the early evening of our arrival in 1975. He was to become a major figure for me and, in time, for my own family.

The precise nature of the activities which my brother and I enjoyed during our five-day stay in July 1975 is not remembered in any detail. No doubt, small boats, dogs and fishing will have been involved and our mother did lead the way in visiting a host of relatives. Knowing her attitude towards smoking, her sons were surprised to hear her enquire, at Finsbay's then one remaining shop, about Uncle Murdo's father's favourite tobacco. She took him a pouch of the right stuff which cheered the elderly gentleman greatly, once he emerged from beneath the 'Stornoway Gazette' which he had apparently placed over his face so he would drop off for his afternoon nap. While I remember his appreciation of the gift of tobacco, the lasting image for me will be the warmth of Norman Macleod's smile when he lifted the newspaper away and saw my mother.

Murdo's 'welcome home' and the general welcome we received during that first return visit had a genuinely profound effect on me. I felt that the connection with my father's people and their island was revitalised and deepened. That feeling of connection has continued and been nurtured ever since. For me, Harris came to mean Quidinish and Quidinish came to mean Uncle Murdo's croft at Number 8.

Murdo became like a Harris grandfather to my sons, John, Seumas and Finlay. I have always stopped short of saying that Auntie Mary Ann is like a Harris granny as she is too young to have a son of my age! Having probably stopped addressing them as 'Uncle' and 'Auntie' in my twenties, I certainly started again once our boys came along.

I spoke to my three sons recently, asking each to give his earliest memory of Harris.

John replied, 'The smoke in the kitchen in Quidinish from Uncle Murdo's pipe.'

Seumas, 'Walking among the lazy beds behind the henhouse at Quidinish with Patch when he was the height of my shoulders.' Patch was, by then, of the retired, elder statesman rank of sheepdog.

Finlay responded, 'Probably Uncle Murdo's magic jumper that would produce a bar of chocolate from nowhere.' That was a reference to Murdo's sleight of hand with chocolate when the wee boy would go for a hug before the family left for the ferry.

~·~ The Bond Deepens ~·~

After the 1975 visit, I started going to Harris as much as possible and it was a particular pleasure if these visits coincided with Auntie Mary or Uncle Roddy, another of Iain Alick's Quidinish cousins, being home on holiday. The latter, with his eldest son, Norman, would make possible three-a-side football. Playing in wellies, Roddy wore the spare pair, steel toe-capped, with a vast age range in the teams just adding to the fun.

Uncle Roddy combined the qualities which led him to become a captain of industry with those of natural wit and kindness. A great storyteller and held in the warmest of high regard, it was of real comfort to me, not long after my father's death, to learn that Roddy had agreed to be a guardian to my brother and me, should the need arise.

Murdo and Mary Ann very quickly invited me to stay at number 8 with family, rather than doing B&B. By that stage, I had graduated and was restricted to four weeks of holiday as a law apprentice. The pay was even less generous than the holiday entitlement, but at least petrol was cheap. The three young boys at no 8, Norman, John and Donald Iain would patiently help me to use my night-class Gaelic. I must have done quite well at the time, because all three of them over-estimate my capabilities now.

Effort was made to arrange my holidays to coincide with busy periods for work with peats or sheep. May often brought good weather and days would be spent at peat banks out beside the Leverburgh road, on the Finsbay side of Loch Langabhat, where Murdo showed me how to use a peat iron, all the while extolling the dexterity, accuracy and speed of his usual cutter, Auntie Mary

Ann. The bar was, therefore, set pretty high from the outset. The slabs cut should not be too thin, as they would break up on drying, nor too thick as they would take too long to dry and would over-tax the cutter's partner who had the more difficult job of bending to catch the slab as it was sliced off the peat bank, before throwing it accurately to join neat rows for drying.

There would be cigarette or pipe smoking breaks, for Murdo that is. The lasting memory of these is the view down towards Finsbay and beyond to the Minch and the mainland. Against a deep blue background, cargo boats would sail quite far in the course of one cigarette. Of course, the whole business was only enjoyable if there was enough breeze to keep the midgies away. The odd cigarette for Murdo was not often quite enough to discourage them completely.

Some days, Mary Ann would bring out a kettle, some rolls, sausages, oatcakes, cheese, crowdie and the like whereupon a few rocks would be gathered to contain a small fire. I have regularly been reminded that I was once reluctant to fill a kettle from the most conveniently located of the moor lochs. I had heard that an elderly lady had fallen in, tragically drowned and been buried right under the rocky overhang which had been her downfall. Was this tragedy a fact or a local tale? The richly green patch of grass by the side of the loch might well have been the old soul's final resting place. On the other hand, it might have pointed to otter activity. Either way, I did not fancy tea made with water taken from the spot, or so they tell me, so I went to the next loch to fill the kettle.

Taking over Uncle Murdo's duties as driver for the local home-helps was another regular feature of a visit. It gave me the pleasure of driving around South Harris, at the same time releasing Murdo to do more specialist work like harvesting seaweed which was once more in reasonable demand. With my much-enjoyed experience at Balavil, helping at fanks came easily to me. Dragging a Harris Blackface to be clipped is much the same as dragging a Speyside Blackface to be clipped. What hadn't been experienced at Balavil was the transporting of lively tups in a very small boat to maroon them on an island until the time was right for them to earn their keep. Blackface rams do not volunteer readily to step down into a rowing boat and have their horns lashed to a thwart; they are even less amenable when it comes to disembarking.

The evenings would be spent knocking a football around with the young Macleod boys. Very quickly, the option of a rugby ball was added and then a retired set of golf clubs. We would take up position out amongst the rocks and lazy beds behind the henhouse where we would pitch golf balls towards each other until bad light stopped play. There would be a dog or two on hand to retrieve ricochets or, worse, balls which had plopped into the soggy drainage ditches between the lazy beds.

Fishing with Murdo and his young sons was another highlight. Years later, these outings would be replicated with John Macleod taking his father's place as adviser/ghillie for me and for my own young boys. Uncle Murdo would lead the fishing party to Loch an Dubhlochan, on his own croft, where two or three rods would be set up to fish for brownies using worms as bait. The fish were by no means huge, but to catch one was still a thrill. Trout in oatmeal would be served for breakfast the next day.

One evening, it was decided to venture further afield, out to the bigger lochs on the moor. That expedition remains vivid in my memory not because of a beautifully marked trout with a tummy the colour of butter, but rather because young Norman caught his even younger brother, John, on a back cast…under the chin. Just for a moment, to my right, I saw John in profile against the evening sky. The image of a startled worm appearing to be wriggling out from John's chin will never leave me. No harm was done, other than to the transfixed watcher's sensibilities.

Many years ago, Murdo introduced me to sea fishing from various rocks around Quidinish Point. Our own boys have taken to it too. Leac a' Bhodaich was probably the most successful casting point and, these days, I can look on my Kindle to find a photo of Leac a' Bhodaich with waves crashing on to the angled slabs and rocky ledges. In the foreground is a life-jacket-clad Seumas, pinning himself back from the edge, spinning rod in hand. The theory recently passed on is that pollack and the like stay well away from the rocks of Quidinish Point at times when the wind is blowing hard and the sea is rough. The family nearest and dearest should follow suit, by the look of it.

Uncle Murdo had shown me how to fish in the traditional style with a bamboo rod of astonishing length. No reel was involved, just a line almost as long as the rod with a bottom weight and three or four hooks on droppers above it. You simply picked your rock according to the state of the tide, swung the weight out and let it sink to the bottom. Once you felt the weight reach the seabed, you raised and lowered the rod which, presumably, made the feathered hooks dance enticingly, inducing the fish to take. Pollack were preferred, or mackerel, if they came close enough in. Some of the catch would always be given away to neighbours, especially those who weren't able to go fishing themselves. Sharing out of any good catch from sea or loch remains a pleasure to this day.

Murdo's sea rod was very long indeed. Goodness knows where it came from or how it was delivered or collected. It was certainly longer than Allan's fifteen-foot salmon rod at Balavil. It could also be used in another method whereby a very much lighter weight was tied on and the rod was swept in an arc with its tip just above or even just below the surface of the sea. The action was broadly similar to mowing with a scythe causing the feathered lures to stream along behind the rod tip. This style was used for cuddies, young coal fish. Uncle Murdo used to claim that, in the good old days, he could fill a creel with fish in twenty minutes or less. That may well have been correct, but the Minch seems to have been 'hoovered' by commercial fishing boats since those times. He also used to say that the best lures were hooks sparsely dressed, especially with white hair; hair plucked from the neck of an unwary sheepdog was the best, of course.

There was a minor triumph not long before Finlay was born. John, Seumas and I had our first sea fishing outing without any native Macleod guidance or advice, just the three of us with spinning rods. Ale came with us and had a cast or two, but she seemed to spend most of her evening unhooking and dispatching fish for her young sons, both of whom were under ten at the time. We struck lucky that evening, the cormorants that expectantly sat on the reefs off Cnoc Eisgean leaving their posts just as the rods were being set up. This was a sure sign that shoals of fish were on their way into the bay. The haul was over sixty fish with a good sprinkling of pollack and mackerel among the plump cuddies. Murdo's 'So, you can fish after all' had the mum and dad very proud of their young sons and, if we are honest, quite pleased with ourselves too. Mary Ann produced a superb platter of mixed grilled fish having displayed speed and dexterity akin to that of her legendary peat-cutting in gutting and cleaning the whole catch. To complement the fish, she produced ceann cropaig which is a coarse fish liver pate. In truth, it is more like skirlie, the stuffing for a chicken, than a pate. The livers of the cuddies are mixed with oatmeal and some flour. Add in onion, salt and pepper then cook inside the heads of the larger pollack. It sounds gruesome, but it tastes great. A large bowl of chips and a bottle of white wine completed a memorable dinner.

I have been very fortunate indeed that my Tuscan wife took to Harris or perhaps more specifically, took to my father's people and they to her. It remains a pleasure to look up from fishing to see Ale and Mary Ann taking a walk out to see how I am getting on. Our boys have grown up with twice yearly visits to Harris and, in 2016, I even had the pleasure of the company of my now daughters-in-law, Catriona and Laura, helping me to celebrate a big birthday in Quidinish.

~•~ Sons, Crabs and Urchins ~•~

A version of what I enjoyed on Mary and Roy's Banffshire farm in my teens was available to our own boys on Harris; more sheep than cattle and certainly no tractors. There is a photo somewhere of a very young Seumas with a container of sheep drench strapped to his back, drenching gun poised, ready to dose his next carefully restrained, nervous ewe. Later, John went off to help the Manish crofters gather their sheep for a fank and came back with the news that he had met a new set of cousins. For him, it is out to fourth cousin degree.

Our sons have taken things to a new level over the last two or three years. Seumas has led the way after his year down at Plymouth University, having there added lobster creels to his array of marine equipment: wetsuit; spear-gun; body board; surfboard; paddle board. Having found and patched up a couple of abandoned creels, he supplemented them by buying a pair of the modern collapsible style.

On a recent visit to Quidinish, Seumas had it in mind to lay his lobster creels in Loch Finsbay. He and Catriona were preparing to go out by kayak on a calm, sunny day during the April holiday, but they were stuck for bait. Norman, at No 8, remembered that there was a tin of mackerel fillets in the fridge. The concern was, however, that tinned fillets, rather than fresh, would likely fall apart and be washed out of the creel before they could attract any crabs or lobsters in. With my high regard for the intellect and dexterity of Harris lobsters, I suggested putting the whole tin into the creel as bait, then offered what I thought was a little more sense by venturing that holes could be punched in the tin to let the mackerel flavoured oil ooze out. I couldn't believe it when my suggestion was taken up.

Seumas and Catriona set out from the little bay near croft no 10, just in front of the Fry's chocolate black house. The sea comes in to within a few yards of the road, making the bay both convenient and very sheltered. They had kayaks, wet suits, creels and tinned mackerel. They also had on board their Jack Russel, Effie, in her wetsuit, a small child-sized version, bought for £1 and carefully altered by Seumas – no sign of a mask or snorkel for her…so far.

The three of them looked as if they took great pleasure in paddling out onto Loch Finsbay, the weather being ideal for their adventure. The water was very clear, allowing them to see right down to the kelp beds, but the real smile came the following day when they went out to retrieve their creel. Only one had been set, as there was only one tin of mackerel fillets. On lifting the creel, they found no fewer than twenty crabs had clambered in to investigate the tinned bait! Admittedly, there was no lobster and none of the crabs was quite up to being kept for the table, but the idea had worked. Ignoring my helpful suggestion of adding a pair of glasses to help the more mature lobster read the instructions on the tin, a further creel was set. This time the lid of the tin was half opened. Only nineteen crabs were caught, but still nothing edible. Success with Solway and North Sea lobsters has come for them since, Seumas now having also perfected the technique of catching lobsters by hand.

On their most recent visit together, John and Seumas tried out a paddle board in the bay right at the very end of Quidinish village, the bay having proved a successful spot for sea trout and pollack. It is also frequented by otters for whom the incoming tide must be like a self-service buffet. As John was making his debut on the paddle board, Health and Safety stuff was provided not just in the form of a buoyancy jacket, but also by Seumas, wet-suited and masked, circling the board, shark-like, while John found his feet. Once his brother had gained confidence, Seumas went down to have a look at what might be living on the seabed.

The answer was sea urchins, lots of them. This was taken as bad news for lobster creeling purposes, as the family marine biologist considered that a high number of sea urchins suggested that there were very few lobsters in the immediate area. That lobsters eat sea urchins, was behind his thinking.

~•~ Two Eagles and an Irritable Seal ~•~

Reflecting quietly on the bank of a loch, during a spell of brown trout inactivity, I concluded that my favourite visit to Harris, in recent years, was a bit of a novelty, at least to begin with. For some time, with a larger, more grown up family, Ale and I had been booking holiday cottages, mostly in Finsbay and Geocrab. Both villages are close to Quidinish which remained, and still remains, the centre of conviviality and activity. Cliff Cottage in Geocrab was the destination on this occasion and the novelty was that I was to be staying there alone for the first couple of days. Seumas and Catriona would arrive with Effie on the Monday and Ale would fly up to Stornoway on the Tuesday. Scudo was allowed to go with the advance party of one, arriving on the Saturday evening.

The Sabbath dawned windy and wet and grey and cold. October can be quite nice up there; this day wasn't, but dogs need to get out, no matter the weather, so the two of us walked south, keeping to the road which was completely deserted. Tourists, if they were braving the weather, would be on the west side. Locals heading for church would not be on the move until later in the morning. It was miserable.

At one point, we ended up sheltering on the leeward side of a sizeable cairn in an emergency of horizontal rain. A great deal more of Harris can be seen on foot, the cairn being not far above the road, but yet passed by the family car hundreds of times without being noticed. Its shelter was not wholly effective, so the morning walk was abandoned and instead we headed in the Land Rover over to the west side, by the northern route rather than via Leverburgh. It would be a run down the improved section of road which reaches almost to the Luskentyre road end and then, back to single track, down as far as the cemetery at Scarista. As I enjoyed the stretch of new roadway, I noticed that we had company to our right in the shape of two eagles cruising south on a course parallel to ours. The road, very nicely upgraded, was totally empty, so the sight could be appreciated, but only briefly, leaving the driver unable to decide whether they were golden or white-tailed sea eagles. I had, however, heard that sea eagles on the west side were hammering the fulmar population so hard that the fulmars were considering a tactical withdrawal back out to St Kilda. I also guessed that the section of improved roadway must be near a regular haunt for the eagles as birdwatchers had been noticed, parked, with binoculars trained. No matter how often eagles of either variety are spotted, they remain a fascinating sight, my most recent being on rounding a corner in Quidinish to find a huge eagle perched on a strainer post, just above the roadside.

Seumas, Catriona and Effie arrived on the Monday ferry, but they only paused long enough to jettison their bags at the cottage before meeting up with Scudo and me at Lingerbay Pier to try some fishing. Wrong state of tide for the location. That was worked out within a matter of a very few minutes and we agreed instead to reconvene at Cnoc Eisgean with its easier access to deeper water.

I called in at No 8 Quidinish on the way past, so by the time I reached the fishing rocks at Cnoc Eisgean, Catriona was seated on a flat rock with Effie beside her. There was no sign of Seumas. As I made my way down to join them, Effie suddenly became most animated. Her high pitched, excited Jack Russell yap was testing on the ears. That is as polite a way as I have ever managed to put it, fond of her as I am. The cause of her excitement was sticking out of the water right in front of her in the shape of Seumas in his wetsuit with mask and snorkel. He had decided that he would have a look underwater and had gone in with his spear-gun, previously well used by Nazareno outside the breakwater at Marina di Pisa. The swell was strong, causing the visibility to be poor, but that was not the only reason for his decision to get out of the water and quickly. His main reason had bobbed up in the sea right behind him; he turned to face it. It was surprising how similar a wet suited Seumas and a seal looked, at least from behind and in fading light. Seals have been known to nip divers who have interrupted their fishing. 'Discretion is the better part of valour' had crossed Seumas's mind and Effie clearly concurred.

By Tuesday afternoon, the novelty factor of Ale's delayed arrival had definitely worn off. If you can have a spring in your step at the wheel of a Land Rover on the Harris and Lewis roads, then that is what I had as I drove up to Stornoway airport. I met Ale off the Edinburgh flight and the two of us stocked up on basic provisions and a few celebratory treats at the Co-op.

Ale just needed to walk into Cliff Cottage to give it the real feeling of home.

~·~ A Six Island Road Trip ~·~

Down the coastline from Cliff Cottage, past Flodabay and Cnoc Eisgean, lies Quidinish Point which extensive headland seems to have a deep-rooted, yet ambivalent fascination for me, in that I both love the place and am wary of it at one and the same time. Perhaps climbers have similar feelings about favourite mountains, not that I would know, never even having attempted a Munro. I am more likely to resort to my hunter-gatherer analogy of feeling at home in my territory, but with spear always at the ready and senses on the alert for danger as well as for prey. Perhaps this distinctive attraction to Quidinish Point has grown from the hours spent with the toes of my Landmasters only inches from the edge of its rocky ledges and only a foot above the waves at Leac a' Bhodaich, where the adrenalin flow on hooking a good fish would mix with cautious respect for the proximity of the formidable swell of the sea. It could be a heady cocktail, especially when there was a young son alongside, holding on to a heavily bent spinning rod.

The direction and strength of the wind always have a bearing on my movements out on the Point, either in trying to guess where the cattle might be grazing or in choosing which fishing spot might be most comfortable and, of course, safe. I was never out there with my dad, so the attraction is not born of childhood memories. My first recollection of being on Quidinish Point is from the return trip in 1975; it must have grown on me from then. Away from the edge of the sea, it is an expanse of varied moorland with a couple of small lochs, a couple of hills, some boggy flat bits and some sharp, rocky slopes. The view is panoramic in places and, if the weather is kind, it is a very peaceful place to be. There have been many happy times out there with immediate family, with Quidinish relatives and on my own.

Ale and I used to try to work out which islands we could see when we looked down the Minch from Quidinish Point, with South Uist being the furthest, we reckoned. There was often talk of, one day, having a trip down to the Uists and there had also been mention, by Uncle Murdo, of a close relative on Berneray. Other than running down the passenger gangway on to the pier at Lochmaddy and back up again, I had never been even to North Uist. The problem had always been that time on Harris was considered so precious that trips to other islands were contemplated, but never taken any further.

All that changed in the strange summer of 2015. The fact that I had stumbled on reference to my father's first cousin on Berneray prompted me to suggest that, finally, there was the chance to look at the islands to the south of the Sound of Harris. In any event, Ale picked up on my vague notion to crack on and, with slightly surprising speed, booked ferries.

Accommodation on Harris was easy. We would be most welcome to stay with friends and then with Mary Ann and my cousins in Quidinish. I surprised the family by proposing the idea of camping on the Uists. That Ale agreed was an even bigger surprise. With us fast approaching our thirtieth wedding anniversary, not one night had been spent in a tent. Ale would be making her debut and I had a whole one night's experience of camping from school days under my belt. Fortunately, all three sons are very experienced. Reviews on two-man tents were read in a hurry and the eventual purchase, at a heavily discounted price, turned out to be a success, especially after Finlay supervised a trial pitching in the back garden and offered well-received advice.

At the last minute, the weather forecast for the first night on North Uist was not great and the camping inexperience was a niggle, so I managed to book a B&B near Sollas for one night only. At least the first night would be dry and comfortable. The ferries had been booked to allow for three nights on the Uists and Berneray. One of the adventuring pair had set their heart on catching a fish so that the other, on one of those nights, could cook it in front of the tent which, of course, would be soundly pitched at an idyllic location and in perfect weather.

The Sound of Harris is beautiful in the right conditions, but it must be very tricky in the wrong. The radio alarm in Craiglockhart is set to Radio Scotland and the frequency of mention of the Leverburgh to Berneray ferry is noticeable. The state of the tide seems to cause as much disruption as the weather. We found out why.

We had a happy journey up from Edinburgh, staying overnight in Uig, but we did find it strange to arrive on Harris only to be leaving again in a matter of a very few hours. Passing through is not something we have ever experienced with the island, but that is exactly what happened. A brief visit to Quidinish was followed by the short and very familiar drive across the 'peat road' to Leverburgh. There was an air of anticipation in the car, probably encouraged by the knowledge that while the weather could do what it liked, the first night would be comfortable come what may.

MV 'Loch Portain' was on time. While not as small as the ferries that crossed from Kyle to Skye in the days before the bridge, it is tiny compared to the ferries which cross the Minch. It was, however, built with the seabed topography of the Sound of Harris in mind. The draught is only 1.5m and it has a water-jet propulsion system so that nothing protrudes below the ship's hull. The idea is that the boat is highly manoeuvrable in the very shallow waters of the Sound. It needs to be, as the 'Loch Portain' changes course eighteen times on its way over to Berneray and seemed to come to a complete halt at one point before doing a ninety-degree turn. The reason is perfectly obvious if you look over the guard rail. Every time we had a look, we could see the seabed clearly.

I have a thing about 'feeling at home' in certain places and Berneray had that effect on me pretty much immediately. The name of the island is sprinkled about amongst the early generations on my family tree, so the place was clearly starting with an advantage. There was also the fact that until 1985 there had been another of my father's full cousins whose circumstances had led to a life on Berneray. The cousin, yet another John MacKenzie, had been born on his maternal grandparents' croft on Berneray in 1906. His mother had then gone back home to No 5 Finsbay where her husband was Dugald, brother of Seocan. Within the year, the mum died and young John, known as Seonaidh Dhùghaill, had been taken back to Berneray to live with his grandparents. More appealing even than any family connection, however, was the compact beauty of the island. It had all the best features of South Harris rolled into a small area of only two miles by three.

We had a quick look round on that first afternoon. General store and café; little harbour with toilets and shower (important); on the west side, acres of multi-coloured machair above a beach as good as any on Harris; on the opposite side, machair above a smaller beach looking back across to Harris; well-known trout loch in Loch Bhrusda. What more could I want? Nothing, really. I would have stayed on Berneray for the whole three days, given the chance.

It took a couple of reminders from Ale, but eventually we left Berneray by driving back south past the little ferry terminal and over the causeway to North Uist which immediately looked and felt very different from both Harris and Berneray. Although the word was that lochs made up one third of North Uist, that was not obvious from the initial route which was down the west side of the island, where the main impression was of green, low lying ground with a sandy coastline.

We found the B&B just south of Sollas and were given a warm welcome by Peggy who was originally from South Uist. Both she and her husband had jobs in addition to their croft and the B&B. Friendly, interested and full of life they were. Their large, modern house on a huge plot at the edge of their croft was absolutely ideal. The outlook was perfect for guests, with bedrooms and a large dining room/lounge all overlooking the bay. To the side and rear it looked set up for modern crofting. It left the travelling party feeling as if they had struck it very lucky; after a bite to eat, we set out to explore a little further down the west coast of the island.

We had hardly turned south when we saw, between the road and the sea, the most immaculately restored black house. Both the chimneys and the stone walls had been whitewashed. It was exactly what could be done with the old house in Quidinish with much funding and access to traditional skills and materials. The thatching on the roof was pristine with a 'fringe' of stones anchoring the network of ropes. It looked a very solid shelter with the deep window recesses suggesting a strength that would withstand a real battering from the Atlantic, with ease.

Further south, we came across a signpost reading 'St Kilda Viewpoint'. Sure enough, there was a steep hill up to the left. Without ever having a great urge to visit St Kilda, we have enjoyed straining to see it with the naked eye, from Harris. The cattle grid just south of Horgabost on the west side of Harris is supposed to be a good spot to catch sight of St Kilda, but the best view we had had previously was from the ancient temple out on Toe Head at Northton, crystal clear on a bright, still day. We were simply not prepared for the view from this North Uist Viewpoint. Not only were the islands which make up St Kilda clearly visible, but there was a panoramic view down towards South Uist too. Again, with the weather kind and no midgies around, there was a chance to enjoy a vantage point with spectacular views. The relative closeness of the island group got us thinking about how much nearer we were to St Kilda from that viewpoint than from Northton. We were still talking about it a week later at the Harris Distillery where we tried to compare the distances on the huge map which is featured in its impressive reception hall.

From the viewpoint, the contrast between North Uist and the Bays of Harris was easy to picture. On the west of North Uist, the ground was flat and dotted with croft houses before it reached the shoreline with its lagoon like bays. To the south, it seemed like the territory was flat as we looked toward Benbecula, before the hills of South Uist rose in the distance. Those hills to the south and the good weather forecast combined to offer an invitation to go for a road trip the following morning.

It had been a long time since we had last explored new ground, at least in Scotland. Wherever the day took us, it was going to be looking its best in the Hebridean sunshine, but there was no prospect of our over-heating all the same, not with that cool breeze. Other than taking in what could be seen from the road, it was just a question of waiting for something to grab the attention.

Trinity Temple at Carinish didn't immediately grab the attention, but fortunately Temple View Hotel did. The possible stop for coffee in the hotel turned into a visit to the temple instead. It is a ruined medieval monastery which was also a college and is said to date from the 13th century. The path to the temple crosses a working croft over which we two solemnly obeyed the very politely written request on the gate that all dogs be kept on a lead. It may well have been the most courteously worded notice we had ever seen, a credit to its crofting author.

Given the age of the ruin, I was very surprised to see, at the gate of the temple's own grounds, a Commonwealth War Graves Commission notice. The first grave was that of Private A. MacAulay of 4th Cameron Highlanders who died on 12 February 1915. He was from Grimsay, North Uist and only seventeen years old. The second was of Private N. Nicholson of 5th Camerons who died two days before Christmas in 1917 at the age of twenty-five. At the time of our visit, Finlay was seventeen and Seumas was twenty-five. The point was not missed and gave rise to moments of quiet reflection.

A much cheerier tone was set at the point furthest south on the road trip where Eriskay on a warm, sunny day was a picture and delighted both Ale and me. The sands were white, the machair highly decorated, the sky was huge and the sea deep blue. Some houses added to the colour with roofs of various shades of red, blue and green dotted around.

The two of us left aside the standard tourist attractions, but noticed, in passing, the pub called 'Am Politician', named after the SS 'Politician' which went down in the Sound of Eriskay in 1941 giving rise to a book, then a film, 'Whisky Galore'. The crew of the vessel were all saved before the locals turned their attention to the cargo which famously included thousands of cases of malt whisky bound for America. The authorities eventually used explosives on the remains of the popular cargo and the criminal justice system on some unfortunate islanders. A sobering thought.

We knew there was also the chance to visit the beach where Bonnie Prince Charlie landed at the start of his ultimately doomed Jacobite rebellion. We gave that a miss too, which was perhaps fortunate, as Ale might have been subjected, yet again, to my usual lecture about MacKenzies having been on both sides in the 1745 rebellion. This had been pointed out to me at a very early age by my father and had been vividly brought to mind at the redeveloped centre at Culloden, where the name of a John MacKenzie appears on a wall as one of the Jacobite slain. Apparently most MacKenzies followed their clan chief in the forming of three MacKenzie Independent Highland Companies raised to fight for the government, but others joined the Earl of Cromartie's Regiment on the Jacobite side. Most of that regiment were absent from the main Jacobite army and, in fact were killed or captured at the Battle of Littleferry or Meikle Ferry in Sutherland by Independent Highland Companies drawn from Clans Mackay and Sutherland, only the remnant fighting at Culloden the next day. I confess to getting frustrated when people speak as if the Battle of Culloden were a Scotland v England, Highland Clans v England or Claymores v Muskets affair. It's history is far from simple.

Happily, we concentrated on the genuine beauty of Eriskay on a day that had it looking spectacular, eventually finding ourselves looking down at the pier where the ferry leaves for Barra. It seemed like a short crossing and Ale was leaning towards extending the road trip with a hop across to Barra on the ferry. The pull of Berneray on me was, however, strong enough for me to 'forget' to mention that my cousin Cathy Ann who is Harris through and through, had told me that she reckoned Barra was the pick of all the Hebridean islands. Barra, we decided, would be visited another day. After meeting a pair of very gentle Eriskay ponies that were obviously used to tourists and were able to ignore an inquisitive dog while enjoying a pat, we turned north again.

The picnic above one of the west coast beaches, not far from Lochboisdale, was a pleasure. South Uist is said to have about twenty miles of machair above its beaches and the panorama of sea, sand and machair soon had two of us enthusing in conversation and the third making it clear he was happy. There was even a picnic table.

A large, new 4x4, with privacy glass, appeared behind us and glided its way over the machair, past our table and down onto the beach below. What followed was a display of how to exercise your dog, but not as we knew it. The automatic tailgate opened and out lolloped a very large dog, breed unknown, before the 4x4 then set off along the deserted beach, the dog galloping along behind. After a few lengths up and down, the vehicle stopped, the tailgate raised, the dog jumped in, the tailgate closed. Job done. Ale and I mused briefly about trying something similar with Scudo. Our dog's thinking on that was written all over his face. 'Aye, right.'

Balivanich, back on Benbecula, was reached in plenty time to return the diesel in the Land Rover to a comfortable level, Lochboisdale's pumps having been sold out. The town, with its airport, hospital and golf club felt more mainland than island. There was plenty life and it looked healthily busy, but Berneray was drawing me back ever more strongly. Balivanich just couldn't compete.

On our return to Berneray, we counted that we had been on six islands in one day being, Eriskay, South Uist, Benbecula, Grimsay, North Uist and Berneray. No ferries had been used and the tyres stayed dry. The string of causeways has opened up the whole of the southern half of the Outer Hebrides, where the roads are excellent and the distances not as great as imagined, allowing a very special day trip which will certainly serve as a taster for future visits.

~•~ Berneray: Camping and Contemplating ~•~

On Berneray, we headed straight for the machair above the east beach, where two or three other groups had decided that this was the place to camp; there was acres of space. A comfortably flat spot was found easily and the practice in the back garden at home allowed the learner campers to pitch the tent without the slightest hiccup. The Land Rover was drawn up alongside as a wind break on what looked like the start of a cool evening and an even cooler night.

The location was excellent. The beach was a few yards in front of the tent with a drop of four or five feet from machair to sand. Beyond that was the Sound of Harris and then Harris itself. I was having another 'feeling at home' episode while Ale was busy preparing for as much comfort as possible. My theory about genealogical roots having an influence on how I felt about the island did not find much favour, but the two of us were certainly in agreement on making the most of our decision to try camping. Ale's preparation had been aimed at raising the tone: glass goblets for wine; a mini kettle to run from the car battery; a lamp to hang up inside the tent. That is far from wild camping, Mrs MacKenzie.

My stated intention to catch a fish for supper had suffered a bit of a blow. Loch Bhrusda turned out to be 'catch and release' only, forcing sights to be lowered in the direction of a pollack, so back we went to the little pier where the ferry comes in. As it is berthed overnight down by the causeway to North Uist, the pier was deserted, as was the sea, it seemed. One small pollack was all we had to show for the best part of an hour of chilling effort. Still, ambition was realised when Ale produced grilled pollack on the Tesco instant barbeque tray, while I lowered the tone a bit by savouring a warming dram from an enamel mug. There had been no real pressure on the fishing, as Ale had brought an abundant selection of food to supplement any disappointing catch. The temperature was a bit of a let-down, with extra layers of clothing being added, in mid-July.

It was a very still evening with hardly any sound other than the gentle lapping of a quiet sea on the beach below and, at one point, a fly past by some swans. The entertainment, a sight which most visitors to the Hebrides would have envied, was provided by a pair of otters playing about at the water's edge, only thirty yards away. They didn't seem in the least interested in the presence of the campers or their dog.

While Ale made ready for as warm and as comfortable a night as possible, I paid scant attention to the temperature and sat down to contemplate the view across to Harris from a new angle. The usual view was from the observation lounge or the stern of the ferry on arrival or departure. This was a view from the south west, from a relatively small piece of land that managed to cram many Harris-like features into its compact form and had emitted an instant and strong appeal to me. It was strange, as I had never looked across from Strond or Leverburgh, on Harris, thinking that Berneray was a place I had to visit. Any appeal of that nature had always been in respect of the bigger islands to the south.

My mind flitted around the islands in the Sound, Ceileagraigh, Grodhaigh, Sgeir Chruaidh to give them the Gaelic version of their names and many more; then beyond, on to Harris itself, still visible late in the evening light. I was thinking of the generations who had gone before, how I felt Harris my spiritual home, how lucky I was that my Tuscan wife had taken to the island. Then I corrected myself as I focussed in on that last thought, recalling yet again that what she had actually told me was that, yes, Harris was a special place to where she would have returned once or twice after discovery, but there were many other places known to her that were just as beautiful and enjoyed much better weather! For her, the people, the relatives had made Harris a special place. They had taken to her and she had taken to them. It warmed me to recall what she had said and to recognise that I could say the same of Tuscany and her people.

My thinking scanned back to the MacKenzies on Harris and how my grandfather's branch had apparently come over to the island from Wester Ross, perhaps as recently as six generations ago. My grandmother's branch of MacKenzies, I knew, went back much further than that. The real depth of Harris roots was, however, to be found in the names of the two great-grandmothers, Morrison and MacLeod. I knew those two names would go back a great deal further in Harris time.

How harsh had life been for the more recent generations on my family tree? Had life been tolerable on the west side and on the little islands? Had they done reasonably well until, as I had heard, they had been cleared to make way for sheep? My mother had told me that my father had a real interest in the era of mistreatment referred to as the 'Highland Clearances.' My father's remark to his very young son, that, as a boy, he hardly had shoes for his feet, had stuck with me. I thought about the contrast with the remarkable new houses at Scarista and Borve, recently featured on national television.

I thought about quite a lot, while Ale carried on doing 'Ale things', recalling the fascination I had enjoyed when coming across a satellite view of Quidinish during a browse and then combining it with reference to Bill Lawson's Croft History; the two worked very well in harness. The extent of lazy bed cultivation which appeared on the satellite image was nothing short of astonishing. It was as if a squadron of massive tanks had been cruising around the Craobhag, leaving swathe upon swathe of deep track marks in its wake. Virtually an island and an area I had often tramped around, the hundreds of lazy beds had not been obvious to me at ground level, perhaps because I usually sought out the higher ground on the lookout for cattle. There were many more around croft number 7 and again as I followed the line of the road past the Macleod and Morrison crofts at 8, 9 and 10. Yes, I had crossed plenty old lazy beds on all of these crofts over the years, but I had never imagined the scale of the work that had been done by previous generations. What intensity, sheer hard graft, what determination… or what desperation? Perhaps it was all of those plus the much higher number of inhabitants which combined both to require and to create these lifelines among the rocks and bogs.

Bill Lawson's Croft History had shown me that the lazy beds were helping to provide for families with six, seven, eight, nine, ten and even eleven children. Many mouths to feed, many pairs of hands and feet to work once they were old enough; it must have been incredibly hard, even if the sea were more bountiful back then.

The combination of satellite image and croft history had drawn me further; out to the main road at Loch Holmsaig, around the corner towards Finsbay bridge and then sharp right up to Sruthmor. I had looked for the ruins of my dad's childhood home, visited once, in the very early days, during a walk on the 'velvet' road to Finsbay. There, near Abhainn na Ciste was the outline of what might have been Iain Alick's family home; my grandfather had been a cottar on croft no 14, my great grandmother had been one of the crofter's nine children. I could only find the one ruin on the satellite view; it did seem rather closer to the two current houses than I had remembered, but I had been very young at the time of the visit. Iain Alick would have worked on these lazy beds that could be seen so clearly, along with his brothers Duncan, Johnnie and Murdo, the Croft History giving its reader the names of my three uncles in age order, my father younger than them all.

I had not known the uncle whose name I was given, but I did know that the eldest of the four MacKenzie brothers had died at the age of twenty-three, long before my own birth. A Quinsy throat had been the cause of death; antibiotics and surgical intervention would not have been available. While that brought to mind that my middle name, William, reflected my mother's loss of a brother too, I had nevertheless smiled to myself as I remembered my mother's comments about the naming of my own brother and, indeed, the name she had thought of… 'It's your choice this time, Margaret, but you know what he should be called,' and he was, John Alexander, after the two grandfathers! So, my mother had suffered the same level of determination in the naming of sons as I myself had visited upon Ale. I had a feeling that my own sons would break new ground when Ale eventually became *nonna*. I hoped so. She would really like an Italian name in there somewhere.

Some three years later, Caspian Azzurro Osborne MacKenzie, born to Seumas and Catriona on 11 September 2018, fitted the bill perfectly.

~·~ Anniversary Trout ~·~

I returned to our camp on that cool July evening, saying little, countering Ale's question on what I had been thinking about down by the shore by telling her I would perhaps write about it for her one day.

The 'Ale things' had included getting heavily wrapped up, so we could stay outside the tent well into the late evening. We didn't attempt to light a fire, but just sat on the camp chairs and took in the peace, the nature and the novelty. The lights on the Harris side grew brighter as did the navigation lights in the Sound. The temperature hadn't risen though and, by the time Scudo was billeted away in the Freelander, Ale looked twice her normal size. She wasn't just dressed for outdoors, but rather for Arctic exploration. Practical, pragmatic even, but some distance away from that Wallabies dress.

In the morning, I reported that I had come to in the middle of the night with the sound of rustling. In my semi-conscious state, I had reached the conclusion that the two otters must have been checking out around the tent for possible scraps. This had to be nonsense. The car would have been rocking to the sound of savage barking if they had come anywhere near. I had more than likely been hearing a slow-cooked Ale trying to struggle quietly out of her two jackets, over trousers and bunnet.

Any pretence of attempting wild camping had gone completely out of the window as we spoiled ourselves in the morning to tea and bacon rolls at the Ardmaree Stores café. There, one of the ladies turned out to have lived very close to Seonaidh Dhùghaill, but even more importantly, told me I'd done quite well after all; many visitors draw a blank when fishing from the ferry pier, so there was nothing to beat myself up about. I did feel better after that.

We had a proper look at the whole of Berneray throughout the rest of the day and had a late picnic lunch on the gentle slopes, above the shore, on the south side of the island, where the view is across to North Uist to the south and over to Boreray to the west. We had just followed the road as it turned south to find that it led to a burial ground, but there was a track heading off across the machair, so we followed that instead. Without knowing it existed, the two of us stumbled on the commemoration of the birthplace of Giant MacAskill. We knew about him, because his family had moved to Quidinish when he was very young, before emigrating to Canada. MacAskill's reef is not far from Quidinish Island and is named after one of the giant's relatives who had to spend the night on it before being rescued. Which relation it was, I cannot be sure, but it seems that I knew more about that story than I knew about Giant Angus MacAskill himself. Seven feet and nine inches (2.36m) he grew to. He was immensely strong and made a living by displaying feats of that strength in shows, both in Europe and America, becoming so famous that Queen Victoria asked him round to Windsor Castle for tea. He was born in a beautiful part of Berneray. I can vouch for that.

The forecast was for rain that evening and into the night. The bold adventurers were having second thoughts about another night in the tent or rather about having to pack it up, soaking wet, and then drying it in a borrowed house on the return to

Harris. We chickened out. Our apprehension about the B&Bs all being booked had proved unfounded, so we decided to opt for that. Peggy at Sollas had a free room, so we were very happy to return there. The delightful bonus was that Peggy's brother-in-law had just visited to share his catch. She gave us crab claws and mayonnaise to enjoy as a starter for our planned indoor picnic dinner.

Ale and I crossed back over to Harris in time to celebrate our thirtieth wedding anniversary. Most of these anniversaries had been celebrated in Italy or Austria, with only a few having been missed by our being in different countries. The pressure on precious school holiday time had sometimes kept me at work, through lack of cover being available, but not very often.

20th July 2015 was a lovely morning; I left it to Ale to suggest how it would be spent. I expected that she would choose a trip to the west side beaches or perhaps all the way to beautiful Husinis. No, she suggested that we go fishing together. What a nice lady. Breakfast was bolted, at least by me, in case of a change of heart.

Loch Dempster was chosen for its proximity. Out to the main road, park, walk through a gate, 100 yards down the old grass road and there was an ideal casting point. We had a laugh at our dog's expense, because he really wasn't sure which one to sit beside. We do have a theory that he always sits beside the least experienced of any fishing party. That morning our canine ghillie diplomatically supported each of us for a little, then sat halfway between us, keeping the landing net company. We were each on our own little rocky promontory only twenty yards apart. For the record, Ale was first to catch, a very nice little brownie on Greenwell's Glory or Kate McLaren. It was a cracking start to our anniversary and much more fun than the chilling hour spent after reluctant pollack on Berneray, but we will soon be back over to that little island. Apparently, I talked about little else for days, make that weeks.

~·~ Quidinish to Bavaria ~·~

Having talked about the possibility for years, Ale and I finally decided to take the Freelander to Italy where there was to be a family wedding. We would then come home via Austria. After another visit together to enjoy my father's island home, where I feel my roots grow ever more strongly, we would head for Tuscany, where Ale's roots really do grow deep and wide. She has the advantage of having been born there, rather than my simply wishing that of Harris.

What a contrast there was between consecutive Sundays.

On the first Sunday we were out on Quidinish Point with Gina, Seocan's granddaughter, her husband Mike, and their chocolate Labrador. I went straight in amongst the Highland cattle, as checking on them was an important part of the walk. As there were visitors, who were unfamiliar to the beasts, and two dogs, I kept everyone well out of the way – at least fifty yards and up a hill. From there, they got a very clear sight of two sea eagles, one of which had been grounded for a while on the high rocks above the Leac a' Bhodaich fishing spot. Ale had thought it was a new cairn until the binoculars revealed what was a large female, regally surveying the rocky shoreline below her chosen perch.

As usual, I was paying more attention to the animals. The truth be told, I was showing off as I called wee Dunc's mum in from some way away to accept, from my hand, the fresh grass I had plucked for her and kept secreted in my jacket. She even licked her lips and it was no doubt perfectly obvious to the others that I was tickled that the cow was happy to make her way gently towards me even though we were all out on open moorland. At the same time, I was keeping a close eye on the bull, as there wasn't enough in my hand for two. A disappointed bull was not high on my wish list.

A week later, Scudo and I were being hurtled along a German autobahn with me at it again, asking Ale please to keep both hands on the wheel of my precious Land Rover. She was nonchalantly flying along at 80mph with one hand on the wheel, running the other through her hair. Very cool, very elegant, very Italian. Oh good, two hands back on. Oh well, that lasted a milli-second before the other one was off, dealing with a minor itch of the chin. I was muttering about light steering being one of the 'cons' I had read in the reviews of the car. Scudo, right at the back, was thinking, 'Go back to sleep, man. She will get us through, no problem. You won't change the habits of a driving lifetime.' I wasn't really concerned, but my recent experienced driver course had rekindled my interest and my instructor would have had a cageful of canaries and a lapful of coffee with this one-handed stuff.

I had driven us down to Newcastle and then, the following day, had taken the first shift out of Amsterdam and well on into Germany. At the first hint of fatigue, we had switched over. From his spacious travel suite in the tailgate section, it was easy for Scudo to tell, without looking, whether we were being driven by

(1) the one who had wanted to grow up to drive tractors and Land Rovers or (2) the one who loves Alfa Romeos and could reverse park into a shoe box, with one hand of course, while noticing everything going on 360 degrees around her and giving a running commentary on it.

We were met by a very kind welcome in Bavaria, where we were spending two or three nights with family friends. This friendship is now into the third generation and had begun with a chance meeting between Ale's parents and Andrea's parents, but this time there was nothing to do with the war. The family cars had been parked up, side by side, waiting for dense fog to clear. Andrea's family had been on holiday in Italy, the kids got playing and Andrea ended up being invited down to Pisa to learn some Italian. She did mention during the Bavarian stopover that her father had been wounded as a very young soldier while serving on the Eastern Front. What he saw on the train, carrying wounded comrades back to hospital, inspired him to change his studies from engineering to medicine. The effect of the war on that generation was all pervading.

The stay with Franz and Andrea Woltering was hugely enjoyable. Their house lies among the hills above the small market town of Holzkirchen. Soon after arrival, we had a large raptor fly over the garden, nothing like as big as the sea eagle of the previous week, but nevertheless impressive. We worked out that it was a red kite, medium-large rather than massive. The surrounding countryside was of the rolling hills variety and heavily wooded too, a complete contrast to the sea, rocks, peat bog, heather and lochs of the Bays of Harris. Franz is a connoisseur of fine malt whisky, so at least there was a hint, but only a hint, of peat when he and I sampled a dram or two.

There was a contrast too when Ale and I drove down towards Holzkirchen. We found ourselves to be in a dairy farming area; dehorned cows, short coats, big udders, in fact, just big all over…. Fleckvieh, the opposite end of the bovine spectrum from our Highland bullock buddies of the previous week.

~·~ Woolly Pigs and an English Garden ~·~

Close to where Franz and Andrea live, Markus Wasmeier, a former alpine ski racer and world and Olympic champion, has created what amounts to a museum farm village using traditional Bavarian methods and materials. Traditional farm implements have been reproduced too. The buildings were still being worked on and Markus seemed to be very much 'hands on'. When we spotted the man himself, he was dressed like a Bavarian farmer, but was having a break. He was talking away on a mobile phone which looked completely out of place in the remarkable surroundings he had created. Wood is the main material. For example, the roof of each building is made from wooden slats which are held in place by longer planks, running both horizontally and diagonally, further secured by Z shaped iron pins. On top of all that lies a selection of heavy stones which are roughly cube shaped. The guttering is crafted out of half of the hollowed-out trunk of a sapling and, in turn, feeds a large wooden barrel at the corner. On one building we noticed hops growing up a long pole at the gable end and guessed correctly that we were looking at the brewery.

My father, Iain Alick in
RAF uniform.
(My Dad's War)

Iain Alick with his young sons.

Nazareno with Dr Gori and the 'Topolino'
(Ale's Dad's War)

Padre John Fletcher at the R.A.P.
Cassenego, nr San Andrea.
During River Senio Battles, Feb 1945.
Courtesy of London Scottish

BAGNO CAVALLO · 1945
(MARCH 21)

F. T. CHAPMAN

TO CAPT. FLETCHER – THE FIRE-EATING PARSON

This card was presented to John F in Italy by an American volunteer ambulance driver, an illustrator in civilian life.

POLA, SEPTEMBER 1945.
Back row L-R: jock Murray, Alf Christie
Front row L-R: Derek Hollebone, Ken Pugh, Alec Murray, John Fletcher
Courtesy of London Scottish

Ale's visit to Scotland. Summer 1983. Isle of Skye.
(Ale and I Meet Again)

My visit to Tuscany. Autumn 1983. San Gimignano.

With my mother, brother and John F.

With Nazareno and Cipria
(The Italian Wedding)

The young Flodabay Five decide that I am OK
(A New Chapter in Harris)

Scudo by Ailie Osborne.

Uisdean by Ailie Osborne.

With my dad in Leverburgh.
Probably at South Harris
Agricultural Show
(Quidinish, Isle of Harris:
Early Memories)

With Seocan MacKenzie
and my mum. 'Fishing'

Painting by Ailie Osborne from
a photo I took on my way to
feed the hens at croft Number 7
(Quidinish: A Continuing Legacy)

I wondered why people were starting to wait along the seafront.
(Marina di Pisa)

Nazareno and Zia Lucilla at Marina di Pisa
(Eat to Stay Young)

Caspian gets to know his great grandfather. Tuscany.

A last look down from the woods beside the 'wee housie' before we left for home.

Painted by Ailie Osborne from my photo of Scudo and the valley of the River Enns.
(Austria)

Tuscany by Ailie Osborne.
(Walking in their Footsteps)

Drenched by an Italian thundery downpour at the celebration for the marriage of Seumas and Catriona.
(Reflection)

Heading for Colinton Dell.
With me from L-R are Catriona, Ale, Caspian, Seumas, John, Laura and Finlay.

Slightly uphill from the brewery was a small enclosure with a shed, again built in traditional style. Within the doorway and only just discernible in the shadows, the two of us made out the remarkable sight of a large pig having a snooze in the shade. Nothing so remarkable in that on first look, but it then became clear that the large snout was protruding from a heavy fleece. While unmistakeably a pig from its snout, the beast's fleece came right over its forehead and also right up to its chin. Even the ears were woolly. Small wonder it looked completely flaked out in the heat of that day.

The animals were Mangalica or Mangalitsa pigs. Originally from Hungary, the breed had nearly died out, but was making a comeback. The name apparently means that the pig is a large hog with lots of lard. Of course, lard went out of favour, but its come-back, as not quite so unhealthy as the scientists once thought, has been good news for these very strange looking animals. A revival is underway and, of course, Harris came to mind; the climate there is more likely to be wet and windy rather than savagely cold. Perhaps they could be a niche opportunity for the Quidinish cousins. Organic pork from woolly pigs? Mangalica Pork Medallions Quidinish Ltd? Maybe not.

Another building caught the eye because of the large water trough near its front door. The trough had been hewn out of a massive tree trunk with both inlet and outflow pipes also crafted from wood. Neatly stacked against the wall was a display of hand implements, again crafted mostly from wood. Hay making tools were to the fore with scythes, broad wide-toothed rakes, drying posts and centre columns for haystacks. Many of these were immediately familiar as cousin John in Quidinish still makes hay in the traditional way.

The main building was a family home, a cowshed, a stable and a hayloft all under the one roof. Between the wood burning stove in the kitchen and the animals close by, there would have been no trouble in staying warm, albeit with an interesting mixture of aromas. People and their animals being together under the same roof to their mutual benefit was a similarity to a Hebridean black house, but the building materials and the fuel burned were in marked contrast. The herb garden, bread bakehouse and a large cheese press made it obvious that, with beer production covered too, this farming community knew how to look after itself.

The next day, Andrea took the three of us, yes, dog too, into the centre of Munich. These German ladies drive quickly, not just on the autobahn either. It would have been another cageful of canaries for my driving instructor. He insists on two hands on the wheel.

Ale and I had been to Munich not long after we were married, my abiding memory of that visit being the earnestly offered advice from my brand-new father-in-law against any attempt to drink a litre stein of the Munich beer!

The centre of Munich greatly impressed us. We walked through an open-air market which gave us the impression of being in a small country town, until, within a few metres we emerged on to the broad streets near the university. It was all very grand indeed.

The plan was for the guests from Scotland to visit the English Garden and we were expecting something like Princes Street Gardens in Edinburgh; not very big, busy, well maintained, but obviously of city centre feel. What we found was very far removed from that. There were acres and acres of parkland with huge trees, both lining the network of pathways and forming large woodland areas. Better still, there was a river. It was also very clear that dogs were welcome in the park with plenty to be seen, both on and off the lead. As it was a glorious, sunny day, Scudo was encouraged to go straight into the river, which was fast flowing, icy cold and generally *wunderbar*.

After he had cooled off, the dog joined the two of us up on a bridge just in time to watch as a girl hurtled below it. She was swimming downstream and taking advantage of the brisk current to reach what looked like a reckless speed. She certainly wouldn't be swimming back upstream, at least not on that stretch of the river.

Ale and I crossed the bridge and started walking upstream on the far bank, finding quieter sections of water with trout plainly visible. There were also spotted, on the other side of the river, several Munich sun enthusiasts who had decided to get as much sun as possible by wearing not a single stitch of clothing. We are talking about a city centre park here, not some secluded beach. It did, however, confirm the MacKenzie thinking – no midgies in Munich.

The English Garden is one of the largest urban parks in the world. Apparently, Prince-Elector Carl Theodor inherited the whole area around the city in the 1700s but was not really enthusiastic about it as he preferred lands elsewhere. The good folk of Munich did not take very kindly to his attitude, so Carl Theodor thought he would try to make things a little better by spending funds on improvements for the city. It seems that his senior military adviser at the time was the American born British soldier, physicist and government administrator Sir Benjamin

Thompson who saw the opportunity of improving matters for both civilians and soldiers. It was thought that soldiers, in times of peace, could learn farming and gardening techniques. The idea was that every town with a barracks should have a military park for soldiers to learn skills for their retirement and for civilians to enjoy too. This seems to have been the origin of the English Garden, created on what was formerly a deer forest.

The walk had been brilliant; plenty other dogs, courteous people, lots of grass and trees, a river with fish, stark-naked sunbathers. Just like Colinton Dell, nearly.

On the way back to the car we enthused to Andrea about the English Garden, but also mentioned our surprise at the naturist style of sunbathing. In fact, we admitted that we couldn't believe our eyes. Andrea explained that this style of sunbathing had been practised in the English Garden for decades, with regulations being brought in relatively recently. Six areas had been set aside for people who wanted to get burned all over, but difficulties had arisen on account of the Eisbach, which is the name of the man-made river. As mentioned, the river has a strong current in places so, when the naked sunbathers went in to cool off, they had a tendency, intentionally or not, to be swept downstream to emerge on the bank well outside their permitted zone. Some of them would then take to the paths, the streets and even the buses to work their way back to where their clothes were waiting for them.

Next, we visited Marienplatz with its Neues Rathaus, New City Hall. This is Munich's historic main square and was crammed with tourists. Ale and I just stood and took it all in while Andrea disappeared for five minutes to collect something from a shop, leaving her guests among visitors from all over the world. The idea was that we were to wait beside the big column in the centre of the square for Andrea's return, but it was so busy that we moved to one side, just to get a little more space. We entertained ourselves by starting to guess all the languages as people passed, so did not immediately notice that a group had gathered round us and were taking photos of the dog from every angle – very enthusiastic Japanese tourists. We managed to keep straight faces at the sight of Scottish being mistaken for Bavarian. Somewhere in Japan, there must be many images of that very Scottish dog, sitting patiently, in the world famous Marienplatz in Munich.

~·~ A Road Well Travelled ~·~

The next morning, the Scottish Land Rover left Holzkirchen in cloud and light rain which provided perfectly comfortable travelling conditions. Near Rosenheim, it was either turn left towards Salzburg or, our route, which was to the right towards Innsbruck. From that turning, Ale and I were on a road which was very familiar to us from all the years of driving between Tuscany and Nazareno's little house in Austria.

Not long after we turned towards Innsbruck, there were serious mountains to our left, seen before, but always with fresh impact. Then, at Innsbruck, it was a left turn and down into Italy through the Brenner Pass. That meant huge mountains on both sides and lots of noting of familiar landmarks emanating from the two in the front of the car. Bressanone; Chiusa; Bolzano; Trento; Rovereto; Verona; Mantova; Carpi; Modena.

Sometimes the place would be in close view, but at other times it was just the signpost that triggered conversation and, inevitably, reminiscence. We had been travelling this route together for over thirty years, but this was our first time on our own, by car. No Nazareno or Cipriana, no John, Seumas or Finlay.

In the early days, the drive would be in Nazareno's now classic Citroen DS estate, which had plenty room for four adults and first one, two and then even three young boys. It lacked modern air conditioning though, which was perhaps just as well, as it would have been impossible to keep both the northern Scot and his Tuscan father-in-law at the right state of cool. Getting agreement on the choice of music had proved difficult enough.

Music and temperature, however, had no influence on the chosen route back in those days. That was dictated by the Citroen's fuel system. Nazareno had converted his car to dual fuel, so he had the choice of running on compressed methane which was incredibly cheap compared to petrol, but its additional tank was unavoidably modest in size. There were regular stops to seek out methane stations which seemed to be situated mostly in industrial zones on the outskirts of towns and cities.

Toll roads were avoided if at all possible, resulting in the journey being more leisurely, the scenery more varied and, if a picnic resulted in the car owner having a snooze in the shade of a tree, so be it. At times, we would be cruising along an A-class road beside a river and would notice that the autostrada, cut along the hillside above us, was ground to a halt. Out would slip a mildly self-congratulatory aside from Nazareno, '*Hai visto*?' ('Did you see that?') It took longer, but it was definitely more relaxed, or so Ale and I were agreeing in our rose-tinted rear-view mirror.

Other than just sounding nice, the above list of places has a couple of names of some significance for the two of us. Carpi is the nearest town to the POW camp where the evidence strongly suggests that my father was held. We had passed it for years without knowing. Trento is mentioned for a very much less sombre reason. Wine! Trento is the capital of Trentino-Alto Adige. The lower slopes of the rugged mountains are clad in terraces of vines. The views are amazing and the two of us are dedicated fans of the area's white wines, in particular.

The signpost for Bolzano triggered a period of enjoyable reminiscence which lasted for quite a few kilometres. Bolzano, it seems, is a very special place. It was recently ranked as the number one city during a survey on quality of life in the provinces of Italy, having consistently been ranked highly. We had not known that when we visited and stayed overnight previously during a marathon train journey from Pisa up to Linz in Austria.

One of the huge gaps in my knowledge of European history had been exposed by that visit. I had noticed over the years that the staff at motorway service stations tended to speak more German than Italian well south of the border with Austria, but I did not know why. Reception staff at the hostel in Bolzano started in German, which was fine, then moved into Italian on seeing Ale's passport and then back into German once they realised that she was completely fluent in their preferred language and that her husband had a decent smattering too. We were staying in what was like brand new halls of residence for students. The air conditioning was a Godsend, especially after one long leg of the journey north had been spent in a crowded rail carriage where the air-conditioning had failed. Reception gave advice on a range of places for dinner and we ventured out for a look around.

I had immediately been struck at how much more like Austria than Italy it felt as we moved around the centre of Bolzano. The streets and squares were much closer to Steyr in style than to Pisa. It was difficult for me to tell about the language until the two of us settled on a place to eat. There, the waiter, a young local, was favouring German and more likely to try out his English than his Italian. The chosen eating place was either a restaurant with its own brewery or a brewery with its own restaurant. Whichever it was, we liked it. The menu was noticeably more Austrian than Italian, with most tables seeming to prefer beer to wine – a telling factor!

Our after-dinner stroll took us past some very fine shops; very slowly in the case of the specialist knife shop whose window display was fascinating, rather more quickly in the case of the clothes shops whose prices were scary. We ended up crossing the bridge over the river Talfer and having a brief look at the Victory Monument, but also noticed other inscriptions in the area which seemed to refer to much more recent strife than the World Wars.

The Bolzano area had an extremely difficult twentieth century history. World War 1 resulted in a predominantly German speaking region becoming part of Italy, but Hitler and Mussolini later imposed an 'Option' on the inhabitants of staying and becoming Italianised or moving into the German Reich. This, apparently, divided society and indeed families. With Italian surrender to the Allies in 1943, the Germans occupied. The Allies then occupied in 1945. The area was returned to Italy, with Austria and Italy being invited to work together on protecting the German speaking population and also those who preferred the third language of the outlying reaches of the area, Ladin. Tensions, however, rapidly grew. Articles described Austria's referring the difficulties to the United Nations. Violence, disruption and even deaths occurred. Agreements were eventually reached by the interested parties and regulations implemented. The Autonomous Province of Bolzano (South Tyrol) seemed not only beautiful but harmonious and thriving to us. Bozen – Südtirol, Bolzano – Alto Adige and Bulsan – Südtirol all surround the provincial coat of arms.

With minds refocussed back on the motorway, our reminiscence about Bolzano had to end as the volume of traffic increased; it was replaced by discussion over whether to head for Florence or towards La Spezia on the west coast. The former route benefited from a new stretch of autostrada, but we were already familiar with the latter. 'Better the devil you know' meant a right turn at Modena for Parma and a serious shock for me at the cost of diesel in motorway service stations in Italy. The note to self was, in future, to arrive in Italy with a full tank and to leave with it almost empty.

Somewhere after Parma, high up in the Appenines, the Freelander came to a complete halt because of major roadworks near a National Park Area. The views were sensational and varied with rock, forest and deep gorge. The driver at the time (tractor man, not *Alfista*) was thoroughly enjoying being stuck, properly at a standstill, engine off and windows wide open. The heat coming in the way was rather ominous for the inquisitive, then apprehensive, senses in the tailgate section.

Once under way again, the Land Rover started eating up the kilometres in thinner traffic and the two in front started chalking up the signposts once more. Castel Nuovo di Garfagnana – caught in a thunderstorm on a tiny golf course deep in the hills; Massa-Carrara – visiting Ale's brother when he was a hospital doctor there; Viareggio – avoiding all the expensive shops (my idea, again) and buying langoustines direct from the fishermen as they berthed their boats at the long pier, Ale's idea and brilliant.

Pisa Centrale was the exit we chose. Instead of crossing the river Arno and turning left, upstream for Pisa, we turned right and headed for the coast and a very warm and humid welcome to Marina di Pisa, now base for Nazareno and, therefore, our home in the Land of Her Father.

~·~ Marina di Pisa ~·~

Having been driven, occasionally one-handed by my wife and mostly one-handed by our dear friend Andrea in her Golf 'flying machine', it had been strictly two hands on the wheel for 440 miles from me. Despite texted 'quips' from my brother, read out by and replied to by Ale, I was close to the speed limit all the way. The text banter, the incoming entirely deprecating, the outgoing mostly self-deprecating, had involved the notion of my being overtaken by tractors in reverse gear, lawnmowers and even a zimmer. He does like his cars very fast.

Now, the real master of steering one-handed round bends on mountain stretches of *autostrada* is Nazareno; one hand on the steering wheel, one eye in the wing mirror and tyres protesting. He made the monumental move to Marina after more than fifty years of having his main home base in the centre of Pisa. Marina di Pisa is just what it says, the marina of Pisa and is right at the mouth of the River Arno.

On turning right after the bridge over the Arno, we drove about six miles along what was mostly a straight road, lined by mature trees. To our left, were fields with the occasional farm steading. To our other side, we could see the Arno, in between gaps in the heavy growth on its banks. The closer we got to Marina, the more evidence of sailing and fishing there was to the right. There were boatyards for pleasure craft and traditional fishing huts some of which had huge square nets hung out over the river from long wooden arms. These nets would be lowered, left in place for a while, then lifted to see what had been caught.

It seems that the main part of Marina was planned in the late 1800s, based on a grid pattern between three squares and built on reclaimed land forming a strip between the sea and the dense pine woods. Put like that, it doesn't sound terribly attractive. It is not a big place and never will be, but with its relatively recent design, the streets are all broad. The promenade along the sea front has no trees, but the two roads running parallel to it are tree lined. Ale, the native and therefore the authority on such matters, would not call it a typical Italian seaside resort as it doesn't have many hotels or expensive beaches, but it does get very busy at weekends, mostly with visitors from Pisa. Nazareno's new home is around the corner from the main street and overlooks a large open area with grass, footpaths and stone benches, beyond which lies the sea, only a hundred yards away.

While Ale was immediately engrossed in giving her father the benefit of her advice on keeping his new kitchen and a large batch of produce from his farm in better balance, Scudo and I went for a walk along the sea front. Having the sea so close was the only common feature with the Harris base that we had left so recently. Again, what a difference in just a few days.

Things soon felt much more familiar on the sea front as Finlay appeared up ahead, walking towards us in the company of sheer elegance! Our youngest son had flown in from Edinburgh earlier in the day and had already transformed from Scottish to Italian - bright vest, cool shorts, flip flops. He was staying only 300 yards away with his aunt Eleonora and her family. One companion was his cousin, Elena. The other was the famous Idi, the nicest German shepherd 'in the world', at least according to Scudo's owners. Scudo tolerated her obvious familiarity with me. Master and hound turned back with the three of them to Nazareno's house, at which point jealousy reared its ugly head. The mutual enthusiasm of greeting between Ale and Idi was a bit much, with Idi lying straight on her back to get her tummy tickled. Unfortunately, Scudo was unable to hold back a curled lip and a flash of dental armoury. He was treated with tolerance by the much bigger dog, which was fortunate, as they were to walk together in the morning.

~·~ Acclimatising for Two ~·~

The Scot started to enjoy the contrasts. It was as if I were seeing Italy anew, simply by having a fresh pair of eyes and ears with me. Last week, we had been looking across at the lights of Skye. On that first evening in Marina, we looked down the coast to the lights of Livorno where it seemed as if half the town had broken off and was floating very slowly out to sea; a massive, luxury cruise liner was leaving port.

On the first morning, another contrast struck, uncomfortably. A week or so earlier, we had left Harris where, on a calm morning, you can experience the bliss of utter stillness. Here, we had cars and people going right past the front door, Vivaldi giving it laldy on the radio and Ale having to raise her voice, as her dad is a little deaf. It was lively stuff.

Nazareno's new home has high ceilings and tiled floors, rather than the low ceilings and wooden floors of Scotland. It all seemed to be designed to help keep cool. The windows had stayed open overnight, albeit with the slatted shutters and mosquito net frames carefully shut.

The main room is entrance hall, living room and dining area all rolled into one. The high ceiling is ornately painted with flowers and vines in the corners, a large eagle in the centre and pairs of herons on each side. The other week's eagle was the real thing and herons had been seen so frequently as barely to rate a mention. The artistic ceiling certainly merited enthusiastic comment from the visitors, but it was strange to look up and see an artist's impressions of what had been available to watch for real only a few days before.

Eleonora arrived on that first morning and gave the impression of seeming very composed for a lady whose daughter was getting married the next day. I left the two sisters to catch up and went out to enjoy the sea air from one of the park benches just across the road.

The sea is the boundary on the west of Marina, La Pineta on the east. It is a National Park Area of dense woodland that stretches for some miles south from the Arno behind both Marina and Tirrenia. There is a similar stretch to the north of the Arno. The Marina Pineta can be entered less than two hundred yards from Eleonora's house.

La Pineta provided plenty shade as I walked with Scudo around the pathways in the dense woods for an hour or so, meeting only a few walkers, joggers and horse riders. The large pinecones were a novelty for the dog to fetch, but the absence of a river was a serious miss.

We left the woods and found a corner near the sea front which provided both shade and a breeze. I waited there for a while, happy just to stand, looking out to sea and letting the breeze cool me down. Parked at the kerb next to us was a strange vehicle which looked like a cross between a scooter and a tractor; it had three wheels. The owner arrived, bulky fellow. He only just managed to squeeze into the cab and, as he drove away, his machine really struggled, sounded like a scooter and was certainly not about to threaten any speed limits. There sat the discerning Scudo, thinking he was going to the land of Ferrari, Maserati and Lamborghini – eyebrows up, eyes wide.

In the early evening, it was back out along the sea front again, but this time in the direction of the new port and its marina. Ale came with me as we took our own dog on one of the routes which had become a favourite for a walk with Idi. We reached a mini lighthouse which, with its partner opposite, signals the entrance from the open sea to the new marina. Naturally, Scudo wanted to have a proper look, so he was quickly up on his hind legs with his front paws resting on the top of the sea wall, a move which drew a comment in Italian to the effect that he was almost human. The speaker must have thought they were safe as Ale and I were conversing in English at the time. The dog that wanted to watch boats and anglers got his two owners into quite a few conversations that evening.

Then came the second part of our traditional Marina evening stroll which is a pre-dinner glass of white wine. The bar we go to is right on the sea front, has tables under large shades and serves tiny pizza bites with the wine. Our plan, now that we were staying with Nazareno, rather than with Eleonora, was to watch the sun go down and then return home for a simple dinner, the timing of the meal being in our own hands.

It never ceases to amaze the Scot that the sun goes down in such a hurry over in Tuscany. Only a few days previously, we could still have been fishing or playing golf in broad daylight.

It was probably strange for our dog to see his two owners looking quite so comfortable in such a different place. Every outside table at Rosa Di Venti had a dog lying by the feet of Italian or visitor owners. An aperitivo while the temperature drops a little and the sun sets is popular. By that time of day, the road at the sea front is closed to vehicles and becomes a true promenade. The sea was to our front, but to our right, in the distance, we could see the Apuan Alps above Massa and Carrara. I mused about marble looking like snow or vice versa and promised myself that I would do some homework on local geography, as I had already been asked for directions three times in the course of that day. I must somehow appear sensible, trustworthy and approachable, at least to the uninitiated, because I certainly don't look like a local; pale skin, blue eyes; white socks under the leather sandals being the cardinal sin and most obvious clue.

In the distance, along the promenade, Ale noticed a cyclist cruising along in our direction. 'That's my dad!'

Out to watch the sunset and enjoy a gentle sea breeze, Nazareno was very happy to park his vintage machine and accept a small, but perfectly chilled, glass of beer.

With the traffic closed off, the area became quieter and we enjoyed a very pleasant end to our first full day. I had been slightly concerned about taking Scudo to Marina di Pisa. There had been some uncomfortable aspects, but with language and some family members already familiar to him plus sea, woods and fishing the dog only really needed to get used to more heat and much more noise. The noise? 'Vitality' was Ale's take on it; I stayed quiet, trusting that I'd feel completely at home in Marina by the time dinner was over.

As it turned out, my acclimatisation took a little longer this time.

After dinner, we were sitting in Ale's dad's main room. Something had caused the traffic to be diverted along Nazareno's little street and there was a constant flow of engines only a few feet from the flat's door and open windows. Compounding all of that, was the loud music coming from the sea front. Perhaps it was a festival or a holiday weekend. Then, without warning, Nazareno started up an electric drill very close to my ears. The famous workshop in the Pisa house had been painstakingly recreated in his new home. The lathe, drawing board and tools had all been set up in the same positions, as had shelves of engineering manuals and scientific journals. I offered Scudo another quick walk.

It was amazing. The place had come to life again. After dinner and long after dark, families were emerging to enjoy the cool end to the day. I could see family groups of three generations, many with dogs too. The variety of dog was quite astonishing with pointers and German shepherds cropping up amongst the smaller breeds. Pan pipes were being played through a powerful sound system. I didn't bother to check whether the music was live or canned; it was just loud and a bit irritating. Then, astonishingly, it segued into 'The Dark Island' and a pretty good job was made of it too. Ian MacLaughlan's much played tune was wafting out on pan pipes over a very busy, late-night sea front in Tuscany.

In Edinburgh or up in Harris, any last trip outside for the dog is usually on his own. In Harris, on a clear night, I might come out to look up at the vast canopy of stars, all the while trying to keep my imagination in check. The awesome sight is mind blowing. There is absolutely no light pollution in Quidinish. Over in Marina, both of us went out with our dog even though it was well after midnight. Yes, the traffic was still on the move, as were couples with grandparents and tiny wee ones in tow. Eventually, just before 1am, Scudo lay down in the bedroom, knowing he would soon be expelled. Nazareno came in looking for some steps. More drilling? Does this place never shut down? The windows were open, cars were still accelerating away from the corner and a generator was running over on the sea front. A sympathetic look down told me that the dog's nose, ears and eyes all felt overworked and that the poor fellow wished Marina di Pisa would please just be quiet and go to sleep.

~·~ Nazareno's Farm
and another Italian Wedding ~·~

The following day was the wedding of Ale's niece, Benedetta, and Daniele so the alarm had been set early, but an ambulance passing by with all alerts blaring had woken everyone anyway. Other traffic was also on the move, but at least the little front street was back to one-way with the lifting of an annoying diversion. I was in the woods with Scudo by 9am, where it felt pleasantly fresh, the other bonus being that it was so quiet that no lead was required.

On the way back I chose the route along the sea front. Although it was hardly past breakfast time, there were already plenty of sun bathers, swimmers and sea anglers. They take their sun very seriously in Tuscany. There are a couple of sandy beaches along by the port, but most of the beaches at Marina are of the stone type which are not particularly comfortable to walk on. Sitting and lying on them can be worse, but the white stones do make a pretty contrast with the blue of the Mediterranean and rattle almost melodically when the waves wash up over them. A few yachts were already on the move. It was Saturday morning, a very fine one at that and the Italians were out to make the most of it.

On the way back to Nazareno's flat, I passed *Il Crudo*. Only two doors away, run by two sisters, this *panineria* is a remarkable licensed sandwich bar where the baguettes are enormous and the fillings both varied and generous. All types of Italian cold meats and salami are available plus a vast range of cheeses and sauces. Any combination can be chosen and, of course, salad can be added. The two sisters are ideal neighbours.

As you might expect, the enjoyment of food is a favourite topic of conversation in the family, especially amongst those with Italian blood. Around the corner from Nazareno's front door, on the main street, are specialist shops for bread, wine, fish and cured meats. If you want all that under the one roof, you simply go to Conad which is only 300 yards away. The couple from Scotland think it is excellent, with an amazing choice for what is a small supermarket in a very small town.

Nazareno, of course, has his own supply of wine, fruit and vegetables from his farm at Certaldo. He also had an olive grove at Buti, just east of Pisa, a source not only of olives, but of olive oil too. He has just transferred Buti to Eleonora whose daughter, Francesca and son-in-law, Mateo, are making a superb job of renovating the traditional Tuscan house which sits amid the terraces of olive trees. The highlight for us is the mantel piece carved from the trunk of a long-fallen olive tree. That length of wood could well be over a thousand years old.

Certaldo is further inland than Pisa, between Siena and Florence. Eleonora's son, Marco, is training to take over the production of grapes, fruit and vegetables. Ale remembers times when her dad had oxen and pigs. In those days, Nazareno could even produce his own prosciutto (air dried ham). Even in my time, rabbits and pigeons were reared for the table. Nazareno's right hand man at the farm, the multi skilled Vestro, whose rural, Florentine accent and vocabulary have long bamboozled me, turned his hand to every aspect of Tuscan farm work, including educating the Gori youngsters. He may well be to thank for my wife's dexterity in skinning a rabbit and plucking a pheasant. He remains regarded with reverence and affection in equal measure.

On my first ever visit to the Gori family, I went on a tour of the farm with Nazareno, just the two of us. Nazareno was using English and told me, with enthusiasm, 'I have many mice.' My response about getting a couple of cats left Nazareno smiling the way he does when my English has left him totally mystified. In a mixture of German and English, Nazareno offered the back-up information that the 'mice' were two metres high.

'MAIZE, Nazareno, not MICE. You need a combine harvester, not cats!'

Another mystified smile.

The two of us have, long since, conversed only in Italian. Sadly, over thirty years later, I still cannot retain the Italian for combine harvester. Nobody is in the slightest interested that I can recall the German… instantly.

Linguistic difficulties continued during that first farm tour when Nazareno pointed to a small brick shed and told me, in English, that he had made it. He offered further information in Italian. The Scottish thought bubble might have been, 'So, you've built a wee brick shed…and?' My underwhelmed look (no mystified smiler here) left Nazareno perplexed until sign language came to the rescue. The little brick shed housed the pump for the irrigation system for the whole farm, but Nazareno's 'I have made this' really meant that he had designed and installed, himself, the complete irrigation system for the whole farm.

Mechanical engineer, farmer, inventor, designer…. the list could go on. A memorable two-week period in July 2017, saw the family gather in Tuscany and Umbria to celebrate the marriage of Seumas and Catriona, the thirtieth birthday of his brother,

John, and the ninetieth birthday of their grandfather, the remarkable Nazareno, who could well have lost his life in his teens had it not been for his family's friendship with Dr Kinsella, John F and the other British soldiers.

Nazareno has twenty-seven grandchildren and, on that sunny Saturday morning in Marina, was preparing to attend granddaughter wedding number three in a light-weight suit. The MacKenzie men, on the other hand, had been determined to wear full Highland dress. I was wavering, trying to persuade Finlay that we could miss out on the black jackets in view of the heat, but Finlay was having none of that. His cousin was expecting the real deal and that was what she would get, hot day or not.

Even before we left for the church, I was complaining about the heat and offering the theory that Finlay was at an advantage in having spent a month in Marina during the height of summer. My kilt was the same one I had worn at my own wedding over thirty years earlier. It seemed to have shrunk, just a little, maybe Scottish dampness meeting Italian heat? Every stage of preparation caused me to overheat and I caught Scudo watching, with head cocked to one side as, at least twice, Ale had to halt her own preparations to flap a towel at her husband to cool him down. The Land Rover's air-conditioning helped greatly and I eventually put on my tie and jacket in the church carpark.

The church was in a small square, not far from the Leaning Tower of Pisa. The pre-arranged Council permits allowed the family members to park almost at the door. Inside, the church was in classic Pisa style, ornate with marble slabs on the floor and a very high ceiling; cool and comfortable, it was not. Many

Italians were already using the order of service as a fan. I thought that rather ominous. Finlay stayed cool.

On arrival, the kilts had generated interest with the groom's family quick to organise an impromptu photo shoot. Daniele himself was immaculate in a fine charcoal-grey suit. His wing-collared shirt with silk brocade waistcoat and matching tie completed a picture of genuine Italian style. No nerves were evident in his broad smile.

After my traditional brogues nearly had me flat out on the smooth church floor, which would have been excruciatingly embarrassing, I ran into even more difficulty. Several of Nazareno's grandchildren were young ladies in their late teens and twenties. I was used to seeing them in t-shirts, jeans and flip flops and normally recognised them all easily, but I found myself receiving hugs and kisses from a bewildering series of stunning young ladies who called me Zio. The problem I had with the nieces was that I wasn't sure which was which. They were all taller than when I had last seen them, only four months earlier. There were high heels for all and platform soles for one or two. The spectacular dresses and hairstyles were even more confusing. I thought it best not to use names and I also steadfastly refrained from initiating any hugging and kissing in case the startled recipient turned out not to be a niece at all – a tricky moment or two, all told.

Once we were seated, Francesca, a sister of the bride, turned around in her pew and whispered, '*Zio, io sofro per te.*' The Italian sounds much better than the English 'Uncle, I'm suffering for you.' Francesca herself was already far too hot in the lightest of dresses.

The Italian orders of service continued to work overtime, unread, as Benedetta, radiant in white and Riccardo, every inch the proud Tuscan dad, walked slowly down the aisle. The music for the occasion was provided and the singing was led by church friends of the bride, who were obviously well accustomed to performing in public. The huge church organ was locked up in its alcove and instead there were acoustic guitars, flute, clarinet and tom-tom. The congregation were well practised in rhythmic clapping.

I had forgotten how much standing was involved in an Italian wedding, as this was my first in many years. When I started thinking about guardsmen keeling over during ceremonial duty, I knew that it might well be time for me to get out of my jacket. Finlay still stayed cool. While the Italians opposite me kept on fanning furiously, I was apparently starting to go a bit pale, so off came the jacket. The distinct possibility of injury, or even worse, severe shame, was averted, with relief immediate. While this mini crisis was going on in my head, Ale was flitting about the place taking photos. She wouldn't even have been close enough to catch me.

The explosion of rice at the church door was avoided with plenty room to spare. Rice is bad for kilt jackets, as the MacKenzies well know from past experience.

Back at the car, the Land Rover party was greeted by the group of young African guys who had, for a couple of euros, issued official looking tickets. There was already a parking pass and Finlay had immediately declared in perfectly audible Italian that the ticket sale was a complete scam. Either way, all was well and one of the Africans, after pointing at the sporran and asking what it was, engaged me in a taxing discussion, in Italian, on the Scottish Independence Referendum, Brexit and the possibility of a second referendum in Scotland. One of the two conversationalists was well-read, well-informed. The other was overheated, kilted and was looking for the best route out of a claustrophobic square in Pisa. The latter claims to have enjoyed the friendly exchange, nevertheless.

The reception was being held deep in the Tuscan countryside, so Ale and her two sisters arranged for the family vehicles to depart together from Piazza san Paolo, the square of the church in which she and I had married. During the convoy's forty-minute drive, nobody matched Cipriana's commanding of junctions, but it was fondly recalled.

The route led in the direction of Florence, before there was a sharp turn straight up into the hills. In the lead was the bride's dad in what is, effectively, a minibus. Riccardo not only knew the way well, but also had many years of experience of driving the wide diversity of Italian roads. One minute it is *superstrada* and the next you can be in ancient hilltop villages whose buildings crowd in on their narrow streets. Nobody had a Ford Tourneo in mind when these villages grew. The nine-seater leading its short column of 4x4s seemed to persuade oncoming vehicles to give way, or even to dive for cover in some cases. The countryside was just as it is depicted in adverts for Tuscan holidays; I could have reached out of the window and touched perfectly formed bunches of black grapes on the vine. We climbed still higher prompting comments about it being cooler with less mosquito risk. The two 'kilties' approved, on both counts.

The destination was what appeared to be a former country estate, with several farm steadings, all of which had been converted into both hotel and *agriturismo* accommodation. The weekend speciality was the hosting of wedding receptions, or so it seemed, with two sets of wedding guests evident before faces were recognised amongst a third. The popularity was understandable, as the location was simply astounding.

The little convoy rolled into a terrace of parking areas from where there was a short uphill walk to the venue. The original building had been extended by the addition of a huge conservatory-style dining area with raised stage and dance floor, all immaculately prepared. That opened out on to an extensive, manicured garden. 'Garden' did not do it justice. It was more like a small park surrounded by sculpted hedges. In the foreground was a large, kidney shaped swimming pool beyond which there had been set up tables with matching arm chairs and sofas plus two buffet stalls and a bar, all in brilliant white which, with the various shades of green of hedges and lawn and the blue of the pool, combined to create the first impression of walking into a film scene.

All of this was on the flat top of a hill. As the high hedges blocked the view down into the surrounding valleys, the venue felt like it was in a world of its own. In the far-left corner of the gardens was a broad gate, again brilliant white. That was where Benedetta and Daniele eventually arrived on a carriage drawn by a single black horse. The spirited animal was easily encouraged to make a first pass at brisk pace, to turn with a flourish beyond, before coming to a halt precisely at the gate. Great style in all respects, but by that stage I already thought I was in the Italian department of Heaven with prosecco, prosciutto, salami, Parmesan cheese and Tuscan bread in apparently limitless supply. I had also worked out which niece was which. Having paid scant attention to the meal at my own wedding, I was determined to be tuned in this time and took note. The highlights were:

First course –

Risotto with flavours of seasonal flowers.
Tortellini with marrow served with a walnut cream sauce.
Little pasta crowns with a ragu of a Tuscan belted pig
in a red wine sauce.

Main courses –

Ham entrecote with roast potatoes.
Duck breast with orange and a pea cream sauce.

These first and main courses were not alternative choices. They were all served one after another.

The banquet continued well into the evening. In contrast with our own tradition, there were no formal speeches. The feasting was accompanied by a live band throughout, their repertoire covering all tastes and ages. In contrast with our own wedding, there was no inter table cork throwing for the bride to admonish, but at one point a table mostly of girls did try to sing louder than a table of boys. It was all definitely more vitality than noise, although it did occur to me at one point that I might be better phoning my sister-in-law who was sat opposite me!

Ale and I arrived back in Marina at about 1am, slightly earlier than we had expected. Finlay had been left enjoying the dancing with his many girl cousins, his kilt holding him back not in the least, although the dance style was far removed from the Dashing White Sergeant and the Gay Gordons.

Nazareno had struggled with the bass, first removing his hearing aid and then turning his famous ingenuity in the direction of improvised ear plugs! Even Nazareno had met his match this time. On leaving the main function room to find peace out by the pool, the poor fellow was dismayed to feel in his chest, rather than hear through his defended ears, bass and drums start up from a hidden speaker. He was soon swallowed up in hordes of young guests as the newly-weds appeared at the water's edge for the cake cutting ceremony. Having enjoyed the day, it was time for him to leave the festivities to the younger generations, so his driver and navigator happily took him home.

Minus jacket and tie, a confident kilt swung its way back and forth along the seafront at Marina until 2am. Lovely wife on his arm, the wearer had a smile in his heart.

~·~ Eat to Stay Young ~·~

'*A tavola, non si invecchia.*' That is 'At the table, you don't grow older,' which might explain why the Italians in the family don't like to rush at mealtime. Certainly, even in the little household in Marina, lunch and dinner can turn into a celebration of Tuscan food, with a glass of wine and some banter added in. A short visit to the supermarket, on the morning after the wedding, produced *alici alla povera* (sprats in vinegar), *insalata di mare* (seafood salad), Tuscan bread and a bottle of very light, slightly sparkling, dry white wine – a first course to savour. Pork cutlets were then served with roasted aubergine and little potatoes in their skins for the main course. There was, of course, Nazareno's masterful salad, containing everything one would expect, but with an emphasis on lemon, onion and peppers. We must not forget *vino di nonno*, grandfather's red wine from Certaldo.

The banter at the table? That is exclusively in Italian and occasionally interspersed with mature, nay philosophical, conversation! Yes, there is plenty Italian in Edinburgh, but it is usually spoken by Ale and Finlay, especially since Finlay started university, but once I have been in Italy for a couple of days, even I plunge in.

One of Nazareno's pleasures is to see his dining companions enjoying his produce. It is such a pleasure that he doesn't readily accept being politely declined. I, on the other hand, not only prefer not to be pressed, but also prefer fruit to be pristine. Bruising from hitting the ground? No, thank you. Evidence of sampling by beasties? No, thank you. That shows the fruit is ripe. Still, no, thank you…and so it goes on. The more often I am pressed, the more stubbornly I decline. On being overly pressed about a pear, I announced that, if it were offered once more, I would never eat pear again in my life. Twice more, would result in my never eating pear in the next life either. What's more, in that next life, if I were asked the reason, I would point the finger at Nazareno. '*Colpa sua!*' 'His fault!' The staged rant with pointing finger appealed to the sense of humour of the genuinely devout father-in-law. Nobody grew older at the table that day.

By the fourth day, the Scottish element was getting more used to the heat. Then, we were hit by the storm.

The visitors had all been away with Eleonora in her 'bus' and thought we had timed the return perfectly as we were dropped off at Nazareno's front door. The rumbling had started and there were flashes out to sea with the wind rising all the while. We noticed that the girls at *Il Crudo* were collapsing the umbrellas and storing away the pavement tables and chairs. No house key had been taken and Nazareno was not answering his doorbell. Unfortunately, the Freelander was parked at his garage about a quarter of a mile away and the sky was about to explode.

Il Crudo came to our rescue. Over a glass of wine in the empty bar, Ale explained our predicament and plans were made as to how permission could be sought for me to cross neighbouring back gardens to access the rear door of Nazareno's house. The main concern was for Nazareno; might he have had a fall?

Conversation stopped for a while as the place erupted; massive crashing, forked lightning and a flash flood took over. It all died down after about ten minutes and, from the front door of *Il Crudo*, Nazareno was spied, bold fellow, marching back around the corner to his own front door. We had reckoned without *l'Inginiere's* curiosity and sense of adventure. From his back garden, he had seen flashing and had heard crashing. He thought a building had been struck, so had gone to investigate round on the main street where, like his guests, he had been obliged to seek shelter when the deluge started. We quickly forgot about the slight panic and carried on getting to know the neighbours a little better.

Il Crudo wine and conversation were finished without undue haste before we went out into the aftermath of the storm. The sun had fought back a little, leaving a narrow, deep-pink strip between a black sky and an even blacker sea. Everything had shut down. There was little enthusiasm for a stroll along the seafront before dinner.

~·~ Nazareno and John F – Walking in their Footsteps ~·~

Ale and I had it in mind that we would drive up to Austria via Tregozzano. There had been talk of a short visit to Austria by Nazareno, followed by a flight back to Pisa, but he decided to stay in Tregozzano instead, as his sister, Lucilla, had a list of jobs for him. Finlay announced that he fancied a trip to Tregozzano too, so Scudo's luxury travel suite was hijacked for my displaced golf clubs and accordion plus bags for four people. His relegation to the front passenger footwell was unavoidable; not much Italian countryside to be seen from down there.

Nazareno's father, Dr Giuseppe Augusto Gori, the doctor in Tregozzano, who had become a friend of Padre John Fletcher, had tragically been killed in a car crash not long after the war. The young doctor, who took over his practice, not only filled his place in the community, but also married one of his daughters, Lucilla. They were Ale's Zio Piero and Zia Lucilla.

Now widowed, Zia Lucilla lives with her daughter, Maria Gaia (Gaia), in a very interesting one and a half storey house set in a huge garden with mature pines and poplars. The garden must be about the size of three football pitches, perhaps more. For the dog, and definitely one other in the party, after the constant bustle of Marina di Pisa, this was a haven of peace and tranquillity. The large trees blocked out much of the outside world, but glimpses could be seen of high hills across the valley of the Arno. It was interesting for me to think that we had driven from the mouth of that river for over two hours without moving far from its course.

The welcome was wonderful. Zia Lucilla and Gaia both speak beautiful English. Gaia teaches and her command of the language is most impressive indeed. My Italian was answered in nothing less than the Queen's English. Everybody was looking to practise their foreign language with a 'tame' native speaker.

At a very early stage of the visit, my conversation with Zia Lucilla turned to the time of my stepfather, John F, being stationed at Tregozzano. I was touched to hear her speak of the fear of living in a war zone, of the huge relief on the success of the Allied advance and then, with real affection, of the subsequent friendship which was formed particularly with my stepfather and with Sergeant Walter Firstbrook. The sharpness of Lucilla's memory and the kindness she described was heart-warming for me, as was the realisation that I was calling Lucilla, who was speaking of those days with such feeling, 'Aunt' in Italian and feeling perfectly natural doing so.

Yet another beautiful speaker of English is Maria Cecilia (Cecilia), Zia Lucilla's elder daughter, who lives on another large plot just above her mum's where her house stands above what will always now be known to Clan MacKenzie as the 'carp lake'. Cecilia has two sons, Alex and Freddy and a recent addition in the shape of Indiana, a very young golden retriever that was a bit bowled over, literally, by Scudo MacKenzie's boisterous arrival.

Indiana and Scudo were soon in the cool water of the carp lake, ignoring accusations of disturbing the fish. She was much more relaxed and playful than Idi who had given the impression of never actually being off duty at all.

Ale, Finlay and I were staying with Cecilia and Nazareno was staying with his sister. A barbeque was planned for dinner, but first, all gathered for prosecco and appetisers down by the edge of the carp lake. A wooden platform area had been built into the bank just below and to the side of the casting point. The platform was for sunbathing and picnics, no doubt, but has potential for fishing which has been noted for the next visit. By the time all three generations were gathered, there were nine plus the two dogs. Indiana's tail was threatening glasses, plates and anti-mosquito candles. There was no way our dog was going to add to that lot, so he took up position on a nearby bridge and kept an eye on us all from up there.

The party moved on to the patio area beside the house and the conversation moved on to the subject of wild boar! A family of them had been marauding in Cecilia's grounds. They lived in the high, wooded hills behind the house and sent regular raiding parties through her defences. That certainly pricked up all Scottish ears and every sound from the surrounding darkness was double checked in case we had wild boar for company. Scudo and I went out last thing that evening when the peace and quiet was far more reminiscent of Harris than Marina di Pisa. No traffic noise was heard at all. The air was still, but fresh. We could even hear fish surfacing in the lake. Not a single wild boar was encountered.

My mind went over Zia's recollections of events seventy years in the past and the bitter struggle for Arezzo. Far from the fear and danger Nazareno and Lucilla had experienced as teenagers, was the fun the pair of them had enjoyed with the younger generations that evening. Those two eighty and ninety-somethings had given everyone another reminder that 'A tavola, non si invecchia.' On the evidence of these two, you actually grow younger!

I mentioned to Zia Lucilla my wish to see the area where, while she and Nazareno were teenagers, her whole family had been driven, at gunpoint, to fend for themselves in the lead up to the battle for Arezzo. She encouraged me to do just that, with Nazareno, and talked of the original family home, which I had presumed was long gone.

After lunch on our last day at Tregozzano, Nazareno and I set off in the Freelander with visions in my head of turning immediately up in to the high, forested hills to the rear, but no, the instruction was to return to the main road and head, instead, for the tiny centre of Tregozzano. Only then did we turn up towards the hills, moving quickly on to rough farm tracks to arrive at a traditional style house, which backed on to a farm steading. The house had an extensive garden to one side and a walled orchard to the front. From there, the view was back over gently falling ground towards Lucilla's home.

A lady came immediately from a house which formed part of the farm steading. Introductions were exchanged from which I understood that I was about to meet the current owners of Nazareno's childhood home. Again, it was the lady of the house who appeared. Further introductions followed which resulted in a generous welcome to visit any part of the grounds and to stay for as long as the two of us might wish.

The owner, *la signora*, was very welcoming and answered every question put to her. Knowing of our particular interest in the war, she mentioned having had work carried out in recent years to a large retaining wall between her garden and her orchard. The work had exposed a cache of WW2 weapons. Handguns, a rifle and ammunition had been discovered, all in pristine condition. Whoever had hidden them in the wall had known what they were doing. The protection afforded to the weapons, using oil, grease and airtight wrapping had been exceptional. The cache had been handed over to 'the authorities' which, I had presumed, meant *Carabinieri or Polizia*. We were told that the presumption made by 'the authorities' was that the cache had been hidden by partisans – very careful partisans, it seemed.

Beyond the substantial boundary wall of the orchard, Nazareno pointed out a flat area of ground which had been a marshalling point for Allied tanks. The war had been parked virtually at his front door.

The two visitors were then invited to have a look around the ground floor of the house itself. This was fifty years after the sale to *la signora* and seventy odd years after the war. Nazareno pointed out where his father's consulting room had been and also the dining room where John F, Dr Kinsella and the captain had enjoyed after-dinner coffee and wine with Dr and Mrs Gori. My father-in-law commented that many of the original features in these rooms had been retained.

The pair of us even visited the garage where Nazareno suffered his life-threatening burns. After what I had heard over the years and, indeed, had recently recorded, to find myself as a guest in the Gori wartime home, I found emotional, although I was not able adequately to describe the feeling afterwards. It wasn't sadness. It was nothing negative in any way, but certainly profound, somewhere between moving and spine-tingling.

What had happened in that building had directly affected my life, but there was more to it than simply a sense of shared history with my wife's family. It was as if I had completed another circle. Getting back to Harris as a teenager had completed one circle. Standing in to look after the crofts in Quidinish had completed another. Visiting the meeting place of my stepfather and the Gori family was one more. My own roots were deep in Harris, Ale's deep and wide in Tuscany, but our combined roots, the roots of our marriage were right there, in that house, in Tregozzano.

Talk of the arms cache brought to Nazareno's mind the capture, by the local partisans, of a German colonel and his staff car. The Germans had rounded up villagers, threatening them that one in twenty would be shot if the colonel were not released immediately. Given what had happened in the area, the threat was viewed as absolutely genuine. The partisans returned the colonel and his staff car to the village square by the appointed time and the Germans kept their word. The staff car was not, in fact, returned entirely intact. Somewhere, Nazareno has a part taken from it. He was slightly evasive when pressed on the nature of the part and how it had come into his possession. The young Nazareno's wartime experiences were genuinely 'hands on', it seems.

The visit to the former Gori home and its grounds had been quite intense. It was a step back in time and a step back too, for me, to memories of my stepfather. At the time of the former padre's marriage to my mother, five years after my father's death, her boys were fifteen and eleven. That cannot have been easy for John F. Looking back, I know now that I was still utterly devastated by the death of my dad and unlikely to have been the most welcoming of stepsons. That difficult thought is made a little easier for me by focussing on the friendship that warmed between my stepfather and me later in life, especially after Ale burst on the scene. His advice to me that I should check the spelling of the Apostle's name in my Gaelic bible before I went to register the birth of Seumas, I will always remember with fondness. Very recently, during a visit to us by Seumas, his wife and baby, I found my son searching through that Gaelic bible to show Catriona the page where the name Seumas had been circled in pencil for thirty years almost to the day. That the bible had been gifted by my father to my mother made the moment even more special for me.

After leaving the former Gori home with Nazareno, our being back out again in the open countryside, with its sprinkling of much more recently built houses, required more imagination. Moving around together in a modern vehicle, the feeling of living history relied entirely on Nazareno's running commentary. He was keen to have us drive up some narrow tracks with steeply banked sides, taking the view that the vehicle could cope easily with the terrain and, of course, he would explain to anyone who he was and why he was visiting. All would be well.

The regular appearance of 'No Entry. Private Road'. in Italian of course, caused hesitation at the wheel. All would not be well if we came nose to nose with a tractor. Yes, it would be fun to take on the steep banks, but no farmer would appreciate the sight of a foreign Land Rover taking evasive action amongst his vines. The rough translation of the exchange between father-in-law and son-in-law would be, 'You really don't want to put anyone out, do you?'

'Eh. Correct.'

We saw plenty anyway.

Nazareno was able to point out the location of the main German defensive positions and the source of the heavy gunfire which brought about the destruction of a jeep close to where he himself had been seeking cover. A German armoured car had been concealed in the wooded slopes above, before itself becoming the target of successful Allied fire. The range of fire was chilling. A nearby farm steading, which had been taken over as a repair depot for Allied tanks immediately after the battle, encouraged me to imagine the sights, sounds and smells.

The grapes on the vines were ready for harvest, the whole setting beautifully peaceful. The main road, which was not busy, by Italian standards anyway, was far below. It was warm and sunny, but the personal recollections of the man seated beside me easily transported this willing listener, on an afternoon I will always remember – back in time to a bloody battle for the Allies against determined, desperate and, in some cases, fanatical defenders.

Our stay in Tregozzano was over too soon and further rounds of fond farewells were suffered. Nazareno was staying on for a few days before returning to Marina. His daughter and son-in-law did not know when they would next see him; a winter visit to Scotland would be unlikely, due to his age and Scotland's weather. Finlay was heading back to Marina by lift, train and bus via Florence and Pisa. We were to meet up with him back in Edinburgh within ten days.

Just before we drove away from Tregozzano, I took myself off down by the carp lake. My mind was full of the previous day

– my late stepfather, John F, and the story which followed his friendship with the Gori family. I was thinking also about my own father. How close might Iain Alick have been to this area on his journey of captivity and deprivation? I thought about the British soldiers who had fallen in thc fight for Arezzo, American and Commonwealth too. My father and the padre who became my stepfather both made it home. In memory of Iain Alick and John F and for all those who did not make it home, I felt like playing a pipe tune on my accordion. There was nobody else around, so I did just that…playing slowly, softly and with all the feeling that had built up during our stay in Tregozzano 'Battle of the Somme', a retreat composed by Pipe Major William Laurie.

AUSTRIA

~·~ Our Favourite Hotel ~·~

As it was Sunday, there were no lorries on the Italian motorways, just loads and loads of cars, all the way up to the Austrian border. Queues for roadworks were encountered, but they were embraced as an opportunity to enjoy the scenery. We were leaving from the Arezzo area rather than from the Pisa area, so for the first stretch, at least, the road was new to Ale and to me. Northwards from Modena, we were in familiar territory.

As it was a case of having to drag ourselves most reluctantly away from Tregozzano, we arrived at Landhotel Forstof in Sierning very late in the evening. We were spending our first night in Austria at the Baumschlager family hotel which had expanded massively since Nazareno and Cipriana had first stayed there on their honeymoon. At that stage, as a *Gasthof*, part of the steading building was still used for agricultural purposes. Tractors were a common sight even when Ale and I stayed there during our own honeymoon.

Having visited the Forstof since she was tiny, Ale knows the hotel like the back of her hand, so knew which door would have been left open for us, knew where to uplift the room key and could even have led us to the room blindfolded. This was most helpful in the middle of the night! With Austria being just as dog friendly as Bavaria, word had been left that, of course,

Scudo was welcome to sleep in our room, not that he gets to do that at home. Very conveniently, the room had a small terrace overlooking the courtyard.

By the time we surfaced in the morning, the hotel was buzzing- with pensioners! The mayor and his town council had invited all the senior citizens of Sierning and its surrounding area to lunch at the Forsthof. With Sierning being in an agricultural area, the practice seems to be for everyone to make a very early start to the day. Main meals are served earlier than they are in Edinburgh and much earlier than in Italy. The Scots/Italian couple had a smile as they left from breakfast to see some Austrians already settling down for their second meal of the day. There were cold beers on the go, too. No wonder the pensioners seemed a cheery lot.

I steered Scudo through the throng of lunch guests, or was it the other way around? There were friendly greetings of '*Grüss Gott*' for me and several stops to allow a pat for the dog. Very smiley, it was. This early to rise and mid-morning beer combination should be available on prescription in Edinburgh.

Mention of Austria in Scotland usually evokes a comment about skiing, but the tourists emerged into gloriously warm sunshine. We have only visited Austria in the summer or early autumn. Sunshine and thunderstorms, that is our impression. The storms can be seen building up in the distance and the locals are very good at predicting the time of arrival. There was no risk of a drop of rain that morning as we headed for Forsthof Wald, which is the Baumschlager wood and farmland about a mile up the road from the hotel. Clear air and trees galore, there are various feeding points to encourage roe deer to make their home in the woods.

Austria must be one of the most mountainous countries in Europe, but despite that, about half of its area is covered by woodland. That doesn't mean the woodland stays untouched – far from it. There is much high-quality woodwork to be seen, but the Austrians are really strict in their control of felling and of replanting. Somehow, they also manage to fell without leaving the area looking as if it had suffered a heavy artillery barrage. How often do you pass a felled forest in the Scottish Highlands without thinking how ugly it looks?

The immediate impression in the Sierning area which is neither built up nor touristy, is of a people who cherish their countryside and its traditions. Their cheery, friendly attitude is definitely not just down to the occasional mid-morning beer. They live in a lovely place which they look after properly. In fact, they do everything properly. There isn't a hint of litter anywhere, but my favourite example of Austrians doing things properly can be experienced as you drive along the tiny hill-top roads which feels akin to walking a tight-rope. If you pull over to let an Austrian come ahead, do not hold your breath while waiting for a wave in thanks. The roads are so narrow, they think it much more important to keep both hands on the wheel. Kindred spirits, at last.

~•~ Nazareno's Wee Housie ~•~

Although we had been kindly offered the use of a flat by our Baumschlager friends, we wanted to stay in Nazareno's little house up on the hill, as much for the pleasure we knew it would give him as anything else. Originally built as a summerhouse, it lies on a wooded ridge in the tiny settlement of Rieglwirt, between Aschach and Garsten. The nearest big town is Steyr which can be reached in about fifteen minutes by car. Officially, Steyr is a city, but by no means a big one. It lies around the meeting point of the rivers Enns and Steyr where its historic importance was ironworking, knives and weapons. It remains well known for tractors and firearms. That makes it sound like an industrial estate, but its cobbled centre is very pretty and a pleasure to visit. Steyr is big enough to have everything we MacKenzies might need, but small enough to have become familiar quite quickly.

On the drive over to the little house, Ale and I were starting to relax after the long trip up from Italy and the late night. We love this area. Even the smell just out of Aschach had us laughing. It was another warm, sunny afternoon and we were driving over hills and between fields, some already harvested and others sporting maize up to eight feet high. The smell? Natural fertilizer, sharn, *Mist* in German; cow dung and all-pervading it was. It might sound extremely odd that two people could celebrate driving into such a powerful pong, but it meant that we were nearly 'home', Austrian style. We likened it to the point, just off Scalpay, on the way into the pier at Tarbert, where you first catch the smell of peat burning in the houses near the Harris shore. An unmistakeable 'welcome back'.

On the linguistic side, I know the German word *Mist* (pronounced 'meest') because I have heard it so often on the golf course in Austria. Like 'shoot' in English, it is the slightly more polite way of expressing disappointment than using the stronger word! A very good Austrian friend of ours can be heard using the word, with feeling, when his tee shots end in the rough or '*gemüse*' (vegetables). As his putting reminds me of the great Seve Ballesteros, the occasional wayward drive is usually recovered by his enviable short game.

On the topic of animal waste, the two in the front seats had received the lesson of a lifetime on that subject during a visit to the *Jagd* (Hunting) *Museum* near St Florian early on during their years of visiting Austria together. Amongst all the hunting exhibits comprising trophies, spears, bows, guns and hugely spiked dog collars, there was a quiet corner where, in an immaculately presented glass case, one could examine the droppings, dung or any other word one might care to use, of all the beasts of the Austrian mountains and woods, hunter and hunted. Fascinating for some it is too.

To one side of the road approaching Rieglwirt, nothing could be seen but maize. To the right, however, the view over the harvested fields was of the valley of the river Enns and was spectacular. On the far side of the river, the valley rose up into rich hillside pasture, dotted with mature trees and flawlessly kept farm steadings. Above that was the higher pastureland, real 'Sound of Music country'. Then, in the haze, were the mountains proper. The two of us now know this view well, but my 'Santo Paradiso, would you look at that,' probably summed up the effect on us succinctly.

Rieglwirt itself comprises only three or four properties. Nazareno's wee house is reached by a narrow road, which becomes a still narrower grass track, running along the boundary of the main property, Gasthaus Rieglwirt, owned by the Mairhofer family. They run a superb Gasthaus in the best Austrian tradition and are very friendly neighbours too. With dining areas inside and out, a very convivial atmosphere and only a few paces away, it is a joy. Even more, the portions are huge. For example, *Backhendl* is fried breaded chicken served with a large portion of chips and a generous side salad. Ale and I reckoned that each of us had been served with one half of the same bird and struggled to finish. Small wonder, as we had started with a bowl of cream of pumpkin soup. These Austrians never risk underfeeding their guests.

Gasthaus Rieglwirt is very popular indeed with families, business guests and the very many walkers of all ages who pass by the gates of the wee house. From the front of the Gasthaus there is a drive of seventy yards of tarmac road followed by seventy yards of grass track to the gates of, what we MacKenzies call, the 'wee house' or more often the 'wee housie', probably because the Italian side of the family refers to it as '*la casetta*', the diminutive of *casa* (house).

The grass track later becomes a footpath and heads off through the woods on its way towards Garsten, which is a delightful market town on the banks of the River Enns. Garsten, like Steyr, has a long history, first appearing in records over one thousand years ago. Oddly enough, it now seems to be best known for its prison, which started out as a monastery around 1100, was fully rebuilt in the 1600s and then converted into a prison in the late 1800s. It was rebuilt in Baroque style in the seventeenth century. Strangely, a list of the fifteen most beautiful prisons on the planet has been drawn up and, at about number four, you can find Garsten, with a comment that it is one of the most beautiful examples of High Baroque architecture in Austria!

As a prison, it is the real thing. Austria's most infamous criminal in recent times is serving his life sentence there.

The valley below the footpath from Rieglwirt to Garsten, lying to the rear of the wee housie, is known as Höllbachtal, which is thought to mean 'Hell stream valley'. The minor road which runs along the valley floor is called Höllstrasse (Hell Street) and that forms part of the official address of Nazareno's house. The road got its name because the locals found the journey through the dense woods hellish scary. It probably was, if a cart got stuck in ruts in the middle of the woods and its driver was there for the night. It is still quite a dark road now, but there are a few nice houses along it and scary it is not.

The view to the front of the wee housie is of the Ennstal, the valley of the River Enns. It is breath-taking, as I well remember from my first visit to Frau Besenreiter, then owner, during the honeymoon. What can be seen from the road outside Aschach is just the *apperitivo* to whet the appetite for this view from the house itself.

On arrival at the wee house itself, I served us a glass of Austrian Grüner Veltliner, then went straight to take in the view from the terrace which runs along the front of the house. The pair of us could sit there for ages, just looking, luxuriating in the taste and beauty of Upper Austria.

While the house is built on the ridge between the two valleys, it is also built into the slope of the land as it starts down towards the Enns. The main floor is at ground level at the rear of the house and at first floor level at the front, sleeping accommodation and a shower room having been created below. The terrace at the front feels quite high, as the ground outside the boundary fence slopes away dramatically in the shape of pasture belonging to Andreas, who farms from the steading far below. The presence of docile dairy cows at the garden fence simply increased the delight felt by one of the MacKenzies and, yes, he did soon persuade them to come to the fence for a gentle pat and a handful of plucked grass. I was caught by the farmer's wife speaking to the cows, in English, with Scudo peeking at them from behind me, his nose poking out from between his master's knees. Well, these beasts were a lot bigger than the Quidinish Highland cattle and probably intimidating if only by their size. While the dog must have looked pretty silly, his owner must have sounded even sillier. Never having met her before, I explained in hesitant German who we were and that I had just spent some weeks looking after cattle on a Scottish island. She was lovely, very happy to suggest the occasional word, when it was needed, and called over her young son to meet us too.

Beyond Andreas's farm steading lies the Enns. It is broad and flows slowly, at this point, between banks which are almost entirely treelined. That evening it was the colour of green olives. There were white specks to be seen on the surface near the far bank – swans, about a dozen of them and hardly moving at all.

In the last few minutes of sunlight, the overall impression was of the colour green, in every shade one could think of. The view to the front was bookended by the dark green of the woodland lying to either side of Andreas's pasture. Beyond the Enns, the ground rose again in a patchwork of huge fields, one or two interrupting the shades of green with brown, where the combine harvester must have already been to visit. I could see a dozen or so farm steadings across the valley with some sited well above the height of our Rieglwirt hill. Straight opposite the wee housie, stood out three high hills, each topped with thick forest. Only above and beyond them began the serious mountains. As darkness fell, the odd pair of headlights showed just how high up the little roads reached on the far side of the valley.

There is a road and a railway line running along the bank of the Enns far below the wee housie. Neither is busy, but hardly any sound reaches up anyway. That evening, insects provided the background. Crickets, grasshoppers, cicada? Whatever they were, they were numerous and very busy. Insects apart, it was totally peaceful without being isolated. By the time we were due to go inside to eat, there was a three-quarter moon above the valley. Down below, ducks had taken fright at something. The sound of their frantic quacking made it all the way up the hill, for me to find myself met by gimlet-eyed reproach on looking down to check on Scudo's whereabouts.

The tiny supermarket in Aschach had been visited on the way over from Sierning. The whole car journey is not much more than ten minutes, with Aschach reachable from the wee housie in under five. My liking for Tuscan bread, prosciutto, salami and cheeses has been documented. I have a similar love for the Austrian version, with the purchase of equivalent provisions immediately essential on arrival. *Salzstangerel*, a long thin roll lightly encrusted with crystals of salt, is a favourite from the vast choice of bread rolls available. From white through to dark-brown, Austrian rolls can include a whole range of nuts and seeds. Once the rolls can be decided upon, there is then a wide variety of cured hams, cold meats and sausages to ponder over, before moving on to the equally difficult choice of cheeses. The Aschach shop is tiny by supermarket standards, but well stocked. The car can be parked right at the front door. What more could one ask?

The Austrians love their beer, with Zipfer Urtyp being a very popular brew and it can be seen being bought by the crate as part of the normal household shopping. Beer, rolls, meats, cheeses plus some tomatoes, onions and gherkins make up what is probably the Austrian equivalent of a Ploughman's Lunch, but often eaten in the evening too. *Jause* is their word for what can be a snack, but if you pile your choices high, especially on a wooden platter, it is a main meal in itself. Lunch or dinner, one of us would even have *Jause* for his breakfast.

The first supper was enjoyed in a truly idyllic setting as we celebrated our return to Austria.

~·~ Highlanders in Austria ~·~

It is small wonder that the view from the front of Nazareno's house is spectacular given that it stands on a ridge in the River Enns Valley Natural Park Region. To the rear, the hills are both closer and lower. Only six farm steadings are in view across 'Hell Stream Valley', one with a sizeable herd of red deer. Again, the ground plunges steeply away from the little house. This time, it is a meadow below the unfenced grass track. Selecting the wrong gear while executing the necessary five-point turn at the garden gates is not advised. For these really steep fields, the local farmers use a walking tractor reaper. It's a two-wheeled cross between a lawn mower and a tractor, with the farmer walking behind, holding on tight – an amazing piece of kit.

Ale and I know the immediate area well, but still enjoy just taking off in the car and seeing where we end up. We visited Ternberg, Trattenbach, Pettenbach, Losenstein, Maria Neustift and many other little places like them. Each was a pretty, pristinely maintained village, set in the grand backdrop of the valley of the Enns and each had something interesting to offer, usually historic. Trattenbach, for example, is famous for knife making. The classic knife is a folding pocketknife with a lathe-turned, wooden handle. Knives have been made here for almost six hundred years, with the first records dating from 1422. Apparently, many of the current residents are descended from the families of either the blade makers or the craftsmen who turned the wooden handles. Dominating the centre of the village, is a huge iron monument in the shape of the classic knife.

My growing enthusiasm, more accurately affection, for Highland cattle led to visits to previously unexplored areas. Our friends had thought we might have reached Austria earlier in the summer. Benedetta's wedding had dictated the timing of the trip, but there was also mention of the 'pet sitting' of the Highland cattle in Quidinish which prompted the response that there were Highland cattle in the near vicinity of Nazareno's wee house. So, there we went, touring round the little roads, among the high hills, between the Enns and Steyr valleys. Wall-to-wall sunshine, verdant pasture galore and beautifully presented farmhouses soon had the two of us believing that farming must be doing very well in Austria. The latest, huge tractor would often be seen parked next to a children's chute, swimming pool or trampoline at the front of a picture-book farmhouse. We stopped at just such a farmhouse for help in our search. Whether there was a flaw in the asking or in our comprehension of the directions, we ended up at a farm where there was all manner of exotic animals on view; dromedary and antelope aplenty, but there was not a single hairy, horned beast in sight.

Another clue led us to a picturesque wooded valley. The farm had various breeds of cattle in its fields plus a trout loch and a *Jause* station serving a broad variety of home reared/produced delights. Yet again, there was a distinct lack of wide, curved horns. Further enquiry was immediately discounted as we realised that we had happened upon the farm which had made the headlines the previous day. The farmer had been working on field drains when earth had collapsed on him. He had been rescued by the emergency services and it was thought that his stay in hospital was precautionary. While we were in the carpark, neighbours stopped by at the farmhouse for an update and to offer their good wishes. This glimpse of kindness and good will was cheering, as was the word that the young farmer had not been seriously hurt. Our wild goose chase was abandoned for the day. No Highland cattle had been seen, but the sights were deemed wonderful, with a black squirrel providing a little novelty for us too.

The question of novelty or otherwise cropped up again later in the evening when I discovered that there were around 13,000 Highland cattle registered in Austria – registered perhaps, but well hidden, it seemed.

On our most recent visit to Austria, another Sierning friend, Hans Artner, remembered our fruitless search. He had been the local bank manager, but to us he is a man of the woods and mountains. Hans guided us along a little road by the banks of the River Steyr and then up into the hills only a couple of miles from the wee house. There they were, about a dozen Highland cattle ranging from a mature bull down to a young calf, enjoying the shade of apple trees in total comfort. As we watched, the bull ignored the lush grass, reaching up instead to pluck an apple from a tree. Goodness knows what the 'Flodabay Five' would have made of it.

~·~ Upper Austria: Courtesy and Tradition ~·~

While the most welcoming and hospitable atmosphere of all is, undoubtedly, to be found at the Baumschlager family homes and at their hotel, mention must be made of Golf Club Herzog Tassilo, which lies just outside Sierning's near neighbour, Bad Hall, a market town and famous for its history of baths and spas. The Baumschlager family were founder members of the golf club and had proudly directed Nazareno and me to it right at the very outset when only the practice ground had been formed. The course has now matured impressively. Trees have grown to full height and doglegs can no longer be cut. Water has to be avoided on almost half of the holes and there are woods, slopes and bunkers everywhere. It is an interesting, challenging golf course with a fantastic clubhouse and first-class practice facilities.

The views, even from the practice ground, are amazing, with a magnificent panorama of what they refer to as the 'foothills of the Alps' available from the driving range and short-game areas. The 'foothills' have always looked like massive mountains to the Scottish side of the family. Where better to hit a bucketful of practice balls under the watchful gaze of a wife who can spot tension in a golf swing instantly?

Even in September, the heat was such that, after my supervised practice, I made use of the excellent guest facilities for a shower and complete change of clothing, leaving my mentor and her dog to enjoy a cooling drink in the shade at the front of the luxurious clubhouse. It was at this point, that the friendliness of Austrians was exemplified beautifully. Certainly, the MacKenzies have visited the club regularly in the twenty-five years since it was founded, both with the Baumschlager family and alone, but we only know a handful of the members. Nevertheless, everyone who passed by the front of the clubhouse greeted Ale with a 'Hello' or a '*Grüss Gott*'.

Even more courtesy emerges if there is any indication that a meal is about to be eaten. When Ale ordered lunch and the place settings were brought to the table, the greeting from those walking past changed to '*Mahlzeit*'. It is a shortened form of the olden '*Gesegnete Mahlzeit*' ('Blessed meal') and means 'Enjoy your meal', which we certainly did.

The Austrians, at least in rural areas, have always impressed and endeared themselves to the MacKenzies as a good-natured and kindly people. The conversations over lunch with golf club members reinforced the opinion, formed years before, that the Austrians are switched on, do things properly and successfully while, at the same time, are happy to enjoy the old traditions of their countryside. It is an enviable combination, flourishing in a beautiful setting.

The visit to Austria coincided with Harvest Thanksgiving in Sierning. Although it is by no means a big town, with a population of nine thousand, Sierning and its surrounding hamlets know how to put on a fantastic celebration of rural tradition and abundance of produce. Top quality soil, real skill and ideal weather seem to join forces in a winning formula.

We had again spent the night as guests in Landhotel Forsthof and stepped outside just after breakfast to find, drawn up at the main entrance, the leading participants in what turned out to be a very long parade. The rear of Landhotel Forsthof seemed to be the assembly point and, once the leaders moved off, a constant stream of groups kept coming around the corner to head in procession for the church square at the far end of the main street. The colourful cavalcade was led by tractors, both vintage and ultra-modern, all prepared to look their very best, their trailers neatly stacked with local produce. Behind them came each organisation and club which formed part of the community. Everyone the MacKenzies knew was in there somewhere in an admirable display of community and tradition. Even the tennis club had prepared a float. Exactly what they had to do with harvest remained unclear, but they kindly lobbed a few tennis balls to the spectators lining the main street. Scudo wasn't allowed to retrieve any – balls or spectators.

Strangely, some elements of the parade seemed reluctant to move off terribly quickly, the reason soon being spotted. A firkin of Forsthof-produced walnut schnapps and a large tray of shot glasses were proving too attractive. Reinhold Baumschlager (junior), now in charge of the Landhotel Forsthof, was also in charge of the firkin. Plenty harvest connection there, at least. That would also be more mid-morning alcohol in happy Austria.

Sheer numbers would prevent mention of all the participants in an amazing spectacle, but the other, younger members of family Baumschlager were certainly picked out. Sophie was with her mum, Siegried, and others wearing their traditional golden hats, her twin brother, Max, was with FC Sierning and his dad, Siegi, was dishing out something, possibly alcoholic, from a horse drawn vehicle. Siegi was dressed in a vintage style military uniform and his comrades were marching with old fashioned rifles, shouldered – the Town Guard, or something like it. It is thought that he is also a member of the Imperial Guard. These Austrians do love their traditions.

We followed the parade down to the main square, beside the church, to find that many stalls had been set up, some with tables and benches. Outside the town hall, the Sierning Orchestra and the town Oompah Band were ready to entertain. Not simultaneously, was the MacKenzie hope.

After a general look around, a plan for lunch was adopted. It began at the Pumpkin Producers' stand. Cream of pumpkin soup has long been a favourite starter at the Forsthof where it stars as *Kürbis Creme Suppe* along with the equally popular *Frittaten Suppe*, which is a clear soup with what looks liked fried tagliatelle in it, *Leberknödel Suppe* – liver dumpling and *Knoblauch Creme Suppe* – cream of garlic. At the Pumpkin Producers' stand, not only was the soup spicy and very tasty, but they also offered pumpkin schnapps which, obviously, had to be sampled. You can begin to see a pattern here, all before Scottish lunchtime.

On we went to the Fire Brigade stall, where the tables looked very popular. On offer were traditional sausage, sauerkraut, rolls and beer. Sauerkraut translates as fermented cabbage which makes it sound disgusting. We liked it. This stall was offering substantial and tasty fare, but it deserved support in its fundraising anyway. Only the very big towns and cities in Austria have full-time, career fire fighters. The rest of the country is served by volunteer units with even the tiniest hilltop communities boasting a pristine (one would expect nothing less), little fire station.

The last stop was with the Golden Hats group of farmers' wives and daughters where Sigrid and Sophie served coffee and things similar to doughnuts in taste, if not in appearance. Ale and I stayed there for quite a while as we were introduced to some local people who were interested to hear how a couple from Scotland and Italy had ended up knowing so well and loving so much, a little, lesser known part of Austria.

Harvest Thanksgiving in Sierning had been a day of memorable sights and tastes for us as we were welcomed to enjoy a small, but vibrant, rural community throwing itself whole heartedly into celebration.

The following day after a last Landhotel Forsthof lunch, the lovely Maria, mother and grandmother Baumschlager, announced her wish that the 'Goodbyes' be '*kurz und schmerzlos*', short and painless. Everyone did their best in that direction as the MacKenzie party set off with the Land Rover brim full of Sierning diesel at less than one euro per litre, the driver wishing out loud that he could take a tankerful home. 630 miles to the ferry terminal. There would be plenty of time for reflection.

REFLECTION

Ale and I had been away for six weeks, other than a two-night break at home in between ferries. It had indeed been a Grand Tour covering Iain Alick's boyhood home on Harris and reaching as far south as Nazareno's boyhood home in Tregozzano. On the way to Harris, we had passed John F's boyhood home at Struanlea, Breakish on Skye and on the return journey, after crossing from Stornoway to Ullapool, we had passed through Balavil Estate, Kingussie. Time had been spent in the Hebrides, Bavaria, Tuscany and Austria, beautiful all, but so different one from the other.

Ale had been seen, dressed in every stitch of anti-midgie clothing she could find, giving a Harris henhouse a thorough clean out and taking pride in the result. I had carted water and feed to hens and ducks before offering beef cattle nuts to my favourite, horned charges. Within a few days of that, the pair of us were sipping chilled white wine at a pavement table while we watched a Mediterranean sunset together.

There were many contrasting sights during the six weeks or so, but also one fundamental theme throughout. Valued friends and relatives alike, the people were lovely, their welcome genuinely affectionate. Hebridean, Tuscan, Bavarian and Austrian were kindness personified.

There had been moments when sadness, loss and fondest memory came very much to the fore: the joint tending of the grave of my father and mother as the sun slowly fell in Scarista, on the west side of Harris, accompanied by Ale's quietly offered Italian prayer for eternal rest; the feeling of the absence of

Uncle Murdo and Uncle Roddy in Quidinish; Nazareno without Cipriana in Marina di Pisa.

As for the coming together of the Scot and the Italian, had the little boy not lost the father he adored, the grown man would not have met the wife he adores. The worst that ever happened to him, to his mother and to his brother had been a *sine qua non* for the best that ever happened to him. Furthermore, had Nazareno not suffered life threatening burns and had the determination to locate the doctor and the other British soldiers, Ale and I would still never have met. These were twists of fate – recognised and acknowledged.

Ale and I had discussed the real affection we had sensed from Lucilla and Nazareno when they spoke of my stepfather. More than seventy years after his stay as the padre in Tregozzano, the impression Rev John Fletcher had made was clear to hear and see.

We had recalled how John F had made a return to Tregozzano, visiting with my mother, Nazareno and Cipriana while the two of us were in Austria on honeymoon. As John F walked around the tiny village, a little old lady had looked up from plucking a chicken at her door to greet the former padre with 'Capitano!' I wish I had witnessed that happy moment. Sadly, John F apparently suffered a minor stroke during that return visit. It may have been pure coincidence, but who knows what memories it had brought back to him and the effect they may have had.

That John F stood at the very heart of our story was clearly set out in his Regimental Obituary in 1990.

'*When at Battalion Headquarters near Arezzo in 1944, he established a friendship with an Italian doctor whose granddaughter married John's stepson, Duncan, in 1985.*'

Ale and I have, long since, each embraced fully the roots of the other and part of that was a natural induction for our sons too. The older boys went on to introduce their fiancées, now wives, both to Harris and to Tuscany and these delightful girls are making progress in learning Italian. Finlay spent his third year at his mum's University of Pisa, graduating in Italian from Edinburgh University with First Class Honours and other awards the following year. Ale made sure that her sons all learned Italian where Uncle Murdo used to say was the best place to learn Gaelic… on the mother's knee. John uses his Italian most days at his work in the world of oil and shipping. Seumas formed his interest in marine biology while snorkelling in the sea off Marina as a young boy, but he has now also visited Italy in connection with his work in tidal energy.

On the face of it, the embracing of each other's roots by Ale and by me even extended to our breakfast fare of cappuccino and porridge. That morning menu, which has almost reached the status of a family motto, could be a daily celebration of the coming together of the two cultures. It isn't. The truth of the matter is that, while I immediately adopted Ale's cappuccino as an essential start to every day, that most beneficial sustenance that is porridge only became part of Ale's breakfast routine following her stay in the highly skilled care of Mr Anderson and his colleagues at Edinburgh's Western General Hospital.

'Cappuccino and porridge': a daily reminder to give thanks and be ever grateful.

SOURCES

Archive material:
The London Scottish Regimental Gazette.
Various excerpts featuring Padre John Fletcher were provided by
Andrew Parsons, Curator and Archivist, London Scottish, initially
to my stepbrother. Mr Parsons then provided me with photographs,
further information and permission on behalf of The Trustees of
the London Scottish Regiment to use any material published or
archival. This was greatly appreciated.

Books

(1) *Croft History, Isle of Harris Volume 3.*
Bill Lawson for Comann Eachdraidh na Hearadh.

(2) *Great Battles*: Culloden. Murray Pittock.

Music

'*Talking with My Father*' Dougie MacLean.
One of my favourite singer-songwriters, I have had the pleasure
of hearing Dougie MacLean introduce and sing his fine song live.
Its title was exactly what I was looking for.

Newspapers

(1) *The Glasgow Herald December 14th December 1996*
Article 'The Europeans'. Jane Scott.

(2) *Badenoch & Strathspey Herald July 2009 and November 2011*
Article 'Kingussie WW II bomber wreckage goes on show'.

Websites:

(1) *Second World War Experience Centre.*
'Not the Image but Reality: British POW Experience in Italian and German Camps'. Peter Liddle and Ian Whitehead.

(2) *World War 2 Today.*
'Shipped out of Tobruk as a POW' with 95 comments.

(3) *Church Times.*
Review by Dr Bernard Palmer of Alan Robinson's
'Chaplains at War': The role of clergymen during World War II.

(4) *The Richest.com.*
'15 Most beautiful and Luxurious Prisons on Earth'.

(5) *Forces War Records*
'German Camps – British and Commonwealth Prisoners of War 1939-45'.

(6) *British Genealogy and Family History Forums.*
Stalag 4D Torgau (Elbe).

(7) *Victoria University of Wellington.*
'Prisoners of War (iv). Evacuation of Prisoners of War by Russian Forces'.

(8) *The Water of Leith Conservation Trust.*

(9) *Heavy Whalley MBE.*
Article in 2017 'July 1944 – Wellington (sic) crash in the Monadhliaths and the very early days of RAF Kinloss Mountain Rescue'.

(10) *Britannica.com*
Sir Benjamin Thompson

(11) *Tempesttintankard.com*
A Beer in thc Park – Beer Gardens in Munich's English Garden.

(12) *Bayerntrips.com*
'Munich's Englishcher Garten'.